# The Perfect Combination of Traditional Chinese Poetry with Classical Music and Contemporary Renowned Compositions

Research on the Commonalities between the Ancient Chinese Traditional Poems, including regulated verse (Lyrics), and Classical Music, including renowned Songs

Liu Kedian

AMERICAN ACADEMIC PRESS

AMERICAN ACADEMIC PRESS

By AMERICAN ACADEMIC PRESS

201 Main Street

Salt Lake City

UT 84111 USA

Email manu@AcademicPress.us

Visit us at http://www.AcademicPress.us

Copyright © 2025 by AMERICAN ACADEMIC PRESS

All rights reserved, including those of translation into foreign languages.

No part of this publication may be reproduced, stored in a retrieval system, or transmitted in any form or by any means, electronic, mechanical, photocopying, recording, or otherwise, now known or hereafter invented, without the prior written permission of the AMERICAN ACADEMIC PRESS, or as expressly permitted by law, or under terms agreed with the appropriate reprographics rights organization. Enquiries concerning reproduction outside the scope of the above should be sent to the Rights Department, American Academic Press, at the address above.

The scanning, uploading, and distribution of this book via the Internet or via any other means without the permission of the publisher is illegal and punishable by law. Please purchase only authorized editions and do not participate in or encourage electronic piracy of copyrighted materials. Your support of the publisher's right is appreciated.

ISBN: 979-8-3370-8947-8

Distributed to the trade by National Book Network Suite 200, 4501 Forbes Boulevard, Lanham, MD 20706

10  9  8  7  6  5  4  3  2  1

# Contents

Introduction .................................................................................................. 1

**1 Research** ................................................................................................. 2

    1.1 Music and poetry should be thoughtfully integrated to enhance and complement each other's expressive qualities ........................................ 2

    1.2 The spiritual essence and material structure of music and lyrics should be mutually expressed ................................................................. 3

    1.3 Scientific nature of the job ................................................................. 6

    1.4 It is some people's interests .............................................................. 7

**2 Collections of New Songs** ..................................................................... 9

    2.01 Song No.01, New Year's day Evening ........................................... 10

    2.02 Song No.02, A Spring morning ..................................................... 16

    2.03 Song No 03, Thoughts on a Quiet Night ........................................ 20

    2.04 Song No.04, To Judge Han Chuo of Yangzhou city ..................... 25

    2.05 Song No.05, Nostalgia ................................................................... 30

    2.06 Song No.06, Joy At Meeting ......................................................... 36

    2.07 Song No.07, Greenish Willows ..................................................... 42

    2.08 Song No.08, Prelude to Water Melody ......................................... 47

    2.09 Song No.09, Visit the villages on the west side of the mountain . 55

    2.10 Song No.10, Memories of the lower reaches of the Yangtze River regions ..................................................................................................... 60

    2.11 Song No.11, Groping For Fish ...................................................... 64

    2.12 Song No.12, Song of Divination ................................................... 71

    2.13 Song No.13, Butterfly Love Flowers ............................................ 75

    2.14 Song No.14, Cooing and Wooing .................................................. 81

    2.15 Song No.15, Go to the frontier ...................................................... 85

    2.16 Song No.16, The Melody of Liangzhou City ............................... 90

    2.17 Song No.17, A Mountain Abode on a Clear Autumn Evening ..... 95

    2.18 Song No.18, Untitled ..................................................................... 99

    2.19 Song No.19, Phoenix Hairpin ..................................................... 107

    2.20 Song No.20, Go Hunting in Mi Zhou ......................................... 117

2.21 Song No.21, Farewell at Jin Ling Tavern ................................. 123
2.22 Song No.22, Plum Blossoms and Willow Leaves ..................... 127
2.23 Song No.23, Chinese Marseillaise .............................................. 132
2.24 Song No.24, Spring night brings joyous rain ............................. 146
2.25 Song No.25, Magnolia ................................................................. 151
2.26 Song No.26, Longing for the imperial capital ........................... 156
2.27 Song No.27, Ferry to Jingmen for farewell ............................... 160
2.28 Song No.28, Song of a Wanderer ............................................... 164
2.29 Song No.29, The Spring Scenery ............................................... 168
2.30 Song No.30, The Long Song ...................................................... 173
2.31 Song No.31, Listen to the flute .................................................. 177
2.32 Song No.32, Moor at Guazhou city ............................................ 183
2.33 Song No.33, New Year's Day ..................................................... 191
2.34 Song No.34, Autumn night ......................................................... 195
2.35 Song No.35, Small Overlapping Mountain ................................ 199
2.36 Song No.36, The wine will be served ........................................ 205
2.37 Song No.37, The peach tree is in full bloom ............................. 212
2.38 Song No.38, Broke the deadlock ................................................ 217
2.39 Song No.39, Magpie Bridge Immortal ...................................... 222
2.40 Song No.40, Nostalgia for Red Cliff .......................................... 227
2.41 Song No.41, The Bodhisattva minority ..................................... 234
2.42 Song No.42, Written the ancient meadow to bid farewell ......... 239
2.43 Song No.43, The fisherman's song ............................................ 243
2.44 Song No.44, Poems on Returning Home ................................... 248
2.45 Song No.45, Seven-character quatrain ...................................... 252
2.46 Song No.46, Climbing Lan Shan Mountain .............................. 256
2.47 Song No.47, Forever yearning .................................................... 261
2.48 Song No.48, Though the turtle lives long .................................. 268
2.49 Song No.49, Enjoy Wines while going down Zhongnan Mountain
.................................................................................................................. 273
2.50 Song No.50, Recording the Dreams on the night ..................... 278
2.51 Song No.51, The reeds ............................................................... 283
2.52 Song No.52, Songs of Eight famous people in Drinking .......... 287
2.53 Song No.53, Song of Divination ................................................ 293

    2.54 Song No.54, Full River Red ........................................................ 298

**3 Discussions** ........................................................................................**304**

    3.1 About the talent ............................................................................304

    3.2 About the translation .................................................................... 304

    3.3 Regarding the pinyin annotation of Chinese characters ............... 305

    3.4 About the sequence arrangement of the songs .............................. 305

**4 Background story of this project** ...................................................**307**

**Postscript and acknowledgments** ......................................................**312**

# Introduction

Classical music reached its zenith prior to the 20th century. By the early 1900s, classical music had achieved its final brilliance, after which it gradually ceased to evolve.

In the 20th century, composers like Dmitri Shostakovich, Jean Sibelius, and Igor Stravinsky continued to innovate within the symphonic form. Shostakovich's symphonies, written under the oppressive Soviet regime, often contain coded political messages and emotional intensity.In my opinion, the composers like Dmitri Shostakovich, Jean Sibelius, and Igor Stravinsky, their names are more famous than their symphonic works.

Ancient Chinese traditional poems are a rich art treasure, as well as a vast, deep, and gorgeous world. However, Chinese traditional poetry reached its peak during the Tang Dynasty (618 - 907 AD), continued to be developed during the Song Dynasty (960 - 1279 AD), began to decline during the Ming Dynasty, and has never recovered since.

Therefore, whether referring to classical music or Chinese classical poetry, the most outstanding works are akin to naturally formed gems, unparalleled, irreplaceable, and un-replicable.

There are both practical reasons and theoretical foundations for these two artistic paradigms to be preserved and passed down through generations, complementing each other harmoniously and forming a perfect combination. Let them join hands and shine together with even more brilliant and dazzling radiance.This book is expected to complete an unprecedented and unparalleled undertaking.

# 1 Research

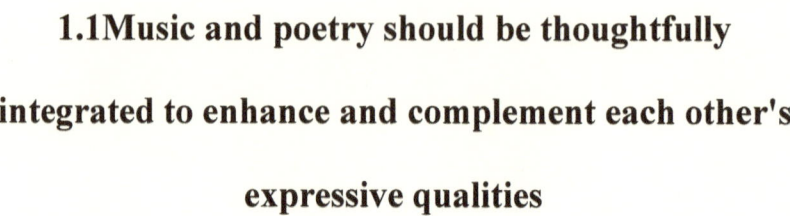

## 1.1 Music and poetry should be thoughtfully integrated to enhance and complement each other's expressive qualities

Poetry represents a refined form of linguistic art, while music embodies a refined form of universal auditory expression. Chinese classical poetry is not primarily intended to expound philosophical doctrines or grand moral principles. It not only conveys specific content clearly but also implies abstract and generalized artistic conceptions, as well as subtle rational insights. Similarly, music possesses both generality and abstraction, along with a relatively defined expressive scope. Music, too, is not created solely for the purpose of conveying philosophical or moral ideas.

Poetry can enrich music by interpreting its emotional depth through lyrical expression. Conversely, music can also enhance the emotional resonance of poetry when lyrics and melody are combined. Classical poetry and classical music share certain characteristics that are more intuitive than verbalizable, as well as common aesthetic sensibilities that can be perceived.

The integration of these two art forms can mutually enhance their expressive power, combining documentary depth with artistic flexibility, thereby amplifying their overall appeal. Moreover, this synthesis possesses enduring artistic value.

Therefore, if either the poetry or the music is of inferior quality, the combination will be counterproductive and diminish the artistic value of both. However, when both are of high quality, they can complement each other beautifully, like dragons and phoenixes soaring together, enhancing each other's brilliance. The result is a refreshing and delightful experience, almost akin to being in a celestial paradise.

## 1.2 The spiritual essence and material structure of music and lyrics should be mutually expressed

The basic expressive structures in poetry include introduction, development, transition, and conclusion. Symphonies typically follow a four-movement structure. Therefore, the structural forms of traditional Chinese poetry and prose are highly comparable to those of Western classical music.

Chinese poetry has a distinct advantage in terms of musicality: each character is composed of a single vowel and consonant, allowing each character to correspond to a single musical note. While this may not offer the same melodic flexibility as Italian opera, however, it proves advantageous for group singing, solo chanting, and small ensemble performances. Thus, setting classical poetry to classical music fully exploits this linguistic-musical compatibility, offering significant aesthetic and practical value.

Classical poetry, especially metrical words (verse), originally had musical forms that could be sung immediately. However, why were these songs not widely disseminated, and why were many of them ultimately lost? One reason is that their musical forms lacked emotional intensity and melodic fluidity, failing to resonate with the general public. Additionally, they often failed to fully and accurately express the rich, nuanced artistic conceptions and subtle emotional layers embedded in the poetry.

The musical talent of ancient Chinese people was by no means inferior. Compared with their Western counterparts of the same era, Chinese musicians were centuries ahead. However, from the 18th century onward, China lagged behind the West in terms of music theory, instrument development, and performance practices.

Another controversial issue is the East Asian emphasis on the pentatonic scale, it is comprising the notes C (Do), D (Re), E (Mi), G (Sol), and A (La), or 1, 2, 3, 5, and 6, while showing little sensitivity to F (Fa) and

B (Si), or 4 and 7, which are rarely used. For example, the traditional Chinese string instrument Guzheng, is based on the pentatonic scale.

Throughout East Asian history, many of the most famous songs have been composed in the pentatonic mode. For instance, several renowned Japanese folk songs and Korean and North Korean traditional melodies, and even Chinese songs from the past century are pentatonic scale music (song).

Such as some famous and popular Japanese and Korean songs:

Japanese song, "Red Dragonfly."

Japanese song, "Spring in the North"

A Japanese song, a netted tune

Korean song Arirang

The Korean song "Flower Girl".

Also as modern Chinese songs:

"Great Road Song" was composed by Nie Er.

(大路歌聂耳曲).

March of the Volunteers (The national anthem of P R China,) Nie Er composed

(义勇军进行曲聂耳曲).

"The Pioneer of the Way" was composed by Nie Er.

(开路先锋聂耳曲).

"battle blade (saber) March" was written and composed by Mai Xin.

(大刀进行曲麦新词曲)

"Tianya Ge Nu," a folk song from Southern Jiangsu, was arranged by He Luting.

(天涯歌女苏南民歌贺绿汀编曲).

"Four Seasons Song" was arranged by He Luting.

(四季歌贺绿汀编曲).

"Ode to the Yellow River" was composed by Xian Xinghai.

(黄河颂冼星海曲).

"The Yellow Water Ballad" was composed by Xian Xinghai.

(黄水谣冼星海曲).

"Little Town Story" was performed by Teresa Teng.

(小城故事邓丽君歌曲)

The song "Nanping Evening Bell" was composed and written

anonymously.

(南屏晚钟佚名词曲).

"Nan Mud Bay" was composed by Ma Ke.

(南泥湾马可曲).

"Kangding Love Song" is a traditional Sichuan folk song.

(康定情歌四川民歌)

"Wusuli Boat Song" was composed by Wang Yuncai and Guo Song.

(乌苏里船歌汪云才,郭颂曲).

"Full River Red" is a Verse written by General Yue Fei and set to music based on ancient compositions.

(满江红岳飞词古曲).

And etc, are all pentatonic compositions, without incorporating the 12-tone equal temperament system.

Therefore, it is impractical to attempt to compose new music using existing Chinese musical frameworks or to compel unskilled composers to create music for classical poetry. Chinese composers, whether temporarily or fundamentally, lack the necessary ability to achieve this effectively. It is akin to forcing ducks to climb shelves or chickens to swim rivers, imposing unnatural tasks that will not yield satisfactory results.

Moreover, in the 20th century, under some oppressive one-party anti-action, antihuman authoritarian system, the creative talents of musicians are often suppressed and distorted, making it difficult to produce truly outstanding artistic works.

It can't even pass the political review. It is impossible to produce excellent works.

For example, composers like Dmitri Shostakovich, his symphonies, written under the oppressive Soviet regime, often contain coded political messages and emotional intensity.

If a music professional is asked to compose music for many poems and verses, first, his or her understanding of the poems and verses may not be accurate. Second, in a rush, there will be no accumulation of creative inspiration, melodic sources and musical melody pieces. At this time, no touching works will be produced.

Even if Schubert composed thousands of songs, only three or four of them have been kept renowned. Similarly, for the operas of the great composers Verdi, Rossini and Puccini, each of them has no more than four or five of their most famous and widely circulated opera pieces. Even the great composers are like this, let alone the mediocre musicians.

Therefore, only by selecting the treasure of human musical works over hundreds of years and combining it with the traditional Chinese poetry, the spiritual wealth accumulated over thousands of years, then a dazzling brilliance can be presented.

## 1.3 Scientific nature of the job

As previously mentioned, the structure of poetry typically follows the pattern of introduction, development, transition, and conclusion. Similarly, a symphony often consists of four movements, with the first movement's three-part structure resembling the poetic structure.

Most classical symphonies adhere to a four - movement structure.

1. The First Movement: Sonata-Allegro Form

This form consists of three main sections:

– Exposition: The composer introduces the main themes of the movement.

– Development: The themes introduced in the exposition are explored, expanded, and transformed.

– Recapitulation: The original themes return, and a coda is added to provide a final sense of closure.

2. The Second Movement: Slow and Lyrical

The second movement offers a contrast to the energetic first movement, providing a slow and lyrical respite. In theme-and-variations, a theme is presented and followed by a series of variations that alter the theme in creative ways.

3. The Third Movement: Dance Forms

The third movement is typically a dance, often in the form of a minuet and trio or a scherzo. The scherzo is similar in structure but faster and more playful, adding a burst of energy to the symphony.

4. The Fourth Movement: Finale

The finale brings the symphony to a rousing conclusion. The finale aims to provide a satisfying sense of closure, leave the listener with a feeling of exhilaration.

Overall, symphonic form closely parallels the structure of poetry. The author believes that the structure of songs and other musical compositions also shares this similarity.

Therefore, the approach adopted in this book is grounded in the methodological principles of scientific. It is unrealistic to expect that the artistic conception conveyed by the musical composition will perfectly match that of the original poetry. The goal is to achieve a degree of similarity or closeness. The perfection is unattainable.

## 1.4 It is some people's interests

It is common practice to rewrite the poem (lyrics) of existing songs or musicl composition. There are many examples, such as:

"Dreaming of Home and Mother" is a song originally composed by the American composer John P. Ordway before the Civil War. The lyrics express a deep nostalgia for childhood and the comfort of home and mother. The song reflects themes of longing and the sweetness of memories associated with family and home life. It has been translated into various languages and remains popular for its emotional resonance: Japanese adaptation "Travel Sorrow" and its Chinese adaptation "Farewell" are typical examples. Chinese musician and poety Li Shutong's (李叔同) Chinese version of "Farewell" has continued to be sung as a school song since 1920s until today.

"Summer Boating on the Sea" or "Over the summer sea," is a light hearted and rhythmic triple-meter song adapted from Verdi's opera "Rigoletto," characterized by a strong sense of motion. The lyrics were arranged by Ferris, based on Verdi's original composition "woman is fickle".

The Great Waltz is a 1972 American biographical musical film directed by Andrew L. Stone, and others, which incorporates lyrics into the segment of the waltz Blue Danub Revier.

Therefore, it is many people's interests to rewrite new poems (lyrics) for renowned songs and incorporate lyrics into renowned musicl composition. This book will reasonably benefit these people.

# 2 Collections of New Songs

# 2.01 Song No.01, New Year's day Evening

### 青玉案　元夕　南宋　辛弃疾

**Tune of the poem: Green jade table. Title of the poem: New Year's day Evening.**
**Author of the poem (lyrics), Southern Song Dynasty, Xin Qi Ji**

#### 2.01.0 About the score and lyrics (poem)

This score (sheet music) is derived (excerpted) from the (pieces) of Offenbach's Orpheus in Hell: Parisians' Joy, and has undergone minor modifications to ensure a better alignment between the musical arrangement and the lyrics (poem).

Offenbach's Orpheus in the Underworld scandalised and delighted 19th century Paris. Offenbach cut a gleeful swathe through political, musical and moral peccadilloes with a dazzlingly tuneful score Offenbach, dubbed by Rossini the Mozart of the Champs Elysées, pokes hilarious fun at po-faced classical opera in general and Gluck in particular as Orpheus is dragged to Hell to rescue an unwilling wife, accompanied by the Gods, in search of Bacchanalian joy.

The cheerful and complex connotations of lyrics (the poem, original text and its translation see the following sections) and music are very similar, so it is quite appropriate for lyrics and music to match each other. Therefore it is well worth to try to combine the lyrics and the music. Thus the author rewrites the poem (lyrics) for the musical score.

## 2.01.1 Sheet music

$1 = C \quad \frac{2}{4}$

| $\underline{5\ 2}$ $\underline{2\ 3}$ | $\underline{2\ 1}$ $\underline{1\ 3}$ | $\underline{4\ 6}$ $\dot{1}\ 6$ | $\underline{6\ 5}$ $5$ |

东 风 夜 放 花 千 树, 更 吹 落, 星 如 雨.

$\underline{6\ 7}$ $\underline{7\ 6}$ | $\underline{5\ 1}$ $\underline{1\ 3}$ | $\underline{3\ 2}$ $\underline{3\ 2}$ | $\underline{3\ 2}$ $\underline{3\ 2}$ |

宝 马 雕 车 香 满 路. 凤 箫 声 动, 玉 壶 光 转,

$\underline{3\ 2}$ $\underline{3\ 2}$ | $\underline{2\ 1}$ $1$ | $\underline{3\ 1}$ $\underline{6\ 5}$ | $\underline{5\ 2}$ $\underline{3\ 4}$ |

一 夜 鱼 龙 舞. 蛾 儿 雪 柳 黄 金

$\underline{3\ 2}$ $1$ $-$ | $\underline{3\ 1}$ $\underline{6\ 5}$ | $\underline{4\ 5}$ $\underline{6\ 7}$ | $\underline{2\ 1}$ $1$ |

缕. 笑 语 盈 盈 暗 香 去.

$3\ 1$ | $6\ 5$ | $\underline{5\ 2}$ $\underline{3\ 4}$ | $\underline{3\ 2}$ $1$ $-$ | $3\ 1$ | $6\ 5$ |

众 里 寻 他 千 百 度. 蓦 然 回 首,

$\underline{4\ 5}$ $\underline{6\ 7}$ | $\underline{1\ 5}$ $\underline{7\ 5}$ | $\underline{1\ 5}$ $\underline{7\ 5}$ | $1$ $1$ | $1$ |

那 人 却 在, 灯 火 阑 珊 灯 火 阑 珊 处.

## 2.01.2 Sheet music with Lyrics marked in Chinese pinyin without tones

| 5 2 | 2 3 | 2 1 | 1 3 | 4 6 | 1 6 | 6 5 | 5 |
|---|---|---|---|---|---|---|---|
| dong feng | ye | fang hua | qian shu |  | geng chui | luo | xing ru | yu |
| 东 风 | 夜 | 放 花 | 千 树. |  | 更 吹 | 落, | 星 如 | 雨. |

| 6 7 | 7 6 | 5 1 | 1 3 | 3 2 | 3 2 | 3 2 | 3 2 |
|---|---|---|---|---|---|---|---|
| bao ma | diao che | xiang man | lu | feng xiao | sheng dong | yu | hu guang zhuan |
| 宝 马 | 雕 车 | 香 满 | 路. | 凤 箫 | 声 动, | 玉 | 壶 光 转, |

| 3 2 | 3 2 | 2 1 | 1 3 | 1 6 | 5 | 5 2 | 3 4 |
|---|---|---|---|---|---|---|---|
| yi ye | yu long | wu |  | e | er | xue liu | huang | jin |
| 一 夜 | 鱼 龙 | 舞, |  | 蛾 | 儿 | 雪 柳 | 黄 | 金 |

| 3 2 | 1 - | 3 | 1 6 | 5 | 4 5 | 6 7 | 2 | 1 1 |
|---|---|---|---|---|---|---|---|---|
| lv |  | xiao | yu ying | ying | an |  | xiang | qu |
| 缕. |  | 笑 | 语 盈 | 盈 | 暗 |  | 香 | 去. |

| 3 1 | 6 5 | 5 2 | 3 4 | 3 2 | 1 - | 3 | 1 | 6 5 |
|---|---|---|---|---|---|---|---|---|
| zhong li | xun ta | qian | bai | du |  | mo | ran | hui shou |
| 众 里 | 寻 他 | 千 | 百 | 度. |  | 蓦 | 然 | 回 首, |

| 4 5 | 6 7 | 1 5 | 7 5 | 1 5 | 7 5 | 1 | 1 1 | 1 |
|---|---|---|---|---|---|---|---|---|
| na ren | que zai | deng huo | lan shan | deng huo | lan shan | chu |
| 那 人 | 却 在, | 灯 火 | 阑 珊 | 灯 火 | 阑 珊 | 处. |

### 2.01.3 Text of the lyrics

东风夜放花千树.更吹落,星如雨.宝马雕车香满路.
凤箫声动,玉壶光转,一夜鱼龙舞.蛾儿雪柳黄金缕.
笑语盈盈暗香去.众里寻她千百度.
蓦然回首,那人却在,灯火阑珊处.

### 2.01.4 Lyrics marked with tones in Chinese pinyin

dōng fēng yè　fang huā qiān shù　gèng chuī luò　xīng　rú　yǔ
东　风　夜　放　花　千　树.更　吹　落,星　如　雨.
bǎo mǎ diāo chē xiāng mǎn　 lù　fēng xiāo shēng dòng
宝　马　雕　车　香　满　路.凤　箫　声　动,
yù hú guāng zhuǎn　yī　yè yú lóng wǔ　é　ér xuě liǔ huáng jīn lǚ
玉　壶　光　转,一　夜　鱼　龙　舞.蛾　儿　雪　柳　黄　金　缕.
xiào yǔ yíng yíng àn xiāng qù zhòng　lǐ xún tā　qiān bǎi dù
笑　语　盈　盈　暗　香　去.众　里　寻　她　千　百　度.
mò rán huí shǒu　nà rén què zài　dēng huǒ lán shān chù
蓦　然　回　首,那　人　却　在,灯　火　阑　珊　处.

### 2.01.5 Literal translation Poetry Tune: Green jade table, title: New Year's Day Evening

A thousand trees are in full bloom at night on the east wind. The wind blows and the stars fall like rain. The precious horse-drawn carving cart fills the road with its fragrance. The sound of the phoenix flute resounds, the light of the jade pot flickers, and the night is filled with the dance of fish and dragons.

Moths, snow willows, golden threads, laughter and a faint fragrance fade away. Looking for her for thousand times in the crowd, looking back suddenly, that person is there, in the dimly lit corner.

## 2.01.6 A more polished and stylistically enhanced translation of the lyrics

A thousand trees are in full bloom at night, illuminated by the gentle breeze of the east wind. Fireworks fall like rain, dazzling the sky. Precious horse-drawn carriages fill the streets with their lingering fragrance. The melodious sound of the phoenix flute echoes, while the flickering light of the jade pot dances across the scene. The vibrant performances of fish and dragon lanterns last for whole night.

Moth-like ornaments, willows adorned with snow, and golden threads embellish the festive atmosphere. Amidst laughter and a faint fragrance, the crowd gradually disperses. I have searched for her countless times among the throng, only to find her after a final glance. She is standing quietly in a dimly lit corner.

### 2.01.7 Translation sentence by sentence

东风夜放花千树.
A thousand trees are in full bloom at night, illuminated by the gentle breeze of the east wind.
更吹落,星如雨.
Fireworks fall like rain, dazzling the sky.
宝马雕车香满路.
Precious horse-drawn carriages fill the streets with their lingering fragrance.
凤箫声动,
The melodious sound of the phoenix flute echoes,
玉壶光转，一夜鱼龙舞.
while the flickering light of the jade pot dances across the scene. The vibrant performances of fish and dragon lanterns last for whole night.
蛾儿雪柳黄金缕.
Moth-like ornaments, willows adorned with snow, and golden threads embellish the festive atmosphere.
笑语盈盈暗香去.
Amidst laughter and a faint fragrance, the crowd gradually disperses.

众里寻她千百度.

I have searched for her countless times among the throng,

蓦然回首，那人却在，灯火阑珊处.

only to find him after a final glance. She is standing quietly in a dimly lit corner.

### 2.01.8 Brief introduction of the author of the poem (lyrics)

辛弃疾（公元 1140 年 - 1207 年），字幼安，号稼轩，山东东路济南府历城县人.南宋豪放派词人.辛弃疾生于金国，少年时代开始抗金后归宋，曾任江西安抚使、福建安抚使等职.

Xin Qi Ji (1140 - 1207 AD), styled You An, with the pseudonym Jiaxuan (Straw pavilion,) was from Licheng County, Jinan, Shandong East Road. He is a bold and unrestrained lyricist and general of the Southern Song Dynasty. Xin Qiji was born in the Jin Dynasty. After resisting the Jin in his youth, he returned to the Song Dynasty and held positions such as the Pacification Commissioner of Jiangxi and Fujian.

# 2.02 Song No.02, A Spring morning

## 春晓　唐　孟浩然

**Title of the poem: A Spring morning**
**Author of the poem (lyrics), Tang Dynasty, Meng Hao Ran**

### 2.02.0 About the score and lyrics (poem)

This score (sheet music) is derived (excerpted) from the (pieces) of Gökvalsen (The Cuckoo Waltz), and has undergone minor modifications to ensure a better alignment between the musical arrangement and the lyrics (poem).

This "Waltz of the Cuckoo" is the most widely spread and has made Jonathan famous throughout the world. A tone imitating the call of a cuckoo appears. The melodious chirping of birds and the relaxed three-beat rhythm create a gentle and charming atmosphere, with a distinct singing quality.

Describing the feelings of spring, the lyrics (the poem, original text and its translation see the following sections) and music are very similar, so it is quite appropriate for lyrics and music to match each other. Therefore it is well worth to try to combine the lyrics and the music. Thus the author incorporates this poem into that renowned musical composition.

## 2.02.1 Sheet music

$1 = C \quad \frac{3}{4}$

| 5 – 3 | 1 – 3 | 1 – 3 | 5  5  7 | 1  3 | 2 – 4 | 7 – 2 | 5 – 2 |
| 春 眠 | 不 觉 | 晓, 处 | 处 | 闻 啼 | 鸟. 春 | 眠 不 | 觉 晓, |

| 4  4  2 | 7  2 | 1 – 3 | 6  6 | 4  6 | 4  6 | 2  1 | 7  2 |
| 处 处 | 闻 啼 | 鸟. | 夜 来 | 风 雨 | 声, | 花 | 落 |

| 1  6 | 5  3 | 1  3 | 6  5 | 0  3 | 2  1 | 0  5 | 5  1 | 0 |
| 知 多 | 少. 春 | 眠 不 | 觉 晓, | 花 | 落 | 知 | 多 少. |

## 2.02.2 Sheet music with Lyrics marked in Chinese pinyin without tones

| 5 – 3 | 1 – 3 | 1 – 3 | 5  5  7 | 1  3 | 2 – 4 | 7 – 2 | 5 – 2 |
| chun mian | bu jue xiao | chu chu | wen ti | niao chun | mian bu | jue xiao |
| 春 眠 | 不 觉 晓, | 处 处 | 闻 啼 | 鸟. 春 | 眠 不 | 觉 晓, |

| 4  4  2 | 7  2 | 1 – 3 | 6  6 | 4  6 | 4  6 | 2  1 | 7  2 |
| chu chu | wen ti niao | ye lai | feng yu | sheng | hua | luo |
| 处 处 | 闻 啼 鸟. | 夜 来 | 风 雨 | 声, | 花 | 落 |

| 1  6 | 5  3 | 1  3 | 6  5 | 0  3 | 2  1 | 0  5 | 5  1 | 0 |
| zhi duo shao | chun mian bu | jue xiao | hua luo | zhi duo shao |
| 知 多 少. | 春 眠 不 | 觉 晓, | 花 落 | 知 多 少. |

### 2.02.3 Text of the lyrics

春眠不觉晓，处处闻啼鸟.
夜来风雨声，花落知多少.

### 2.02.4 Text of the lyrics marked with tones in Chinese pinyin

chūn mián bù jué xiǎo　chǔ chù wén　tí　niǎo
　春　　眠　不　觉　晓，处　处　闻　啼　鸟.
yè lái fēng yǔ shēng huā luò zhī duō shǎo
夜来　风　雨　声，花　落　知　多　少.

### 2.02.5 Literal translation of the lyrics

In spring, one sleeps without realizing dawn; everywhere one hears the chirping of birds. Hearing the sounds of wind and rain in the night, who knows how many flowers have fallen.

### 2.02.6 A more polished and stylistically enhanced translation of the lyrics

In spring, one may fall asleep without realizing that dawn has arrived, and the chirping of birds can be heard everywhere. Hearing the sounds of wind and rain during the night raise the question and regret of how many flowers have fallen.

### 2.02.7 Translation sentence by sentence

春眠不觉晓，
In spring, one may fall asleep without realizing that dawn has arrived,
处处闻啼鸟.
and the chirping of birds can be heard everywhere.
夜来风雨声，花落知多少.
Hearing the sounds of wind and rain during the night raise the question and regret of how many flowers have fallen.

## 2.02.8 Brief introduction of the author of the poem (lyrics)

孟浩然（公元 689 - 740），名浩，字浩然，号孟山人，襄州襄阳（现湖北襄阳）人，世称孟襄阳。因他未曾入仕，又称之为孟山人，是唐代著名的山水田园派诗人.

Meng Haoran (689 -740 AD), whose given name was Hao, courtesy name was Haoran, and pseudonym was Meng shan ren (Hermit Meng), was from Xiangyang, Xiangzhou, and was known as Meng Xiangyang. As he never entered public service, he was also called Meng Shanren and was a renowned poet of the landscape and pastoral school in the Tang Dynasty.

# 2.03 Song No 03, Thoughts on a Quiet Night

静夜思　唐　李白

**Title of the poem: Quiet Night Thought**
**Author of the poem (lyrics), Tang Dynasty, Li Bai**

### 2.03.0 About the score and lyrics (poem)

This score (sheet music) is derived (excerpted) from the (pieces) of Brahms' lullaby, and has undergone minor modifications to ensure a better alignment between the musical arrangement and the lyrics (poem). Brahms' Lullaby is classic, beautiful.

Adults who are homesick are like children. The expressing styles of lyrics (the poem, original text and its translation see the following sections) and music are similar, so it looks appropriate for lyrics and music to match each other. Therefore it is well worth to try to combine the lyrics and the music. Thus the author rewrites the poem (lyrics) for the musical score.

## 2.03.1 Sheet music

$1 = C \quad \frac{3}{4}$

| 3 3 - | 5 3·3 | 5 - 3 5 | i̇ 7 6 | 6 5 - |
|---|---|---|---|---|
| 床 | 前 明 月 | 光， 疑 是 | 地 上 | 霜. |

| 0 0 2 3 | 4 2 2 3 | 4 - 2 4 | 7 6 5 7 |
|---|---|---|---|
| 床 前 | 明 月 光， | 疑 是 地 | 上 |

| i̇ - - | 0 0 1 1 | i̇ - 6 4 | 5 - 3 1 |
|---|---|---|---|
| 霜. | 举 头 | 望 明 月， | 低 头 |

| 4 5 6 | 3 5 5 - | 0 0 1 1 | i̇ - 6 4 |
|---|---|---|---|
| 思 | 故 乡 | 举 头 | 望 明 |

| 5 - 3 1 | 4·5 4 3 2 | 1 - - |
|---|---|---|
| 月， 低 头 思 | 故 乡. | |

## 2.03.2 Sheet music with Lyrics marked in Chinese pinyin without tones

```
| 3  3   -   | 5   3· 3 | 5   -   3  5 | 1̇  7  6 | 6  5   -   |
  chuang       qian ming yue guang     yi shi di shang   shuang
  床           前   明   月  光，     疑 是 地 上       霜.

| 0  0   2  3 | 4   2   2  3 | 4   -   2  4 | 7  6  5  7 |
          chuang qian   ming yue guang     yi shi di shang
          床   前       明   月  光，     疑 是 地 上

| 1̇  -   -   | 0   0   1  1 | 1̇  -   6  4 | 5   -   3  1 |
  shuang             ju tou   wang ming yue       di tou
  霜.                举 头    望   明   月，      低 头

| 4  5  6 | 3  5  5  -  | 0  0  1  1 | 1̇  -   6  4 | 5
  si gu xiang                  ju tou   wang ming yue
  思 故 乡                     举 头    望  明   月，

|  -   3  1 | 4· 5  4 | 3  2 | 1   -   -   |
      di tou si     gu xiang
      低 头 思    故 乡.
```

### 2.03.3 Text of the lyrics

床前明月光，疑是地上霜.
举头望明月，低头思故乡.

### 2.03.4 Text of the lyrics marked with tones in Chinese pinyin

chuáng qián míng yuè guāng　　yí shì dì shàng shuāng
　床　　前　　明　月　光，疑是 地　上　　霜.
jǔ tóu wàng míng yuè　　dī tóu　　sī gù xiāng
举头　　望　明　月，低头　　思故 乡.

### 2.03.5 Literal translation of the lyrics

The bright moonlight before the bed seems to be frost on the ground. Looking up at the bright moon, bowing my head, I miss my home town.

### 2.03.6 A more polished and stylistically enhanced translation of the lyrics

The bright moonlight shining before my bed resembles frost lying upon the ground. As I raise my gaze to contemplate the luminous moon, and then bow my head in reflection, thought of and miss my hometown.

### 2.03.7 Translation sentence by sentence

床前明月光，疑是地上霜.
The bright moonlight shining before my bed resembles frost lying upon the ground.
举头望明月，
As I raise my gaze to contemplate the luminous moon,
低头思故乡.
and then bow my head in reflection, thought of and miss my hometown.

## 2.03.8 Brief introduction of the author of the poem (lyrics)

　　李白（公元701年－762年），字太白，号青莲，出生于西域碎叶，祖籍甘肃省秦安县.唐朝伟大的浪漫主义诗人.人爽朗大方，乐于交友，爱好饮酒作诗.天宝三年（公元744年），李白到东都洛阳遇到杜甫，中国文学史上最伟大的两位诗人即为挚友.曾经得到唐玄宗李隆基赏识，担任翰林供奉，赐金放还后，游历全国，唐肃宗李亨即位后，卷入永王之乱，流放夜郎，辗转到达当涂县.著有《李太白集》.白所作词赋，艺术成就享有极为崇高的地位，后世誉为"诗仙"，与诗圣杜甫并称"李杜".

　　Li Bai (701 - 762 AD), courtesy name Taibai and pseudonym Qinglian, was born in Suiye of the Western Regions. His ancestral home was located in Qinan County, Gansu Province. He is the most prominent romantic poet of the Tang Dynasty. Known for his vivacious and generous personality, Li Bai was passionate about poetry and wine, and enjoyed cultivating friendships. Tianbao era (744 AD), Li Bai met Du Fu in Luoyang, which was then the eastern capital. The encounter marked the beginning of a close friendship between two literary giants whose works continue to influence Chinese culture. He was once favored by Emperor Xuanzong of Tang (Li Longji) and served as a Hanlin Academician. After being granted compensation and dismissed from court service, he embarked on extensive travels across the country. During the reign of Emperor Suzong of Tang (Li Heng), he became involved in the rebellion led by Prince Yong and was exiled to Yelang. Eventually, he found refuge at Dangtu County. He authored the "Collected Works of Li Tai Bai". His poetic and literary achievements hold an esteemed place in Chinese literary history. Revered as the "Poet Immortal," he is often paired with Du Fu, known as the "Poet Sage," and together they are referred to as "Li and Du."

# 2.04 Song No.04, To Judge Han Chuo of Yangzhou city

寄扬州韩绰判官　　唐　杜牧

**Title of the poem: To Judge Han Chuo of Yangzhou city**
**Author of the poem (lyrics), Tang Dynasty, Du Mu**

### 2.04.0 About the score and lyrics (poem)

This score (sheet music) is derived (excerpted) from the (pieces) of Schumann's Moonlit Nights, and has undergone minor modifications to ensure a better alignment between the musical arrangement and the lyrics (poem).

The romantic tones of lyrics (the poem original text and its translation see the following sections) and music evoke similar imagination and appeal in people, they are quite match each other. Thus the author incorporates this poem into that renowned musical composition.

## 2.04.1 Sheet music

$1 = C \quad \dfrac{3}{8}$

| 0 6̲ 6 | 6 6̲ 6̲ 7 | 1̲̇ 2̇ | 2 5̲ | 0 0̲ 5̲ | 1 5̲ |
|---|---|---|---|---|---|
| 青 山 隐 | 隐 水 迢 迢， | | 秋 尽 江 | | |

3̲ 2̲ 1 | 5̲ 0̲ 0 | 0 0̲ 6̲ | 6 0̲ 6̲ | 6 6̲ 7̲ | 1̲̇ 2̇ |
南 草 木 | 凋. | 二 十 | 四 | 桥 明 | 月

2̇ 5̲ | 0 0̲ 5̲ | 1̲̇ 5̲ | 3̲ 2̲ 1 | 5·̲ 5̲ | 0 0̲ 0̲ 6̲ |
夜， | 玉 人 | 何 处 | 教 吹 箫. | | 青

6 6̲ | 6 6̲ 7̲ | 1̲̇ 2̇ | 2 5̲ | 0 0̲ 5̲ | 1 5̲ | 3̲ 2̲ 1 |
山 | 隐 隐 水 | 迢 迢， | 秋 尽 | 江 南 | 草 木 |

5̲ 0̲ 0̲ 6̲ | 6 6̲ | 6 6̲ 7̲ | 1̲̇ 2̇ | 2 5̲ | 0 0̲ 5̲ |
凋. | 二 十 | 四 | 桥 明 | 月 夜， | 玉

1̲̇ 5̲ | 3̲ 2̲ 1 | 5·̲ 5̲ | 5̲ 5̲ 5̲ | 5̲ 2̲ | 1̲ 2̲ | 4̲ 3̲ | 5̲ 0̲ |
人 何 | 处 教 | 吹 箫. | 青 山 | 隐 隐 水 | 迢 迢，

5̲ 5·̲ 5̲ | 1̇ 5̲ | 6 1̲ | 6 0̲ | 6 6̲ | 6 6̲ | 6̲ 7̲ | 1̲̇ 2̇ |
秋 尽 江 | 南 | 草 木 凋. | 二 十 | | 四 桥 | 明 月

2̇ 5̲ | 0 0̲ 5̲ | 1̇ 5̲ | 0 5̲ | 0 2̲ | 1̲ 5·̲ | 5̲ | 1 5̲ |
夜， | 玉 人 何 | 处 | 教 | 吹 箫， 玉 人 何

0̲ 5̲ 0̲ | 4̲ 0̲ | 4̲ 3̲ 1 |
处 教 | 吹 | 箫.

## 2.04.2 Sheet music with Lyrics marked in Chinese pinyin without tones

| 0 6 | 6 6 | 6 6 7 | 1̇ 2̇ | 2 5 | 0 0 | 5 | 1̇ 5 |
|---|---|---|---|---|---|---|---|
| qing | shan yin yin | shui tiao | tiao | | qiu | jin jiang |
| 青 | 山 隱 隱 | 水 迢 | 迢， | | 秋 | 盡 江 |

3 2 1 5 | 0 6 0 0 6 | 6 6 7 | 1̇ 2̇ | 2 5 |
nan cao mu diao    er shi    si    qiao  ming yue    ye
南 草 未 凋． 二 十    四    橋   明 月    夜，

0 0 5 | 1̇ 5 3 2 | 1 5· | 5 | 0 0 | 0 6 | 6 6 |
    yu ren he chu jiao chui xiao            qing shan
    玉 人 何 處 教 吹 簫．         青 山

6 6 7 | 1̇ 2̇ | 2 5 | 0 0 | 5 | 1̇ 5 | 3 2 | 1 |
yin yin shui tiao   tiao       qiu  jin  jiang nan  cao mu
隱 隱 水 迢   迢，       秋  盡  江 南  草 未

5· | 0 0 6 | 6 6 6 7 | 1̇ 2̇ | 2 5 | 0 0 | 5 |
diao    er shi   si qiao ming yue    ye       yu
凋．    二 十   四 橋 明 月    夜，       玉

1̇ 5 3 2 | 1 5 5 | 5 5 | 5 2 | 1̇ 2̇ 4 | 3 5 | 0 |
ren he chu jiao chui xiao    qing shan yin yin shui tiao tiao
人 何 處 教 吹 簫．    青 山 隱 隱 水 迢 迢，

5 5· 5 | 1̇ 5 | 6 1 | 0 | 6 6 | 6 6 | 6 7 | 1̇ 2̇ |
qiu jin jiang nan cao mu diao    er shi  si    qiao  ming yue
秋 盡 江 南 草 未 凋．    二 十 四    橋   明 月

2̇ 5 | 0 0 | 5 | 1̇ 5 | 0 | 5 | 0 2 | 1 5· | 5 | 1̇ 5 |
ye         yu ren he    chu      jiao chui xiao yu ren he
夜，       玉 人 何    處      教 吹 簫． 玉 人 何

0 5 | 0 4 | 0 4 3 | 1 |
chu    jiao    chui    xiao?
處    教    吹    簫．

### 2.04.3 Text of the lyrics

青山隐隐水迢迢，秋尽江南草未凋.
二十四桥明月夜，玉人何处教吹箫.

### 2.04.4 Text of the lyrics marked with tones in Chinese pinyin

qīng shān yǐn yǐn shuǐ tiáo tiáo　qiū jǐn jiāng nán cǎo mù diāo
　青　山　隐 隐　水　迢 迢，秋 尽 江　南 草 木　凋.
er shí　sì qiáo míng yuè yè　yù rén hé chǔ jiào chuī xiāo
二 十　四 桥　明　月 夜，玉 人 何 处　教　吹　箫.

### 2.04.5 Literal translation of the lyrics

The green mountains are faintly visible and the water stretches far away. As autumn fades, the grass in the south of the Yangtze River remains withered. On a bright moonlit night over the Twenty-four Bridges, where could the beautiful lady teach someone to play the flute?

### 2.04.6 A more polished and stylistically enhanced translation of the lyrics

The verdant mountains appear faint in the distance, while the waters extend far beyond the horizon. As autumn wanes, the grasslands south of the Yangtze River remain desolate and withered. On a bright moonlit night above the Twenty-Four Bridges, one might wonder where the graceful lady imparts someone flute-playing skills.

### 2.04.7 Translation sentence by sentence

青山隐隐水迢迢，
The verdant mountains appear faint in the distance, while the waters extend far beyond the horizon.
秋尽江南草未凋.
As autumn wanes, the grasslands south of the Yangtze River remain desolate and withered.

二十四桥明月夜，
On a bright moonlit night above the Twenty-Four Bridges,
玉人何处教吹箫．
one might wonder where the graceful lady imparts someone flute-playing skills.

### 2.04.8 Brief introduction of the author of the poem (lyrics)

杜牧（公元 803 - 852 年），字牧之，号樊川居士，京兆万年（今陕西西安）人．杜牧是唐代杰出的诗人，散文家．唐文宗大和二年 26 岁中进士，授弘文馆校书郎．后赴江西观察使幕，理人国史馆修撰，等职．

Du Mu (803 AD - 852 AD), was styled Mu Zhi and with the pseudonym Fan Chuan Jushi, was from Wan Nian, Jingzhao (now Xi 'an, Shaanxi Province). Du Mu was an outstanding poet and essayist of the Tang Dynasty. In the second year of the Taiwa era of Emperor Wenzong of Tang, at the age of 26, he passed the imperial examination and was appointed as a librarian at the Hongwen Academy. Later, he went to Jiangxi to observe the military etc. He was in charge of the compilation of the National History Museum.

# 2.05 Song No.05, Nostalgia

## 苏幕遮　怀旧　北宋　范仲淹

**Tune of the poem: Shielding curtain made in Suzhou.**
**Title of the poem: Nostalgia**
**Author of the poem (lyrics), Northern Song Dynasty Fan Zhong Yan**

### 2.05.0 About the score and lyrics (poem)

This score (sheet music) is derived (excerpted) from a former Soviet Union song: The Nightingale Song and has undergone minor modifications to ensure a better alignment between the musical arrangement and the lyrics (poem).

The sorrowful, sentimental and melancholy mood of lyrics (the poem, original text and its translation see the following sections) and music are very match each other. Thus the author rewrites the poem (lyrics) for the song.

## 2.05.1 Sheet music

$1 = C \quad \frac{4}{4}$

| 6 3 2 6 | 4 5 4 3 2 3 - | 2 3 2 1 2 |
碧云 天,红　　叶 地, 秋色 连波,

3 1 | 7 3 6 - | 6 3 3 2 6 | 4 5 4 3 2 |
波上寒烟翠,　山映 斜阳天　　接

3 2 | 1 5 6 5 4 | 3 2 7 3 | 6 0 4 3 4 |
水,芳草无情,　更在斜阳外. 黯乡

5 3 1 6 | 6 5 4 3 4 | 5 3 1 - | 2 3 5 4 |
魂,追旅思,夜夜除非, 好梦留 人　　睡.

3 5 3 6 - | 2 1 2 3 3 2 | 6 - - - | 2 3
明月楼高 休　独　倚,　　　酒入

5 4 | 3 5 3 6 - | 2 1 2 3 3 2 | 6 - - -
愁肠,化　作 相　思　泪.

## 2.05.2 Sheet music with Lyrics marked in Chinese pinyin without tones

```
6·  3   2   6 | 4  5  4   3  2   3   —  | 2   3   2   1   2 |
bi  yun     tian hong        ye     di      qiu     se      lian bo
碧  云      天,  红           叶     地,    秋      色,     连   波,

3   1   7·  3   6·  —  | 6  3   3   2   6 | 4  5  4   3   2
bo  shang han shan cui      shan yin     xie yang tian      jie
波  上   寒  烟  翠.         山   映     斜  阳   天        接

3·  2 | 1   5   6   5  4 | 3   2   7   3 | 6   0   4   3  4 |
      shui fang cao wu  qing     geng zai xie yang wai      an xiang
      水,  芳   草  无  情,      更   在  斜  阳   外.      黯  乡

5   3   1   6·  6   5   4   3  4 | 5   3   1   —  | 2   3   5
hun zhui lv  si  ye  ye  chu fei      hao meng liu      ren
魂, 追   旅  思, 夜  夜  除  非,     好   梦  留       人

4 | 3   5   3   6   —  | 2   1   2   3   3   2 | 6   —  —  — |
shui ming yue lou gao       xiu         du           yi
睡, 明   月  楼  高        休          独           倚,

2   3   5   4 | 3   5  3   6   —  | 2   1   2   3   3   2   |
jiu ru  chou chang hua         zuo         xiang       si
酒  入  愁  肠,  化            作          相         思

6·  —  —  — |
lei
泪.
```

### 2.05.3 Text of the lyrics

碧云天，红叶地，秋色连波，波上寒烟翠.
山映斜阳天接水，芳草无情，更在斜阳外.
黯乡魂，追旅思，夜夜除非，好梦留人睡.
明月楼高休独倚，酒入愁肠，化作相思泪.

### 2.05.4 Text of the lyrics marked with tones in Chinese pinyin

bì yún tiān hóng yè   dì   qiū sè lián bō bō shàng hán yān cuì
碧 云   天, 红 叶   地, 秋 色 连 波, 波  上   寒  烟 翠.
shān yìng xià yang tiān jiē shuǐ   fāng cǎo wú qíng gèng zài xià yang wài
山   映  斜  阳  天  接  水,   芳   草  无  情, 更   在  斜  阳  外.
àn xiāng hún   zhuī lǚ sī   yè yè chú fēi   hǎo mèng liú rén shuì
黯  乡   魂,   追   旅 思, 夜 夜 除 非,   好   梦   留  人  睡.
míng yuè lóu gāo xiū dú yǐ   jiǔ rù chóu cháng huà zuò xiāng sī lèi
明   月   楼 高  休  独 倚, 酒  入 愁   肠,    化  作  相   思 泪.

### 2.05.5 Literal translation of the lyrics

The sky is blue with clear clouds, the ground is red with leaves, the autumn colors stretch on the waves, and the cold smoke on the waves is green. The mountains reflect the setting sun, the sky meets the water, the fragrant grass is heartless, and it lies beyond the setting sun. The homesick soul and the yearning for the journey worry me every night, unless, sweet dreams keep one asleep. The bright moon is shining on the high tower, so I don't lean alone. Wine flows into my heart full of sorrow, turning into tears of longing.

### 2.05.6 A more polished and stylistically enhanced translation of the lyrics

The sky is a clear blue with scattered clouds, while the ground is adorned with red leaves; autumn hues extend across the water, and a faint greenish mist hovers above the waves. Mountains mirror the glow of the setting sun, where sky and water meet seamlessly. The fragrant grass appears indifferent, stretching beyond the horizon beneath the fading light. The homesick soul and the yearning for the journey worry me every night, unless, sweet dreams keep one asleep. High above the tower shines a bright moon, yet I find no solace in leaning upon the railing alone. Wine flows into my sorrow-laden heart, ultimately transforming into tears of longing.

### 2.05.7 Translation sentence by sentence

碧云天，红叶地，
The sky is a clear blue with scattered clouds, while the ground is adorned with red leaves;
秋色连波，波上寒烟翠.
autumn hues extend across the water, and a faint greenish mist hovers above the waves.
山映斜阳天接水，
Mountains mirror the glow of the setting sun, where sky and water meet seamlessly.
芳草无情，更在斜阳外.
The fragrant grass appears indifferent, stretching beyond the horizon beneath the fading light.
黯乡魂，追旅思，夜夜除非，好梦留人睡.
The homesick soul and the yearning for the journey worry me every night, unless, sweet dreams keep one asleep.
明月楼高休独倚，
High above the tower shines a bright moon, yet I find no solace in leaning upon the railing alone.
酒入愁肠，化作相思泪.
Wine flows into my sorrow-laden heart, ultimately transforming into tears of longing.

### 2.05.8 Brief introduction of the author of the poem (lyrics)

范仲淹（公元989年－1052年），字希文.居苏州吴县. 北宋初年政治家，文学家.大中祥符八年（1015年），范仲淹苦读及第，授广德军司理参军.后历任兴化县令，等职，因秉公直言而屡遭贬斥.皇祐四年（1052年），改知颍州.

  Fan Zhongyan (989 - 1052 AD), was styled Xiwen. Home: Su state Wu county. He was a politician and litterateur in the early Northern Song Dynasty. In the eighth year of the Dazhong Xiangfu era (1015 AD), Fan Zhongyan studied hard and passed the imperial examination, being appointed as the commander of the Guangde Army. Later, he held positions such as the magistrate of Xinghua County, etc. However, he was repeatedly demoted for his fair and straight forward speech. In the fourth year of the reign of Emperor Huangyou (1052 AD), he was transferred to the position of governor of Yingzhou.

# 2.06 Song No.06, Joy At Meeting

## 相见欢　五代　李煜

**Tune of the poem: Joy At Meeting**
**Author of the poem (lyrics), Song Tang Dynasty, Li Yu**

### 2.06.0 About the score and lyrics (poem)

This score (sheet music) is derived (excerpted) from the (pieces) of Fleece's Lullaby (This piece was once mistakenly believed to be composed by Mozart), and has undergone minor modifications to ensure a better alignment between the musical arrangement and the lyrics (poem). The author rewrites the (poem) lyrics for the song.

## 2.06.1 Sheet music

$1 = C \quad \frac{2}{4}$

| 3 4 3 2 1 2 | 1 0 0 | 1 4 4 4 5 6 | 5 — |
| 无 言 独 上 西 楼, | 月 | 如 | 钩. |

2 1 2 2 1 2 | 4 0 0 | 3 3 3 4 3 4 | 5 —
寂 寞 梧 桐 深 院 锁 清 秋.

6 6 6 6 5 6 | i 0 0 | 5 5 5 5 4 5 | i —
剪 不 断, 理 还 乱,

4 5 4 3 4 5 | 2 0 0 | 3 4 3 2 1 2 | 1 —
是 离 愁, 别 是 一 般

5 5 4 4 3 4 2 | 1 —
滋 味 在 心 头

3 4 3 2 1 2 | 1 0 | 1 4 4 4 5 6 | 5 —
林 花 谢 了 春 红, 太 匆 匆

2 1 2 2 1 2 | 4 0 | 3 3 3 4 3 4 | 5 —
无 奈 朝 来 寒 雨 晚 来 风.

6 6 6 6 5 6 | i 0 | 5 5 5 5 4 5 | i —
胭 脂 泪 相 留 醉

4 5 4 3 4 5 | 2 0 | 3 4 3 2 1 2 | 1 —
几 时 重 自 是 人 生

5 5 4 4 3 4 2 | 1 — |
长 恨 水 长 东

## 2.06.2 Sheet music with Lyrics marked in Chinese pinyin without tones

```
3  4  3   2  1  2  | 1  0 | 1   4  4   4  5  6 | 5  —
wu yan du shang xi    lou    yue         ru       gou
无  言  独   上   西    楼，   月          如        钩.

2  1  2   2  1  2  | 4  0 | 3  3  3  | 4  3  4 | 5  —
ji mo     wu          tong   shen yuan  suo qing   qiu.
寂 寞     梧           桐     深   院    锁  清     秋.

6  6  6  | 6  5  6 | 1  0 | 5  5  5 | 5  4  5 | 1  —
jian       bu          duan   li       hai       luan
剪         不          断，   理       还        乱，

4  5  4 | 3  4  5 | 2  0 | 3  4  3 | 2  1  2 | 1  —
shi       li          chou.  bie shi   yi        ban
是        离          愁.    别  是    一        般

5  5  4  4 | 3  4  2 | 1  —  |
zi   wei     zai xin    tou
滋   味     在  心     头.

3  4  3   2  1  2  | 1  0 | 1   4  4   4  5  6 | 5  —
lin hua   xie le chun hong   tai         cong     cong
林  花    谢 了  春   红，   太          匆       匆.

2  1  1   2     1  2  | 4  0 | 3  3  3  | 4  3  4 | 5  —
wu    nai zhao       lai      han yu      wan lai    feng
无    奈  朝          来      寒  雨      晚  来     风

6  6  6  | 6  5  6 | 1  0 | 5  5  5 | 5  4  5 | 1  —
yan zhi                lei    xiang     liu       zui
胭  脂                 泪，   相        留        醉

4  5  4 | 3  4  5 | 2  0 | 3  4  3 | 2  1  2 | 1  —
ji         shi        chong  zi   shi   ren       sheng
几        时         重     自   是   人        生

5  5  4  4 | 3  4  2 | 1  —  |
chang hen   shui chang  dong
长    恨    水   长     东
```

### 2.06.3 Text of the lyrics (a)

无言独上西楼，月如钩. 寂寞梧桐深院锁清秋.
剪不断，理还乱，是离愁. 别是一般滋味在心头.

### 2.06.4 Text of the lyrics marked with tones in Chinese pinyin (a)

wú yán dú shàng xī lóu yuè rú gōu jì mò wú tong shēn yuàn suǒ qīng qiū
无　言 独　上　 西楼， 月 如钩. 寂寞 梧 桐　深　 院 锁 清　秋.

jiǎn bù duàn　 lǐ hái luàn shì lí chóu bié shì yì bān zī wèi zài xīn tóu
剪　不 断，理还　乱, 是离 愁. 别 是一 般 滋 味 在 心 头.

### 2.06.5 Literal translation of the lyrics (a)

I climbed up the Western tower alone in silence, and the moon was like a hook. The lonely paulownia trees lock the clear autumn in the deep courtyard. Unbreakable and tangled, it is the sorrow of parting. It's a special taste lingering in the heart.

### 2.06.6 A more polished and stylistically enhanced translation of the lyrics (a)

I ascended the western tower in solitude, where the moon hung like a hook. The solitary parasol trees enclosed the crisp autumn air within the depths of the courtyard. Inseparable and entangled, the sorrow of parting lingers. A unique emotion that remains deeply etched in the heart.

### 2.06.7 Translation sentence by sentence of lyrics (a)

无言独上西楼，月如钩.
I ascended the western tower in solitude, where the moon hung like a hook.
寂寞梧桐深院锁清秋.
The solitary parasol trees enclosed the crisp autumn air within the depths of the courtyard.
剪不断，理还乱，是离愁.

Inseparable and entangled, the sorrow of parting lingers,
别是一般滋味在心头.
A unique emotion that remains deeply etched in the heart.

### 2.06.8 Text of the lyrics (b)

林花谢了春红，太匆匆.无奈朝来寒雨晚来风.
胭脂泪,相醉,几时重.自是人生长恨水长东.

### 2.06.9 Text of the lyrics marked with tones in Chinese pinyin (b)

lín huā xiè le chūn hóng tài cōng cōng wú nài zhāo lái hán yǔ wǎn lái fēng
林 花 谢 了 春 红, 太 匆 匆. 无 奈 朝 来 寒 雨 晚 来 风.
yān zhī lèi xiǎng liú zuì   jǐ shí zhòng
胭 脂泪, 相 留 醉, 几时 重.
zì shì rén shēng cháng hèn shuǐ zhǎng dōng
自是 人 生 长 恨 水 长 东.

### 2.06.10 Literal translation of the lyrics (b)

The spring flowers in the forest have withered, too quickly. Alas, cold rain comes in the morning and wind in the evening. The crimson tears, I wish to stay intoxicated, when will they ever return? Of course, as people, they always regret the water flowing eastward.

### 2.06.11 A more polished and stylistically enhanced translation of the lyrics (b)

The spring flowers in the forest have withered， far too quickly. Unfortunately, cold rain arrives in the morning, and evening brings strong winds. I long to remain immersed in their sorrow，as for the crimson tears. When could they ever return? Indeed, as people, they always regret the passage of time, just as water flows inevitably eastward.

## 2.06.12 Translation sentence by sentence of lyrics (a)

林花谢了春红，太匆匆.
The spring flowers in the forest have withered, far too quickly.
无奈朝来寒雨晚来风.
Unfortunately, cold rain arrives in the morning, and evening brings strong winds.
胭脂泪，相醉，几时重.
I long to remain immersed in their sorrow, as for the crimson tears. When could they ever return.
自是人生长恨水长东.
Indeed, as people, they always regret the passage of time, just as water flows inevitably eastward.

## 2.06.13 Brief introduction of the author of the poem (lyrics)

李煜，五代十国时南唐国君，公元961年 - 975年在位，字重光.于宋建隆二年（961年）继位，史称李后主.开宝八年，宋军破南唐都城，李煜降宋，被俘至汴京.后因作感怀故国的词《虞美人》被宋太宗毒死.李煜书法，绘画，音律，诗和文均有造诣，尤以词的成就高.

Li Yu, the ruler of the Southern Tang during the Five Dynasties and Ten Kingdoms period, reigned from 961 AD to 975 AD, and his courtesy name was Chongguang. He ascended the throne in the second year of Jianlong of the Song Dynasty (961) and was historically known as Li Houzhu. In the eighth year of Kaibao, the Song army captured the capital of the Southern Tang. Li Yu surrendered to the Song Dynasty and was captured and taken to Bianjing. Later, he was poisoned to death by Emperor Taizong of Song for writing the poem "Yu Meiren" expressing his feelings for his homeland. Li Yu was accomplished in calligraphy, painting, music, poetry and prose, with his achievements in ci poetry being particularly outstanding.

# 2.07 Song No.07, Greenish Willows

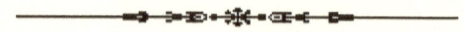

## 竹枝词　唐　刘禹锡

**Tune of the poem: Greenish Willows.**
**Author of the poem (lyrics), Tang Dynasty, Liu Yu Xi**

### 2.07.0 About the score and lyrics (poem)

This score (sheet music) is derived from the famous folk song of Australia: Shearling (Click Go the Shears), and has undergone minor modifications to ensure a better alignment between the musical arrangement and the lyrics (poem).

Shearling "Click Go the Shears" is one of the most famous and iconic folk songs of Australia. With its Australian theme and wide popularity, it has become part of Australia's folk music tradition.

The ups and downs of young people's emotions along with the rhythm of labor movements during their work is the singing here implies and expresses the emotions between young men and women, it happens that there is a similar case, the poem as well. Accordingly, the author rewrites the poem (lyrics) for the song.

## 2.07.1 Sheet music

$1 = C \quad \frac{3}{4}$

| 3 3  3 2  1 3 5 | i̇ i̇  i̇ 7  6 | 5 5 6 |
|---|---|---|
| 杨 柳  青 青  江 水 平, 闻 郎 |

| 5 3 1 | 2  2 3  2 | 3 3  3 2  1 3 5 | i̇ |
| 岸 上  踏 歌  声. 东  边  日  出 西 |

| i̇ 7 6 | 2̇ i̇  7 6  5 4  3 2 | 1 i̇  i̇ i̇  i̇ |
| 边  雨, 道 是 无 晴 却 有 晴, 却 有 晴. |

| 2̇  2̇ i̇  7  2̇ | i̇ 3  i̇ | 6  6̇ 7  i̇ 6 | 5 5 |
| 杨 柳  青 青 江 水 平, 闻 郎  岸 上 踏 |

| i̇ i̇  2 2 | 3 3  3 3  3 2  1 3 5 | i̇ i̇  i̇ 7 |
| 歌  声. 东  边  日  出 西 边 |

| 6 | 2̇ i̇  7 6  5 4 | 3  2  1 | i̇ i̇  i̇ i̇  i̇ | |
| 雨, 道 是 无 晴 却 有 晴, 却 有  晴. |

## 2.07.2 Sheet music with Lyrics marked in Chinese pinyin without tones

```
3  3   3  2 | 1  3  5 | 1̇  1̇   1̇  7 | 6 | 5   5  6
yang   liu   qing   qing  jiang  shui   ping  wen  lang
杨     柳    青     青    江     水,    平,   闻    郎

5  3   1 | 2   2  3  2 | 3  3   3  2 | 1   3  5 | 1̇
an shang   ta  ge    sheng dong   bian    ri chu    xi
岸 上      踏  歌.    声.   东     边     日 出     西

1̇  7   6 | 2̇  1̇   7  6 | 5  4 | 3  2 | 1 | 1̇  1̇ | 1̇
bian   yu   dao shi   wu qing  que    you   qing  que  you   qing
边     雨,  道 是    无 晴    却    有    晴.   却    有    晴.

2̇  2̇   1̇ | 7  2̇ | 1̇  3  1̇ | 6 | 6̇  7 | 1̇ | 6   5  5
yang liu   qing qing   jiang shui ping,  wen lang    an  shang ta
杨   柳    青   青     江    水   平,    闻  郎      岸  上    踏

1̇  1̇ | 2   3  3  3 | 3  2 | 1   3  5 | 1̇  1̇   1̇  7
ge    sheng  dong       bian    ri chu   xi         bian
歌.   声.    东         边     日 出    西         边

6 | 2̇  1̇   7  6   5  4 | 3  2 | 1 | 1̇  1̇ | 1̇  1̇ | 1̇ |
yu    dao shi   wu qing   que you   qing    que  you   qing
雨,   道 是    无 晴     却  有    晴.    却   有    晴.
```

### 2.07.3 Text of the lyrics

杨柳青青江水平，闻郎岸上踏歌声，
东边日出西边雨，道是无晴（情）却有晴（情）．

### 2.07.4 Text of the lyrics marked with tones in Chinese pinyin

yang liǔ qīng qīng jiāng shuǐ ping wén láng ān shàng tà gē shēng
　杨　柳　青　青　江　水　平，闻　郎　岸　上　踏歌　声．
dōng biān rì chū xī biān yǔ　dào shì wú qíng què yǒu qíng
　东　边　日　出西　边　雨，道　是　无　晴　却　有　晴．

### 2.07.5 Literal translation of the lyrics

The willows are green and the river water is flowing with the same level of banks. One can hear the singing of youth just following on his stepping on the bank of the river. The sun rises in the east while it rains in the west. It seems there is no clear weather (no affection), but there is clear weather (affection).

### 2.07.6 A more polished and stylistically enhanced translation of the lyrics

The willows are verdant, and the river water is at bank level. Hearing the young boys are singing that are synchronizing with their rhythm of walking steps on the riverbank. The sun rises in the east, while rain falls in the west. It appears that there is no clear weather (no affection), yet there is clarity in both weather and emotion.

### 2.07.7 Translation sentence by sentence

杨柳青青江水平，
willows are verdant, and the river water is at bank level.
闻郎岸上踏歌声，
Hearing the young boys are singing that are synchronizing with their rhythm of walking steps on the riverbank.

东边日出西边雨,
The sun rises in the east, while rain falls in the west.
道是无晴（情）却有晴（情）.
It appears that there is no clear weather (no affection), yet there is clarity in both weather and emotion.

### 2.07.8 Brief introduction of the author of the poem (lyrics)

刘禹锡（公元 772 – 842）字梦得，洛阳人，为匈奴族后裔. 他和柳宗元一同参与永贞年间短命的政治改革，结果一同贬谪远郡，晚年回到洛阳. 他的诗以精炼含蓄的语言表达对人生和历史的深刻理解.他在远谪湖南，四川时受到当地民歌的一些影响，创作出竹枝词，浪淘沙诸词.

Liu Yuxi (772 - 842 AD), was styled Mengde, was from Luoyang and a descendant of the Huns. He and Liu Zongyuan jointly participated in the short-lived political reforms during the Yongzhen period, and as a result, they were both demoted to distant prefectures and returned to Luoyang in their later years. His poems express a profound understanding of life and history in concise and implicit language. When he was exiled to Hunan and Sichuan, he was influenced by some local folk songs and composed poems such as Bamboo Branch and Sand Washed by Waves etc.

# 2.08 Song No.08, Prelude to Water Melody

水调歌头　　北宋　　苏轼

**Tune of the poem: Prelude to Water Melody**
**Author of the poem (lyrics), Northern Song Dynasty, Su Shi**

### 2.08.0 About the score and lyrics (poem)

This score sheet music (a) is derived (excerpted) from the (pieces) of Haydn's Serenade for strings which is one of the most delightful pieces by the Austrian composer. The score has undergone minor modifications to ensure a better alignment between the musical arrangement and the lyrics (poem).

The score sheet music (b) is derived (excerpted) from the (pieces) of Drigo's Serenade, and has undergone minor modifications to ensure a better alignment between the musical arrangement and the lyrics (poem).

For a poem or a piece of music, different people have different feelings and understandings. Even for the same person, when he or she is under different thoughts and emotions, his or her feelings and understandings may still be very different.

However, there is no doubt that this poem is very suitable to be set in a serenade. Therefore the author rewrites the poem (lyrics) for the two renowned serenades separately.

## 2.08.1 Sheet music (a) (derived from Haydn's serenade)

$1 = C \quad \frac{4}{4}$

```
| 3̇ 4̇ | 5̇ 3̇  1̇ -  | 5̇ 3̇ | 6̇ 4̇  1̇ -  | 4̇ 6̇ | 6̇ 5̇  4̇ 3̇ |
  明 月   几 时 有，   把 酒   问 青 天，    不 知   天 上 宫

  2̇ 0  i 7 | 7 i  5 - | 5 5 | 5 6  5 4  3 2 |
  阙，  今 夕 是 何 年，  我 欲  乘 风 归 去， 又 恐

  i 7 | 7 i -  | i 2 | 3  i  5 3  2 - | 2̇ i | 3̇ i  6 |
  琼 楼   玉 宇，   高     处   不 胜 寒，  起 舞  弄 清 影，

  i | 7  2̇ 2̇ - | i 7 | 7 6  6 7  5 2̇ | 0  i 7  6 5 |
  何    似 在 人  间.    在 人  间.     转     来

  2̇ | 6  i 7  6 5  5 | 0 5  4 - | 2̇ 2̇ | 2̇ 2̇  3̇ 2̇ |
  阕，  低    绮     户，   照 无   眠. 照 无   眠. 不 应

  i 7  i  i  7 | 6 7  i 7  6 5  6 | 2̇ 2̇  2̇ 7  i |
  有 恨，       何 事  长 向  别 时  圆.  人 有

  2̇ 7 | 3̇ i  5  0  2̇ 7 | 3̇ i  2̇ 7  5  0 | i̇ 5 |
  悲 欢   离 合，    月 有   阴 晴  圆  缺， 此 事

  4̇ 2̇  0 4̇ 3̇ i | 0 3̇  0  2̇ i  7 6 | 5 -  5 5 |
  古 难    全. 古 难    全.    但 愿  人 长   久，  此 事

  5̇ | 6̇ 5̇  0  5̇ 4̇  4̇ 5̇ | 4̇ 6̇  6̇ 4̇  4̇ 3̇ | i̇ - - - |
  古   难 全.    但 愿  人 长   久，  千 里   共 婵  娟.
```

## 2.08.2 Sheet music (a) with Lyrics marked in Chinese pinyin without tones

| 3 4 | 5 3 | 1 - | 5 3 | 6 4 | 1 - | 4 6 | 6 5 | 4 3 |
ming yue ji shi you ba jiu wen qing tian bu zhi tian shang gong
明 月 几 时 有, 把 酒 问 青 天. 不 知 天 上 宫

| 2 0 | 1 7 | 7 1 | 5 - | 5 5 | 5 6 | 5 4 | 3 3 | 2 |
que jin xi shi he nian wo yu cheng feng gui qu you kong
阙, 今 夕 是 何 年. 我 欲 乘 风 归 去, 又 恐

| 1 7 | 7 1 - | 1 2 | 3 1 | 5 3 | 2 - | 2 1 | 3 1 | 6 |
qiong lou yu yu gao chu bu sheng han qi wu nong qing ying
琼 楼 玉 宇, 高 处 不 胜 寒. 起 舞 弄 清 影,

| 1 | 7 2 | 2 - | 1 7 | 7 6 | 6 7 5 | 2 | 0 1 7 | 6 5 |
he si zai ren jian zai ren jian zhuan zhu
何 似 在 人 间. 在 人 间. 转 朱

| 2 6 | 1 7 | 6 5 | 5 | 0 5 | 4 - | 2 2 | 2 2 | 3 2 |
ge di qi hu zhao wu mian zhao wu mian bu ying
阁, 低 绮 户, 照 无 眠 照 无 眠. 不 应

| 1 7 | 1 1 | 7 | 6 7 | 1 7 | 6 5 | 6 | 2 2 | 2 7 | 1 |
you hen he shi zhang xiang bie shi yuan ren you
有 恨, 何 事 长 向 别 时 圆. 人 有

| 2 7 | 3 1 | 5 0 | 2 7 | 3 1 | 2 7 | 5 0 | 1 5 |
bei huan li he yue you yin qing yuan que ci shi
悲 欢 离 合, 月 有 阴 晴 圆 缺, 此 事

| 4 2 | 0 4 | 3 1 | 0 3 | 0 | 2 1 | 7 6 | 5 - | 5 5 |
gu nan quan gu nan quan dan yuan ren chang jiu ci shi
古 难 全. 古 难 全. 但 愿 人 长 久, 此 事

| 5 6 | 5 0 | 5 4 | 4 5 | 4 6 | 6 4 | 4 3 | 1 - - - |
gu nan quan dan yuan ren chang jiu qian li gong chan juan
古 难 全. 但 愿 人 长 久, 千 里 共 婵 娟.

## 2.08.3 Sheet music (b) (derived from Drigo's serenade)

```
3· 5  5 | 6 7 6  5  3 | 5· 5  6  5  4 3 | 3  2
明    月   几 时   有.       把 酒   问   青

2  1  1 | 3· 5  5 | 6 7 6  5  3 | i· i  3  4  5  7
天.   不   知    天   上 宫 阙,  今 夕   是   何

7  4 | 6 7 6  5  0 | 5 4  3 | 4  5  6  3 3 | 3
年.   今 夕 是   何    年.   我 欲   乘   风  归 去,  又

5  4  3  2  6 | 0· 7· 2 | 6 7 | 5· 5 | 0· 5  4 3 | 4
恐   琼   楼   玉 宇,  高    处  不     胜  寒.    起    舞  弄

5  6 | 6  3  3 | 3· 7  2  3 | 4  3  4 | 4· 7  3  4 |
清     影,   何  似   在    人    间.   转   朱 阁,

5  4  5 | 5· 5  4  5 | 5· i· i | 7  6  7 | i  7  6· 3 |
低    绮  户,  照   无   眠.  不  应   有       恨,

6· 7· 7 | 6  5  6  7 | 6  5· 2 | 5  4  3· | 3  3  2
何   事   长  向   别    时   圆.   人   有    悲

3  4 | 3  2  6 | 0  0 | 1  2  1  7  6 | 5  5  6  1  7
欢    离   合,          月   有   阴 晴   圆       缺,

4  3 | 3  2  1  1 | 0  0 | 1  6  5 | 4· 1 | 3  4  5 |
此  事  古  难   全.              但   愿  人    长 久,   千 里  共

5  0 | 6  i | i  0 |
婵   娟.
```

## 2.08.4 Text of the lyrics

明月几时有，把酒问青天.不知天上宫阙，今夕是何年.
我欲乘风归去，又恐琼楼玉宇，高处不胜寒.
起舞弄清影，何似在人间.转朱阁，低绮户，照无眠.
不应有恨，何事长向别时圆.
人有悲欢离合，月有阴晴圆缺，此事古难全.
但愿人长久，千里共婵娟.

## 2.08.5 Text of the lyrics marked with tones in Chinese pinyin

míng yuè jǐ shí yǒu bǎ jiǔ wèn qīng tiān bù zhī tiān shàng gōng què
　明　月 几时 有，把酒 问　青　天.不 知 天　　上 宫　阙，
jīn xī shì hé nián　wǒ yù chéng fēng guī qù　　yòu kǒng qióng lóu yù yǔ
今夕是 何　年. 我 欲 乘　　风　归 去，又　恐　　琼　　楼 玉宇，
gāo chù bù shèng hán　qǐ wǔ nòng qīng yǐng　hé sì zài rén jiān
高　处 不 胜　　寒．起舞 弄　清　　影，何似 在 人　间.
zhuǎn zhū gé　dī qǐ hù zhào wú mián　bù yīng yǒu hèn
　转　　朱 阁，低绮户，照 无　眠. 不 应　 有　恨，
hé shì zhǎng xiàng bié shí yuán rén yǒu bēi huān lí hé
何 事　长　　向　别 时　圆.人 有 悲　欢　离合，
yuè yǒu yīn qíng yuán quē　cǐ shì gǔ nán quán
月　有 阴　晴　　圆　缺，此事 古 难　全.
dàn yuàn rén cháng jiǔ qiān lǐ gong chán juān
但　愿　人　长　　久，千里 共　　婵　娟.

## 2.08.6 Literal translation of the lyrics

When will the bright moon appear? Raise the wine and ask the blue sky. I wonder what year it is in the heavenly palace tonight. I wish to return with the wind, but I'm afraid that the pavilions and palaces will be too beautiful and the high places will be too cold. Dancing and understanding, how could it be like being in this world? Turning around the vermilion pavilion and lowering the brocade door, I can't sleep. There should be no hatred about why should parting last forever? People have joys and sorrows, partings and reunions; the moon waxes and wanes. Such is the way of the world since ancient times. We wish each other a long life so as to share the beauty of this graceful moonlight, even though miles apart.

## 2.08.7 A more polished and stylistically enhanced translation of the lyrics

When will the bright moon appear? I raise my cup of wine and inquire of the azure sky. I wonder what time it is tonight in the celestial palace above. I long to return on the wind, yet fear that its pavilions and towers may be too magnificent, and the heights too cold. Dancing and appreciating the scene, how could it compare to being here in this world? Turning around the vermilion pavilions and passing through the lowered silken curtains, it shines me make me unable to sleep.   There should be no resentment about why must separationendures so long? People experience joy and sorrow, parting and reunion; the moon waxes and wanes. Such has been the nature of the world since time immemorial. May we all enjoy a long life, sharing the beauty of this gentle moonlight, even if separated by thousands miles.

## 2.08.8 Translation sentence by sentence

明月几时有,
When will the bright moon appears,
把酒问青天.
I raise my cup of wine and inquire of the azure sky.
不知天上宫阙, 今夕是何年.
I wonder what time it is tonight in the celestial palace above.
我欲乘风归去,
I long to go there by the wind,
又恐琼楼玉宇, 高处不胜寒.
yet fear that its pavilions and towers may be too magnificent, and the heights too cold.
起舞弄清影, 何似在人间.
Dancing and appreciating the scene, how could it compare to being here in this world?

转朱阁，低绮户，照无眠.
Turning around the vermilion pavilions and passing through the lowered silken curtains, it shines me make me unable to sleep.
不应有恨，何事长向别时圆？
There should be no resentment about why must separationendures so long?
人有悲欢离合，月有阴晴圆缺，此事古难全.
People experience joy and sorrow, parting and reunion; the moon waxes and wanes. Such has been the nature of the world since time immemorial.
但愿人长久，千里共婵娟.
May we all enjoy a long life, sharing the beauty of this gentle moonlight, even if separated by thousands miles.

### 2.08.9 Brief introduction of the author of the poem (lyrics)

苏轼，（公元 1037 - 1101）字子瞻、号东坡，四川省眉山人，北宋著名文学家，书法家，画家.与父苏洵，弟苏辙三人并称"三苏".苏轼是北宋中期文坛领袖，在诗词，散文，书画等方面取得很高成就.词开豪放一派，与辛弃疾并称"苏辛"；散文为"唐宋八大家"之一.嘉祐二年（1057年），参加殿试中乙科，赐进士及第.嘉祐六年（1061年），参加制科考试，授大理评事、签书凤翔府判官.宋神宗时，曾在杭州等地任职.元丰三年（1080年），因"乌台诗案"，被贬为黄州团练副使.宋哲宗即位后，出任兵部尚书，礼部尚书等职，外放治理杭州，扬州等地.随着新党执政，又被贬惠州，儋州.宋徽宗时，获赦北还，病逝于常州.

Su Shi (1037 - 1101 AD), styled Zizhan and with the pseudonym Dongpo, was from Meishan, Sichuan Province. He was a renowned literary figure, calligrapher and painter of the Northern Song Dynasty. He was known as the "Three SUS" along with his father Su Xun and his younger brother Su Zhe. Su Shi was a literary leader in the middle of the Northern Song Dynasty and achieved remarkable accomplishments in poetry, lyrics, prose, calligraphy and painting. Ci Kai was a representative of the bold and unrestrained school, and together with Xin Qiji, they were known as "Su Xin". Prose is one of the "Eight Great Prose Masters of the Tang and Song Dynasties". In the second year of the Jiayou reign (1057), he passed the second round of the palace examination and was awarded the title of Jinshi. In the sixth year of the Jiayou reign (1061), he took the imperial examination and was appointed as a judge of the Dali Department and signed the title of Judge of Fengxiang Prefecture. During the reign of Emperor Shenzong of the Song Dynasty, he held positions in Hangzhou, Mizhou, Xuzhou, Huzhou and other places. In the third year of the Yuanfeng era (1080), he was demoted to the position of deputy commander of the Huangzhou Militia due to the "Wutai Poetry Case". After ascending the throne, Emperor Zhezong of the Song Dynasty held positions such as Minister of War and Minister of Rites, and was exiled to govern Hangzhou, Yangzhou and other places. With the new Party coming to power, he was demoted to Huizhou and Danzhou again. During the reign of Emperor Huizong of the Song Dynasty, he was pardoned and returned north, and died of illness in Changzhou

# 2.09 Song No.09, Visit the villages on the west side of the mountain

### 游山西村　南宋　陆游

**Title of the poem: Visit the villages on the west side of the mountain.
Author of the poem (lyrics), Southern Song Dynasty, Lu You**

### 2.09.0 About the score and lyrics (poem)

This score (sheet music) is derived from the Czech Folk Song and has undergone minor modifications to ensure a better alignment between the musical arrangement and the lyrics (poem).

　　The author believes that this song depicts the festive life scenes in the Czech countryside (It is exactly the same as the poem). A cheerful rhythm and mood of the music is quite similar to the lyrics (the poem, original text and its translation see the following sections). Therefore the author rewrites the poem (lyrics) for the song.

## 2.09.1 Sheet music

$1 = C \quad \dfrac{2}{4}$

| 3 3 | 5 5 | 5 <u>4 4</u> | 5 <u>4 4</u> | 2 2 | 4 4 | <u>3 3</u> |
|---|---|---|---|---|---|---|
| 莫 笑 | 农 家 | 腊 酒 浑, | 腊 酒 浑, | 丰 年 | 留 客 | 鸡 豚. |

| 4 <u>3 3</u> | 1 1 | 3 3 | 3 <u>2 2</u> | 3 <u>2 2</u> | 5 5 | 6 7 |
|---|---|---|---|---|---|---|
| 足 鸡 豚. | 山 重 | 水 复 | 疑 无 路, | 疑 无 路, | 柳 暗 | 花 明 |

| 2 <u>1 1</u> | 2 <u>1 1</u> | 3 1 | 5 5 | 4 2 | 7 6 | 5 5 |
|---|---|---|---|---|---|---|
| 又 一 村. | 又 一 村. | 箫 鼓 | 追 随 | 春 社 | 近, | 衣 冠 |

| 6 7 | 2 <u>1 1</u> | 2 <u>1 1</u> | 3 1 | 5 5 | 4 2 | 7 6 |
|---|---|---|---|---|---|---|
| 简 朴 | 古 风 存. | 古 风 存. | 从 今 | 若 许 | 闲 乘 | 月, |

| 5 5 | 6 7 | 2 <u>1 1</u> | 2 <u>1 1</u> |
|---|---|---|---|
| 拄 杖 | 无 时 | 夜 叩 门. | 夜 叩 门. |

## 2.09.2 Sheet music with Lyrics marked in Chinese pinyin without tones

| 3 3 | 5 5 | 5 <u>4 4</u> | 5 <u>4 4</u> | 2 2 | 4 4 | <u>3 3</u> |
|---|---|---|---|---|---|---|
| mo xiao | nong jia | la jiu hun | la jiu hun | feng nian | liu ke | zu ji tun |
| 莫 笑 | 农 家 | 腊 酒 浑, | 腊 酒 浑, | 丰 年 | 留 客 | 鸡 豚. |

| 4 <u>3 3</u> | 1 1 | 3 3 | 3 <u>2 2</u> | 3 <u>2 2</u> | 5 5 | 6 7 |
|---|---|---|---|---|---|---|
| zu ji tun | shan zhong | shui fu | yi wu lu | yi wu lu | liu an | hua ming |
| 足 鸡 豚. | 山 重 | 水 复 | 疑 无 路, | 疑 无 路, | 柳 暗 | 花 明 |

| 2 <u>1 1</u> | 2 <u>1 1</u> | 3 1 | 5 5 | 4 2 | 7 6 | 5 5 |
|---|---|---|---|---|---|---|
| you yi cun | you yi cun | xiao gu | zhui sui | chun she | jin | yi guan |
| 又 一 村. | 又 一 村. | 箫 鼓 | 追 随 | 春 社 | 近, | 衣 冠 |

| 6 7 | 2 <u>1 1</u> | 2 <u>1 1</u> | 3 1 | 5 5 | 4 2 | 7 6 |
|---|---|---|---|---|---|---|
| jian piao | gu feng cun | gu feng cun | cong jin | ruo xu | xian cheng | yue |
| 简 朴 | 古 风 存. | 古 风 存. | 从 今 | 若 许 | 闲 乘 | 月, |

| 5 5 | 6 7 | 2 <u>1 1</u> | 2 <u>1 1</u> |
|---|---|---|---|
| zhu zhang | wu shi | ye kou men | ye kou men |
| 拄 杖 | 无 时 | 夜 叩 门. | 夜 叩 门. |

### 2.09.3 Text of the lyrics

莫笑农家腊酒浑，丰年留客足鸡豚.
山重水复疑无路，柳暗花明又一村.
箫鼓追随春社近，衣冠简朴古风存.
从今若许闲乘月，拄杖无时夜叩门.

### 2.09.4 Text of the lyrics marked with tones in Chinese pinyin

mò xiào nóng jiā　là jiǔ hún fēng nián liú kè zú jī tún
莫　笑　农　家　腊酒浑，丰　年　留客　足鸡豚.
shānc chòng shuǐ fù yí wù lù　liǔ àn huā míng yòu yī cūn
山　重　水复疑　无路，柳暗花　明　又　一　村.
xiāo gǔ zhuī suí chūn shè jìn　yì guān jiǎn pu gǔ fēng cún
箫　鼓　追　随　春　社近，衣冠　简朴古　风　存.
cóng jīn ruò xǔ xián chéng yuè　zhǔ zhàng wú shí yè kòu mén
从　今　若许　闲　乘　月，拄　杖　无时夜叩　门.

### 2.09.5 Literal translation of the lyrics

Don't laugh at the muddiness of the rural cured wine; in a bountiful year, it will retain enough guests, chickens and pork. When the mountains and rivers seem to have no way out, a bright and beautiful village appears. As the activities of spring worshipping festival approaches, the flute and drum follow, and the simple dress and ancient style remain. From now on, if I allow myself to leisurely ride the moon, leaning on a walking stick, I will knock at the door at night all the time.

### 2.09.6 A more polished and stylistically enhanced translation of the lyrics

Do not mock the rustic appearance of homemade village wine; in times of abundance, it can still generously entertain guests, with ample provisions of chickens and pork. When the mountains and rivers appear to block all paths, a bright and picturesque village emerges unexpectedly. As the ritual observance of the vernal for spring season approaches, music from flutes and drums fills the air, while villagers don traditional attire, preserving ancient customs. From this moment onward, if I am granted the leisure to wander beneath the moonlight, stick in hand, I shall eagerly visit my neighbor's home even in the late hours of the night.

### 2.09.7 Translation sentence by sentence

莫笑农家腊酒浑,
Do not mock the rustic appearance of homemade village wine;
丰年留客足鸡豚.
in times of abundance, it can still generously entertain guests, with ample provisions of chickens and pork.
山重水复疑无路,
When the mountains and rivers appear to block all paths,
柳暗花明又一村.
a bright and picturesque village emerges unexpectedly.
箫鼓追随春社近,
As the ritual observance of the vernal for spring season approaches, music from flutes and drums fills the air,
衣冠简朴古风存.
while villagers don traditional attire, preserving ancient customs.
从今若许闲乘月,
From this moment onward, if I am granted the leisure to wander beneath the moonlight,
拄杖无时夜叩门.
stick in hand, I shall eagerly visit my neighbor's home even in the late hours of the night.

### 2.09.8 Brief introduction of the author of the poem (lyrics)

陆游（公元 1125 - 1210），字务观，号放翁.越州山阴（今浙江绍兴）人，南宋爱国著名诗人.少时受家庭爱国思想熏陶，高宗时应礼部试，为奸相秦桧所黜.孝宗时赐进士出身.中年入蜀，投身军旅.

Lu You (1125 - 1210 AD), styled Wuguan, with the pseudonym

Fangweng, was a renowned patriotic poet from Shaoxing, Zhejiang Province during the Southern Song Dynasty. Born into a family with strong patriotic values, he was deeply influenced by these ideals from an early age. During the reign of Emperor Gaozong, Lu You passed the imperial examination conducted by the Ministry of Rites but was later dismissed due to political conflicts involving the treacherous primer minister Qin Hui. Under Emperor Xiaozong's rule, he was reinstated and awarded the prestigious Jinshi degree. In his middle age, he traveled to Sichuan and participated in military activities.

# 2.10 Song No.10, Memories of the lower reaches of the Yangtze River regions

忆江南　唐　白居易

**Tune of the poem: Memories of the lower reaches of the Yangtze River regions.
Author of the poem (lyrics), Tang Dynasty, Bai Ju Yi**

### 2.10.0 About the score and lyrics (poem)

This score (sheet music) is derived from the Danish Folk Song: Harvest Song, and has undergone minor modifications to ensure a better alignment between the musical arrangement and the lyrics (poem).

The cheerful and joyful mood is in perfect harmony with the poem, the author rewrites the poem (lyrics) for the song.

### 2.10.1 Sheet music

$1 = C \quad \frac{2}{4}$

| $\dot{1}$ 5 3 | 1 3 5 | 1 3 5 | $\dot{1}$ - | 4 6 6 6 | 3 5 |
江 南 好，风　　景　　旧 曾 谙，日 出 江 花 红 胜

| 3 5 | 2 4 3 2 | 1 0 | $\dot{1}$ 5 3 | 1 3 5 | 1 3 5 |
火，　红　　胜　　火，江 南 好，风　　景　　旧 曾

| $\dot{1}$ - | 4 6 6 6 | 3 5 5 5 | 2 4 3 2 | 1 0 |
谙，日 出 江 花 红 胜 火，　红　　胜　　火，

| $\dot{1}$ $\dot{1}$ | 7 $\dot{2}$ | 5 | 2 2 | $\dot{1}$ $\dot{3}$ | 5 | 4 6 6 6 | 3 5 |
春 来 江　　水　　绿　　如　　蓝，春 来 江 水 绿 如

| 5 5 | 2 4 3 2 | 1 0 |
蓝，　能 不 忆 江 南。

### 2.10.2 Sheet music with Lyrics marked in Chinese pinyin without tones

| $\dot{1}$ 5 3 | 1 3 5 | 1 3 5 | $\dot{1}$ - | 4 6 6 6 | 3 5 |
jiang nan hao　feng jing　　jiu zeng　　an　　ri chu jiang hua hong sheng
江 南 好　风 景　　旧 曾　　谙　　日 出 江 花 红 胜

| 3 5 | 2 4 3 2 | 1 0 | $\dot{1}$ 5 3 | 1 3 5 | 1 3 5 |
huo　　hong　　sheng　　huo　　jiang nan hao feng　jing jiu　zeng
火　　红　　胜　　火　　江 南 好，风　　景 旧　曾

| $\dot{1}$ - | 4 6 6 6 | 3 5 5 5 | 2 4 3 2 | 1 0 |
an　　ri chu jiang hua hong sheng huo　　hong　　sheng　　huo
谙　日 出 江 花 红 胜 火　　红　　胜　　火

| $\dot{1}$ $\dot{1}$ | 7 $\dot{2}$ | 5 | 2 2 | $\dot{1}$ $\dot{3}$ | 5 | 4 6 6 6 | 3 5 |
chun lai jiang　　shui　　lv　　ru　　lan chun lai jiang shui lv ru
春 来 江　　水　　绿　　如　　蓝，春 来 江 水 绿 如

| 5 5 | 2 4 3 2 | 1 0 |
lan　　neng bu yi jiang nan.
蓝。　能 不 忆 江 南。

### 2.10.3 Text of the lyrics

江南好，风景旧曾谙.日出江花红胜火，
春来江水绿如蓝.能不忆江南.

### 2.10.4 Text of the lyrics marked with tones in Chinese pinyin

jiāng nán hǎo　　fēng jǐng jiù zēng ān　　rì chū jiāng huā hóng shèng huǒ
　江　南　好，　风　景　旧　曾　谙.　日　出　江　花　红　　胜　火，
chūn lái jiāng shuǐ lǜ rú lán néng bù yì jiāng nán
　春　来　江　水　绿 如 蓝.能 不 忆 江　　南.

### 2.10.5 Literal translation of the lyrics

The southern part of the eastern section of the Yangtze River Basin is beautiful, and its scenery is familiar to me. At sunrise, the river flowers are redder than fire; when spring comes, the river water is greener than blue. How could one not recall Jiangnan?

### 2.10.6 A more polished and stylistically enhanced translation of the lyrics

The southern part of the eastern Yangtze River Basin is picturesque, its scenery familiar to me. At sunrise, river flowers blaze redder than fire; when spring arrives, the waters turn greener than blue. How could one not recall the southern part of the eastern Yangtze River Basin?

### 2.10.7 Translation sentence by sentence

江南好，风景旧曾谙.
The southern part of the eastern Yangtze River Basin is picturesque, its scenery familiar to me.
日出江花红胜火，
At sunrise, river flowers blaze redder than fire; when spring arrives,
春来江水绿如蓝.
The waters turn greener than blue.

能不忆江南.

How could one not recall the southern part of the eastern Yangtze River Basin?

### 2.10.8 Brief introduction of the author of the poem (lyrics)

白居易（公元772年 - 846年），字乐天，号香山，生于河南新郑.是唐代伟大的现实主义诗人,唐代三大诗人之一.白居易的诗歌题材广泛,形式多样,语言平易通俗.官至翰林学士.公元846年，白居易在洛阳逝世，葬于香山.代表诗作有《长恨歌》,《卖炭翁》,《琵琶行》等

Bai Juyi (772 - 846 AD), whose courtesy name was Letian and pseudonym was Xiangshan. He was born in Xinzheng, Henan. He was a great realist poet of the Tang Dynasty and one of the three great poets of the Tang Dynasty. Bai Juyi's poems cover a wide range of subjects, have diverse forms and use plain and popular language. He rose to the position of Hanlin Scholar. In 846 AD, Bai Juyi died in Luoyang and was buried in Xiangshan. Representative poems include "The Song of Everlasting Regret" and "The Pipa Player", etc

# 2.11 Song No.11, Groping For Fish

摸鱼儿　南宋　辛弃疾

**Tune of the poem: Groping For Fish.**
**Author of the poem (lyrics), Southern Song Dynasty, Xin Qi Ji**

### 2.11.0 About the score and lyrics (poem)

This score (sheet music) is derived (excerpted) from the (pieces) of Saint-Saëns'Thoughts of the Swan，（Saint-Saëns's 'The Swan'）, and has undergone minor modifications to ensure a better alignment between the musical arrangement and the lyrics (poem).

This poem is the most solemn and sorrowful one by Xin Qi Ji, a poet of the Southern Song Dynasty. She fits the melody of the music very well, thus the author incorporate this poem into that renowned musical composition.

## 2.11.1 Sheet music

$1 = C \quad \frac{3}{4}$

| $\dot{1}$ 7 3 | 6 5 1 | 2 - 2 3 | 4 - - | 6 - 7 1 | 2 3
更 能 消 几 番 风 雨， 匆 匆 春 又 归 去.

4 5 6 7 | 3 3 0 | $\dot{1}$ 7 3 | 6 5 1 | 2 - 2 3 |
春 又 归 去.  惜 春 长 怕 花 开 早, 何 况 落 红

4 - - | 7 1 2 3 | 4 5 6 7 | $\dot{1}$ 2 | 5 - - | 5 3 $\dot{1}$
无  数. 落 红 无 数 春 且 住. 见 说 道,

6 7 $\dot{1}$ | 5 - 5 6 | 7 - - | 4 2 7 | 5 6 7 | 4 5
天 涯 芳 草 无 归 路. 怨 春 不 语. 算 只 有 殷 勤,

6 - - | 6 2 3 | 4 - 5 6 | 7 - - | 6 - - | 6 2 3 | 4 -
 画 檐 蛛 网, 尽 日 惹 飞 絮. 长 门 事, 准拟

5 6 | 7 - - | $\dot{1}$ 7 3 | 6 5 1 | 2 - 2 3 | 4 - - | 6 -
佳 期 又 误. 蛾 眉 曾 有 人 妒. 千 金 纵 买 相

7 1 | 2 3 4 5 6 7 | 3 3 0 | 3 2 6 | $\dot{1}$ 7 4 |
如 赋, 脉 脉 此 情 谁 诉. 君 莫 舞, 君 不 见 玉 环

6 5 1 | 2 3 1 0 | 3 4 5 3 | 6 - 7 5 | $\dot{1}$ $\dot{1}$ - |
飞 燕 皆 尘 土. 闲 愁 最 苦. 闲 愁 苦.

$\dot{1}$ 7 3 | 6 5 1 | 2 - 2 3 | 4 - - | 7 1 2 3 | 4 5
休 去 倚 危 栏, 休 倚 危 栏, 斜 阳 正 在 烟 柳

6 7 $\dot{1}$ 2 | 5 5 0 |
断 肠 处.

## 2.11.2 Sheet music with Lyrics marked in Chinese pinyin without tones

```
i  7   3  | 6   5   1 | 2 -   2  3 | 4 - -   | 6 -   7   1 | 2   3 |
geng neng xiao  ji  fan feng yu   cong cong   chun         you gui  qu
更   能   消    几   番   风   雨,  匆    匆     春           又   归   去

4   5   6   7 | 3   3   0 | i   7   3 | 6   5   1 | 2 -   2   3 |
chun you gui  qu            xi  chun      zhang    pa  hua    kai
春   又   归   去,           惜   春       长       怕   花     开

4 - -   | 7   1   2   3 | 4   5   6   7 | i   2 | 5 - -   | 5   3   i |
zao       he kuang luo    hong  wu  shu chun qie  zhu      jian shuo dao
早,       何   况   落    红   无   数   春   且   住,      见   说   道,

6   7   i | 5 -   5   6 | 7 - -   4   2 | 7   5   6 | 7   4   5 |
tian ya fang cao     wu gui  lu     yuan chun bu yu suan zhi you yin qin
天   涯   芳   草     无   归   路,    怨   春   不   语, 算   只   有   殷   勤,

6  | 6   2   3 | 4 -   5   6 | 7 - -   | 6 - -   | 6   2   3 | 4 -
    hua yan zhu wang  jin  ri re fei   xu         chang men shi zhun ni
     画   檐   蛛   网, 尽   日  惹  飞   絮,       长   门   事,   准   拟

5   6 | 7 - -   i   7   3 | 6   5   1 | 2 -   2   3 | 4 - -   | 6 -
jia  qi  you wu   e  mei ceng you ren du  qian jin zong      mai       xiang
佳   期   又  误, 蛾   眉   曾   有   人  妒, 千   金   纵       买       相

7   1 | 2   3   4   5 | 6   7   3   3   3 | 3   2   6 | i   7   4 |
ru  fu  mo  mo   ci qing shui  su jun mo wu jun bu jian yu        huan
如  赋, 脉  脉   此   情   谁   诉, 君   莫  舞, 君   不   见   玉     环

6   5 | 1   2   3   1 | 0   3   4   5   3 | 6 -   7   5 | i   1 - |
fei     yan jie chen tu       xian chou  zui      ku    xian chou  ku
飞,    燕   皆   尘   土,      闲   愁    最       苦,   闲   愁    苦,

i   7   3 | 6   5   1 | 2 -   2   3 | 4 - -   | 7   1   2   3 | 4   5 |
xiu      qu  yi wei lan xiu    yi wei lan       xie yang zheng zai yan liu
休       去  倚  危   栏, 休     倚  危   栏,      斜   阳   正    在   烟   柳

6   7 | 1   2 | 5   5   0 |
duan    chang  chu
断      肠     处。
```

### 2.11.3 Text of the lyrics

更能消几番风雨，匆匆春又归去.惜春长怕花开早，何况落红无数.春且住.见说道，天涯芳草无归路.怨春不语.算只有殷勤，画檐蛛网，尽日惹飞絮.长门事，准拟佳期又误.蛾眉曾有人妒.千金纵买相如赋，脉脉此情谁诉.君莫舞，君不见，玉环飞燕皆尘土.闲愁最苦.休去倚危栏，斜阳正在，烟柳断肠处.

### 2.11.4 Text of the lyrics marked with tones in Chinese pinyin

gèng néng xiāo　jǐ fān fēng yǔ　cōng cōng chūn yòu guī qù
　更　能　消　几番风雨，匆匆　春又归去.
xī chūn zhǎng pà huā kāi zǎo　hé kuàng luò hóng wú shù
惜春　长 怕花开早，何况　落 红 无数.
chūn qiě zhù jiàn shuō dào　tiān yá fāng cǎo wú guī lù
　春 且住.见 说 道，天涯芳草无归路.
yuàn chūn bù　yǔ suàn zhǐ yǒu yīn qín　huà yán zhū wǎng
　怨　春不语.算只 有 殷 勤，画 檐 蛛 网，
jǐn rì rě fēi xù cháng mén shì　zhǔn nǐ jiā qī yòu wù
尽日惹飞絮.长　门 事，准 拟佳期又 误.
　é méi céng yǒu rén dù qiān jīn zòng mǎi xiàng rú fù
蛾眉 曾 有 人 妒.千 金 纵 买　相　如赋，
mò mò cǐ qíng shuí sù jūn mò wǔ　jūn bú jiàn
脉 脉 此 情　谁 诉.君 莫 舞，君 不 见，
yù huán fēi yàn jiē chén tǔ　xián chóu zuì kǔ xiū qù yǐ wēi lán
玉　环 飞 燕 皆 尘 土.闲 愁　最 苦.休 去倚 危 栏，
xié yang zhèng zài　yān liǔ duàn cháng chù
斜 阳　正 在，烟 柳 断 肠　处.

### 2.11.5 Literal translation of the lyrics

How many more storms can it dispel? Spring has gone in a hurry. I cherish the long spring and fear the early blooming of flowers, let alone the countless fallen red petals. Stay in spring. It is said, "The fragrant grass in the ends of the earth has no way back." Complaining that spring remains silent. All that can be said is diligence, painting cobwebs on the eaves, and all the flying fluff of Yogyakarta. A long and important matter was scheduled at a wrong time. There was once someone jealous of Mei Mei. Even a thousand pieces of gold would buy a prime minister like a rhapsody, but who would express this sentiment of Maimai? Do not dance, lady! Have you not seen that both the Flying Swallows around the Jade Ring are just dust? Idle worries are the most bitter. Don't lean against the perilous railing, where the setting sun is still shining and the willows are weeping.

## 2.11.6 A more polished and stylistically enhanced translation of the lyrics

How many more storms can it withstand? Spring has returned in haste. I value the prolonged spring yet fear the premature blossoming of flowers, let alone the countless fallen petals. Let us remain in spring. It is said, "The fragrant grass reaches the ends of the earth, yet there is no path back." Complaining that spring remains indifferent and silent, all one can do is diligently paint cobwebs on the eaves, while the flying fluff drifts through the air. An important and lengthy matter was unfortunately scheduled at an inappropriate time. There was once jealousy toward Mei Mei. Even a thousand pieces of gold could not buy a minister as invaluable as her, yet who would express such feelings for her? Do not dance, lady! Have you not seen that both the Concubine Flying Swallows and the Concubine Jade Ring are but dust in the wind? Idle worries bring the deepest bitterness. Do not lean upon the precarious balustrade, where the setting sun still shines and the willows seem to weep.

## 2.11.7 Translation sentence by sentence

更能消几番风雨,
How many more storms can it withstand?
匆匆春又归去.
Spring has returned in haste.
惜春长怕花开早,
I value the prolonged spring yet fear the premature blossoming of flowers,

何况落红无数.
let alone the countless fallen petals.
春且住.见说道，天涯芳草无归路.
Let us remain in spring. It is said, "The fragrant grass reaches the ends of the earth, yet there is no path back."
怨春不语.
Complaining that spring remains indifferent and silent,
算只有殷勤，画檐蛛网，尽日惹飞絮.
all one can do is diligently paint cobwebs on the eaves, while the flying fluff drifts through the air.
长门事，准拟佳期又误.
An important and lengthy matter was unfortunately scheduled at an inappropriate time.
蛾眉曾有人妒.
There was once jealousy toward Mei Mei.
千金纵买相如赋，
Even a thousand pieces of gold could not buy a minister as invaluable as her,
脉脉此情谁诉.
yet who would express such feelings for her?
君莫舞，君不见,玉环飞燕皆尘土.
Do not dance, Lady! Have you not seen that both the Concubine Flying Swallows and the Concubine Jade Ring are but dust in the wind?
闲愁最苦.
Idle worries bring the deepest bitterness.
休去倚危栏，
Do not lean upon the precarious balustrade,
斜阳正在，烟柳断肠处.
where the setting sun still shines and the willows seem to weep.

## 2.11.8 Brief introduction of the author of the poem (lyrics)

辛弃疾（公元 1140 - 1207），字幼安，号稼轩，山东东路济南府历城县人.南宋官员、文学家，豪放派词人.与苏轼合称"苏辛".辛弃疾出生时，中原已为金兵所占.21 岁参加抗金义军，不久归南宋.历任湖北、浙东安抚使等职.一生力主抗金.由于辛弃疾的抗金主张与当政的主和派政见不合，后被弹劾落职，退隐江西带湖.

  Xin Qiji (1140 - 1207 AD), styled You 'an and with the pseudonym Jiaxuan, was from Licheng County, Jinan Prefecture, Shandong East Road. An official and literary figure of the Southern Song Dynasty, a bold and unrestrained lyricist. He is known together with Su Shi as "Su Xin". When Xin Qiji was born, the Central Plains had already been occupied by the Jin army. At the age of 21, he joined the anti-Jin rebel army and soon returned to the Southern Song Dynasty. He successively held positions such as pacification Commissioner of Hubei and Eastern Zhejiang. He strongly advocated against the Jin throughout his life. As Xin Qiji's anti-Jin stance was at odds with the political views of the ruling pro-peace faction, he was later impeached and removed from office, and retired to Daihu, Jiangxi Province.

## 2.12 Song No.12, Song of Divination

卜算子　北宋　李之仪

**Tune of the poem: Song of Divination.**
**Author of the poem (lyrics), Northern Song Dynasty, Li Zhi Yi**

### 2.12.0 About the score and lyrics (poem)

This score (sheet music) is derived (excerpted) from the (pieces) of Toseri's Serenade Serenata, Op.6 (Toselli, Enrico), and has undergone minor modifications to ensure a better alignment between the musical arrangement and the lyrics (poem).

Toseri's Serenade Serenata, is a song about a broken heart. The meaning of this poem is slightly more hopeful than Toseri's Serenade Serenata, hoping to maintain deep affection that never fades. Prevent a broken heart before it happens, but the mood is somewhat quite similar, therefore the author rewrites the poem (lyrics) for the song.

## 2.12.1 Sheet music

$1 = C \quad \dfrac{3}{4}$

| $\dot{1}$ | 5 | 6 3 | 5 — | 1 | 1 3 | 7 | 6 — | 5 | 2· | $\dot{3}$ | $\dot{4}$ | $\dot{1}$ |

我 住 长 江 头, 君 住 长 江 尾. 日 日 思 君

| 7 | $\dot{1}$ | $\dot{2}$ 6 | 5 6 | 7 5 | 2 3 | 1 | 1 — | 1 2 | 3 | 5 |

不 见 君, 共 饮 长 江 水. 此 水 几 时

| 5 | 2 | 2 — | 2 3 | 4· 6 | 6 3 | 3· 1 | $\dot{1}$ — | 7 6 | 5 3 |

休, 此 恨 何 时 已. 只 愿 君 心 似 我

| 1 2 | 3 5 | 3 — | 2 2 | 5 — — | 6· $\dot{1}$ | $\dot{2}$ $\dot{1}$ | $\dot{3}$ — — |

心, 定 不 负 相 思 意. 此 水 几 时 休

| $\dot{3}$ $\dot{1}$ | 7 6 | 5 1 | 4 — | 2 3 | 4 | 5· 6 | 7 2 | $\dot{1}$ |

只 愿 君 心 似 我 心, 定 不 负 相 思 意.

## 2.12.2 Sheet music with Lyrics marked in Chinese pinyin without tones

| $\dot{1}$ | 5 | 6 3 | 5 — | 1 | 1 3 | 7 | 6 — | 5 | 2· | $\dot{3}$ | $\dot{4}$ | $\dot{1}$ |
| wo | zhu | chang jiang | tou | | jun | zhu | chang jiang | wei | | ri | ri | si | jun |

我 住 长 江 头, 君 住 长 江 尾. 日 日 思 君

| 7 | $\dot{1}$ | $\dot{2}$ 6 | 5 6 | 7 5 | 2 3 | 1 | 1 — | 1 2 | 3 | 5 |
| bu | jian | jun | gong yin | chang jiang | | shui | | ci | shui ji | shi |

不 见 君, 共 饮 长 江 水. 此 水 几 时

| 5 | 2 | 2 — | 2 3 | 4· 6 | 6 3 | 3· 1 | $\dot{1}$ — | 7 6 | 5 3 |
| xiu | | | ci | han he | shi | yi | zhi yuan | jun xin | si wo |

休, 此 恨 何 时 已. 只 愿 君 心 似 我

| 1 2 | 3 5 | 3 — | 2 2 | 5 — — | 6· $\dot{1}$ | $\dot{2}$ $\dot{1}$ | $\dot{3}$ — — |
| xin | ding bu | fu | xiang si | yi | ci | shui ji | shi xiu |

心, 定 不 负 相 思 意. 此 水 几 时 休,

| $\dot{3}$ $\dot{1}$ | 7 6 | 5 1 | 4 — | 2 3 | 4 | 5· 6 | 7 2 | $\dot{1}$ |
| zhi yuan | jun xin | si wo | xin | ding bu | fu | xiang si | | yi. |

只 愿 君 心 似 我 心, 定 不 负 相 思 意.

### 2.12.3 Text of the lyrics

我住长江头，君住长江尾.日日思君不见君，共饮长江水.
此水几时休，此憾何时已.只愿君心似我心，定不负相思意.

### 2.12.4 Text of the lyrics marked with tones in Chinese pinyin

wǒ zhù cháng jiāng tóu   jūn zhù cháng jiāng wěi   rì rì   sī jūn bú jiàn jūn
我  住  长   江   头，君 住  长    江  尾.日日 思君 不 见 君，
gòng yǐn cháng jiāng shuǐ   cǐ shuǐ   jǐ shí xiū   cǐ hàn hé shí yǐ
共   饮   长    江   水. 此 水   几 时 休, 此 憾 何 时 已.
zhǐ yuàn jūn xīn shì wǒ xīn   ding bù fù xiāng sī yì
只  愿  君 心  似 我 心，定  不负  相 思意.

### 2.12.5 Literal translation of the lyrics

I live at the head of the Yangtze River, while you live at the tail. Every day I think of you but can't see you, and we drink the water of the Yangtze River together.

When will this water cease? When will this regret end? I only hope that your heart is like mine, and I will surely live up to your longing.

### 2.12.6 A more polished and stylistically enhanced translation of the lyrics

I reside at the source of the Yangtze River, while you dwell at its mouth. Each day I think of you yet cannot see you, and we both drink from the same waters of the Yangtze. When will these waters recede? When will this regret come to an end? I can only hope that your heart holds the same sentiments as mine, and I shall certainly prove worthy of your longing.

### 2.12.7 Translation sentence by sentence

我住长江头，君住长江尾.
I reside at the source of the Yangtze River, while you dwell at its mouth.
日日思君不见君，

Each day I think of you yet cannot see you,
共饮长江水.
and we both drink from the same waters of the Yangtze.
此水几时休，此憾何时已.
When will these waters recede? When will this regret come to an end.
只愿君心似我心，
I can only hope that your heart holds the same sentiments as mine,
定不负相思意.
and I shall certainly prove worthy of your longing.

### 2.12.8 Brief introduction of the author of the poem (lyrics)

李之仪（公元 1048 - 1117）北宋词人，字端叔.山东沧州无棣人.哲宗元祐初为枢密院编修官，判原州.元祐末从苏轼于定州幕府，朝夕酬和.

Li Zhiyi (1048 - 1117 AD) was a lyricist of the Northern Song Dynasty. Uncle Zi Duan. From Wudi, Cangzhou, Shandong Province. In the early years of the reign of Emperor Zhezong, he served as a compiler in the Secretariat and was in charge of the jurisdiction of Yuanzhou. At the end of the Yuanyou period, he followed Su Shi in the Dingzhou military camp, writing poems day and night to exchange with each other.

# 2.13 Song No.13, Butterfly Love Flowers

## 蝶恋花　北宋　苏轼

**Tune of the poem: Butterfly Love Flowers.**
**Author of the poem (lyrics), Northern Song Dynasty, Su Shi**

### 2.13.0 About the score and lyrics (poem)

This score (sheet music) is derived (excerpted) from the (pieces) of Antonín Dvořák' Humoresques, Op.101 (Alternative title Humoresky, Humoresken) and has undergone minor modifications to ensure a better alignment between the musical arrangement and the lyrics (poem).

The witty and humorous rhythm and melody are very much like the strange behavior of great literary figures seeking entertainment in their spare time, therefore the author incorporate this poem into that renowned musical composition.

## 2.13.1 Sheet music

$1 = C \quad \frac{2}{4}$

| 1· 2 | 1· 2 | 3· 5 | 6· 5 | 1̇· 7 | 2̇· 1̇ | 7· 2̇ | 1̇· 6 |

花 褪 残 红 青 杏 小. 燕 子 飞 时, 绿 水 人 家

5· 5   6· 5 | 1̇· 6   5 ·3 | 2 — | 6 5 | 4 0 | 1· 2

绕. 绿 水 人 家 绕. 人 家 绕. 枝 上

1· 2 | 3· 5   6· 5 | 1̇· 7   2̇· 1̇ | 7· 2̇   1̇· 6 | 5· 5

柳 绵 吹 又 少, 天 涯 何 处 无 芳 草. 何 处

1̇ 1 | 2 5 | 1 — | 0 3̇ 2̇ | 2 1̇ | 1̇ 7· 6 | 6 5 |

无 芳 草. 墙 里 秋 千 墙 外 道.

5 4 6 | 5 4 | 3 2 | 1 0 | 1 2 | 3 3· 2̇ | 2̇ 1̇ |

墙 外 行 人, 墙 里 佳 人 笑. 笑 渐 不 闻

1̇ 7 6 | 6 5 | 5 4 5 6 | 3 2 | 3 4 | 3 3 2 | 1

声 渐 悄, 多 情 却 被 无 情 恼.

## 2.13.2 Sheet music with Lyrics marked in Chinese pinyin without tones

```
1· 2  | 1· 2  | 3· 5  | 6· 5  | i· 7  | 2· i  | 7· 2  | i· 6  |
hua tui  can    hong qing xing   xiao      yan  zi  fei shi  lv  shui ren jia
花  褪   残    红   青   杏    小.       燕   子  飞  时,  绿  水  人  家

5· 5  | 6· 5  | i· 6  | 5 ·3  | 2  -  | 6  5  | 4  0  | 1· 2  |
rao       lv   shui ren jia         rao         ren jia rao       zhi shang
绕       绿   水  人  家           绕         人  家  绕       枝  上

1· 2  | 3· 5  | 6· 5  | i· 7  | 2· i  | 7· 2  | i· 6  | 5· 5  |
liu mian chui you shao         tian ya   he  chu   wu  fang cao    he  chu
柳  绵   吹   又  少,          天  涯   何  处   无  芳  草    何  处

i  1  | 2  5  | 1  -  | 0  3· 2 | 2   i  | i  7· 6 | 6   5  |
wu fang        cao              qiang li  qiu qian qiang wai  dao
无  芳        草.                墙   里  秋  千   墙   外  道

5  4  | 6  5  | 4  3  | 2  1  | 0  1  | 2  3  | 3· 2  | 2  i  |
qiang wai     xing ren qiang li  jia     ren     xiao  xiao jian  bu  wen
墙   外       行   人, 墙  里  佳     人     笑.  笑   渐    不  闻

i  7  | 6  6  | 5  5  | 4  5  | 4  5  | 6  3  | 2  3  | 4  3  | 2  1  |
sheng jian qiao        duo qing que bei  wu          qing                 nao
声    渐   悄,         多  情   却  被   无          情                   恼.
```

### 2.13.3 Text of the lyrics

花褪残红青杏小.燕子飞时，绿水人家绕.
枝上柳绵吹又少，天涯何处无芳草.
墙里秋千墙外道.墙外行人，墙里佳人笑.
笑渐不闻声渐悄，多情却被无情恼.

### 2.13.4 Text of the lyrics marked with tones in Chinese pinyin

huā tuì cán hóng qīng xìng xiǎo　yàn zi fēi shí　lù shuǐ rén jiā rào
花　褪　残　红　青　杏　小.　燕 子 飞　时,　绿 水 人 家 绕.
zhī shàng liǔ mián chuī yòu shǎo tiān yá hé chǔ wú fāng cǎo
枝　上　柳 绵　吹　又　少,　天 涯 何 处 无　芳　草.
qiáng lǐ qiū qiān qiáng wài dào qiáng wài xing rén qiáng lǐ jiā rén xiào
　墙　里　秋　千　墙　外 道.　墙　外　行　人,　墙　里佳 人 笑.
xiào jiàn bù wén shēng jiàn qiāo duō qíng què bèi wú qíng nǎo
笑　渐　不 闻　声　渐 悄,　多　情 却 被 无　情　恼.

### 2.13.5 Literal translation of the lyrics

The red flowers fade and, green apricots are small. When swallows fly, green water surround the houses. The willow catkins on the branches are few and far between; everywhere in the world, where is no fragrant grass? Swing inside the wall and walk outside the wall. A traveler is outside the wall, a beauty inside smiling. Laughter fades away, voices fall silent; the affectionate is tormented by the heartless.

### 2.13.6 A more polished and stylistically enhanced translation of the lyrics

Red petals of flowers wither and green apricot blossoms small. Swallows flying while green waters surrounding dwellings. Sparse willow catkins drift from the branches; fragrant grass grows everywhere. Ther swings within the garden wall, while walks surrounding it. A wandering traveler stands outside, while a fair maiden smiles within. Her laughter fades, her voice falls silent; the loving heart is left to suffer at the hands of indifference.

### 2.13.7 Translation sentence by sentence

花褪残红青杏小.
Red petals of flowers wither and green apricot blossoms small.
燕子飞时，绿水人家绕.
Swallows flying while green waters surrounding dwellings.
枝上柳绵吹又少,
Sparse willow catkins drift from the branches,
天涯何处无芳草.
across the land, fragrant grass grows everywhere.
墙里秋千墙外道.
There are swings within the garden wall, while walks surrounding it.
墙外行人，墙里佳人笑.
A wandering traveler stands outside, while a fair maiden smiles within.
笑渐不闻声渐悄,
Her laughter fades, her voice falls silent,
多情却被无情恼.
the loving heart is left to suffer at the hands of indifference.

### 2.13.8 Brief introduction of the author of the poem (lyrics)

苏轼，（公元 1037 年 - 1101 年）字子瞻、号东坡居士，世称苏东坡，汉族，眉州眉山人，北宋著名文学家，书法家，画家，与父苏洵，弟苏辙三人并称"三苏".苏轼是北宋中期文坛领袖，在诗、词、散文、书、画等方面取得很高成就.词与辛弃疾同是豪放派代表，并称"苏辛"；散文与欧阳修并称"欧苏"，为"唐宋八大家"之一.苏轼善书，"宋四家"之一；擅长文人画.

Su Shi (1037 – 1101 AD), styled Zizhan and with the pseudonym Dongpo Jushi, was known as Su Dongpo. He was of Han ethnicity and originated from Meishan, Meizhou. Su Shi was a renowned literary figure, calligrapher and painter of the Northern Song Dynasty. He was known as the "Three SUS" along with his father Su Xun and his younger brother Su Zhe.

Su Shi was a literary leader in the middle of the Northern Song Dynasty and achieved remarkable accomplishments in poetry, lyrics, prose, calligraphy and painting. Ci and Xin Qiji were both representatives of the bold and unrestrained school and were collectively known as "Su Xin". His prose is known as "Ouyang and Su" along with Ouyang Xiu, and he is one of the "Eight Great Prose Masters of the Tang and Song Dynasties". Su Shi was good at calligraphy and was one of the "Four Great Calligraphers of the Song Dynasty". Good at literati painting.

# 2.14 Song No.14, Cooing and Wooing

## 关雎　先秦　孔子

**Title of the poem: Cooing and Wooing**
**Author of the poem (lyrics), Pre-Qin Dynasty, Confucius**

### 2.14.0 About the score and lyrics (poem)

This score (sheet music) is derived (excerpted) from the (pieces) of Wagner's Wedding March, and has undergone minor modifications to ensure a better alignment between the musical arrangement and the lyrics (poem).

The sincere expression of national style of The Book of Songs is lustful but not lewd, it is also serious about the relationship between men and women. The author incorporates this poem into that renowned musical composition.

## 2.14.1 Sheet music

$1 = C \quad \frac{2}{4}$

5 $\underline{\dot{1}\cdot\ \dot{1}}$ | $\dot{1}$ - | 5 $\underline{\dot{2}\cdot\ 7}$ | $\dot{1}$ - | 5 $\underline{\dot{1}\cdot\ 4}$ | 4 $\underline{\dot{3}\cdot\ \dot{2}}$ |
关 关 雎 鸠, 在 河 之 洲. 窈 窕 淑 女,

$\dot{1}$ $\underline{\dot{2}\cdot\ \dot{1}}$ | $\underline{7\cdot\ \dot{1}}$ $\underline{2\ 5}$ | $\underline{\dot{1}\cdot\ \dot{1}}$ | $\dot{1}$ - | 5 $\underline{\dot{2}\cdot\ 7}$ | $\dot{1}$ - |
君 子 好 逑. 关 关 雎 鸠, 在 河 之 洲.

5 $\underline{\dot{1}\cdot\ 3}$ | 5 $\underline{\dot{3}\cdot\ \dot{1}}$ | 6 $\underline{\dot{2}\cdot\ \dot{3}}$ | $\dot{1}$ - | 4 $\underline{\dot{3}\ \dot{2}}$ | 6 6 |
窈 窕 淑 女, 君 子 好 逑. 求 之 不 得,

7 $\underline{\dot{1}\cdot\ \dot{2}}$ | $\dot{2}\cdot$ 0 | 4 $\underline{\dot{3}\ \dot{2}}$ | 6 6 | 6 $\underline{7\cdot\ \dot{1}}$ | $\dot{1}$ - |
寤 寐 思 服. 悠 哉 悠 哉, 辗 转 反 侧.

## 2.14.2 Sheet music with Lyrics marked in Chinese pinyin without tones

5 $\underline{\dot{1}\cdot\ \dot{1}}$ | $\dot{1}$ - | 5 $\underline{\dot{2}\cdot\ 7}$ | $\dot{1}$ - | 5 $\underline{\dot{1}\cdot\ 4}$ | 4 $\underline{\dot{3}\cdot\ \dot{2}}$ |
guan guan ju jiu zai he zhi zhou yao tiao shu nv
关 关 雎 鸠, 在 河 之 洲. 窈 窕 淑 女,

$\dot{1}$ $\underline{\dot{2}\cdot\ \dot{1}}$ | $\underline{7\cdot\ \dot{1}}$ $\underline{2\ 5}$ | $\underline{\dot{1}\cdot\ \dot{1}}$ | $\dot{1}$ - | 5 $\underline{\dot{2}\cdot\ 7}$ | $\dot{1}$ - |
jun zi hao qiu guan guan ju jiu zai he zhi zhou
君 子 好 逑. 关 关 雎 鸠, 在 河 之 洲.

5 $\underline{\dot{1}\cdot\ 3}$ | 5 $\underline{\dot{3}\cdot\ \dot{1}}$ | 6 $\underline{\dot{2}\cdot\ \dot{3}}$ | $\dot{1}$ - | 4 $\underline{\dot{3}\ \dot{2}}$ | 6 6 |
yao tiao shu nv jun zi hao qiu qiu zhi bu de
窈 窕 淑 女, 君 子 好 逑. 求 之 不 得,

7 $\underline{\dot{1}\cdot\ \dot{2}}$ | $\dot{2}\cdot$ 0 | 4 $\underline{\dot{3}\ \dot{2}}$ | 6 6 | 6 $\underline{7\cdot\ \dot{1}}$ | $\dot{1}$ - |
wu mei si fu you zai you zai zhan zhuan fan ce
寤 寐 思 服. 悠 哉 悠 哉, 辗 转 反 侧.

### 2.14.3 Text of the lyrics

关关雎鸠，在河之洲.窈窕淑女，君子好逑.
求之不得，寤寐思服.悠哉悠哉，辗转反侧

### 2.14.4 Text of the lyrics marked with tones in Chinese pinyin

guān guān jū jiū　zài hé zhī zhōu yǎo tiǎo shū nǚ
　关　关 雎鸠，在 河之　洲. 窈 窕　淑女，
jūn zǐ hǎo qiú　qiú zhī bù dé　wù mèi sī fú
君 子 好 逑. 求 之 不 得，寤 寐 思服.
yōu zāi yōu zāi　zhǎn zhuǎn fǎn cè
悠　哉悠　哉， 辗　转　反 侧.

### 2.14.5 Literal translation of the lyrics

The turtle dove birds is chirping on the river island. A graceful and virtuous lady is the ideal match for a gentleman. The desire is unattainable, and one long for it day and night. Leisurely, leisurely, tossing and turning.

### 2.14.6 A more polished and stylistically enhanced translation of the lyrics

The turtle dove is Guan-Guan chirping upon the island in the river. A graceful and virtuous lady is deemed the ideal companion for a gentleman. Though the object of desire lies beyond reach, it is yearned for tirelessly, both day and night. Restless and contemplative, one tosses and turns endlessly.

### 2.14.7 Translation sentence by sentence

关关雎鸠，在河之洲.
The turtle dove is Guan-Guan chirping upon the island in the river.
窈窕淑女，君子好逑.
A graceful and virtuous lady is deemed the ideal companion for a gentleman.
求之不得，寤寐思服.

Though the object of desire lies beyond reach, it is yearned for tirelessly, both day and night.

悠哉悠哉，辗转反侧。

Restless and contemplative, one tosses and turns endlessly.

### 2.14.8 Brief introduction of the author of the poem (lyrics)

孔子（公元前 551- 479 年），山东鲁国曲阜人，中国最著名的教师，文学家，（相传诗经为其编撰）哲学家和政治理论家，他的思想深刻地持续两千余年影响了中国持续两千余年和其他东亚国家的文明.

Confucius (551- 479 BC), a native of Qufu, the State of Lu in Shandong Province, was the most renowned teacher in China. A literary figure (it is said that the Book of Songs was compiled by him), philosopher and political theorist. His thoughts profoundly influenced the civilizations of China and other East Asian countries for over two thousand years.

# 2.15 Song No.15, Go to the frontier

### 出塞 唐 王昌龄

**Title of the poem: Go to the frontier**
**Author of the poem (lyrics), Tang Dynasty, Wang Chang Ling**

### 2.15.0 About the score and lyrics (poem)

This score (sheet music) is derived (excerpted) from the (pieces) of Tchaikovsky's March (From The Nutcracker) and has undergone minor modifications to ensure a better alignment between the musical arrangement and the lyrics (poem).

The poetry is reflection and thought on a military life at the frontier, it ismatch the music of march. Therefore the author incorporates this poem into that renowned musical composition.

## 2.15.1 Sheet music

$1 = C \quad \frac{4}{4}$

| $\dot{1}$ $\dot{1}$ $\dot{1}$ $\dot{1}$ $2$ $2$ | $\dot{3}$ $\dot{1}$ $2 -$ | $\dot{1}$ $\dot{1}$ $\dot{1}$ $\dot{1}$ $\dot{2} \cdot \dot{2}$ |

秦 时　　明 月 汉 时 关，万 里　　长 征

$3$ $\dot{1}$ $2 \cdot 2$ | $\underline{7 \cdot 1}$ $\underline{7 \cdot 6}$ $\underline{5 \cdot 4}$ $\underline{3 \cdot 5}$ | $\underline{6 \cdot 7}$ $\underline{6 \cdot 5}$

人 未 还，但 使 龙 城 飞 将 在，　不 教 胡 马

$\underline{4 \cdot 3}$ $\underline{2 \cdot 4}$ | $\underline{3 \cdot 2}$ $\underline{1 \cdot 5}$ $\underline{4 \cdot 3}$ $\underline{2 \cdot 6}$ | $\underline{7 \cdot 6}$ $\underline{5 \cdot 4}$

度 阴 山　但 使 龙 城 飞 将 在，　不 教 胡 马

$\underline{7 \cdot 1}$ $\dot{1}$ | $\dot{1}$ $\dot{1}$ $\dot{1}$ $\dot{1}$ $2$ $2$ | $\dot{3}$ $\dot{1}$ $2 -$ | $\dot{1}$ $\dot{1}$ $\dot{1}$

度 阴 山，秦 时　　明 月 汉 时 关，万 里

$\dot{2}$ $\dot{2}$ | $\dot{3}$ $\dot{1}$ $\dot{2} \cdot \dot{2}$ | $\underline{7 \cdot 1}$ $\underline{7 \cdot 6}$ $\underline{5 \cdot 4}$ $\underline{3 \cdot 5}$ | $\dot{1} \cdot \dot{2}$

长 征 人 未 还，但 使 龙 城 飞 将 在，　不 教

$\underline{\dot{1} \cdot 7}$ $\underline{6 \cdot 5}$ $\underline{4 \cdot 6}$ | $\underline{\dot{2} \cdot \dot{1}}$ $\underline{7 \cdot \dot{2}}$ $\underline{\dot{3} \cdot \dot{2}}$ $\underline{\dot{1} \cdot \dot{3}}$ | $\underline{\dot{4} \cdot \dot{3}}$

胡 马 度 阴 山，但 使 龙 城 飞 将 在，　不 教

$\underline{\dot{2} \cdot \dot{3}}$ $\underline{\dot{4} \cdot \dot{2}}$ $\dot{5}$ |

胡 马 度 阴 山。

**2.15.2 Sheet music with Lyrics marked in Chinese pinyin without tones**

```
1  1  1  1   2  2 | 3  1  2 - | 1   1  1  1   2· 2 |
qin shi         ming yue    han shi guan  wan  li           chang zheng
秦  时           明   月     汉  时   关，  万   里          长     征

3  1  2· 2 | 7· 1   7· 6   5· 4   3· 5 | 6· 7   6· 5
ren wei huan    dan shi  long cheng fei jiang zai    bu jiao  hu ma
人  未  还.     但  使   龙   城    飞  将   在，   不 教   胡 马

4· 3  2· 4 | 3· 2   1· 5   4· 3   2· 6 | 7· 6   5· 4
du yin shan    dan shi  long cheng fei jiang zai    bu jiao  hu ma
度 阴  山.     但  使   龙   城    飞  将   在，   不 教   胡 马

7· 1  1  1   1  1   2  2 | 3  1  2 - | 1   1  1
du yin shan qin shi       ming yue  han shi guan   wan li
度 阴  山. 秦  时         明   月   汉  时   关，  万  里

2  2 | 3  1  2· 2 | 7· 1   7· 6   5· 4   3· 5 | 1· 2
chang zheng ren wei huan    dan shi  long cheng fei jiang zai    bu jiao
长   征   人  未  还.       但  使   龙   城    飞  将   在，   不 教

1· 7  6· 5  4· 6 | 2· 1   7· 2   3· 2   1· 3 | 4· 3
hu ma  du yin shan    dan shi  long cheng fei jiang zai    bu jiao
胡 马  度 阴  山      但  使   龙   城    飞  将   在，   不 教

2· 3  4· 2  5 |
hu ma  du yin shan
胡 马  度 阴  山
```

### 2.15.3 Text of the lyrics

秦时明月汉时关，万里长征人未还.
但使龙城飞将在，不教胡马度阴山.

### 2.15.4 Text of the lyrics marked with tones in Chinese pinyin

qín shí míng yuè hàn shí guān wàn lǐ cháng zhēng rén wèi huán
秦　时　明　月　汉　时　关，万　里　长　　征　人　未　还.
dàn shǐ long chéng fēi jiàng zài　bù jiào hú mǎ dù yīn shān
但　使　龙　城　　飞　将　在，不　教　胡　马　度　阴　山.

### 2.15.5 Literal translation of the lyrics

The bright moon of the Qin Dynasty and the pass of the Han Dynasty; the long March of ten thousand miles has yet to return. But as long as the flying generals of Dragon City remain, the northern barbarian tribes will not be allowed to the Yin Mountain.

### 2.15.6 A more polished and stylistically enhanced translation of the lyrics

The luminous moon over the Qin Dynasty and the Han frontier passes; the arduous March of ten thousand miles has still not brought our troops home. Yet as long as the valiant generals of Dragon City remain vigilant, the cavalry of the northern barbarian tribes shall not dare to cross the Yin Mountains.

### 2.15.7 Translation sentence by sentence

秦时明月汉时关，
The luminous moon over the Qin Dynasty and the Han frontier passes,
万里长征人未还.
the arduous March of ten thousand miles has still not brought our troops home.
但使龙城飞将在，

Yet as long as the valiant generals of Dragon City remain vigilant,

不教胡马度阴山.

the cavalry of the northern barbarian tribes shall not dare to cross the Yin Mountains.

### 2.15.8 Brief introduction of the author of the poem (lyrics)

王昌龄（公元 698 - 757），字少伯，汉族，河东晋阳人，盛唐著名边塞诗人.王昌龄早年依靠农耕维持生活，30 岁左右进士及第.初任秘书省校书郎等职，后被贬岭南.其诗以七绝见长，尤以登第之前赴西北边塞所作边塞诗最著.

Wang Changling (698 - 757 AD), styled Shaobo, was of Han ethnicity and from Jinyang, Hedong. He was a renowned frontier poet in the prosperous Tang Dynasty. Wang Changling made a living by farming in his early years and passed the imperial examination at around the age of 30. He was initially appointed as a librarian in the Secretariat and other positions, but was later demoted to Lingnan. His poems are renowned for their seven-character quatrains, with the frontier poems he composed during his journey to the northwest frontier before ascending the imperial examination being the most remarkable.

# 2.16 Song No.16, The Melody of Liangzhou City

### 凉州曲　唐　王翰

**Tune of the poem: The Melody of Liangzhou City.**
**Author of the poem (lyrics), Tang Dynasty, Wang Han**

### 2.16.0 About the score and lyrics (poem)

This score (sheet music) is derived (excerpted) from the (pieces) of Bizet's Habanera, and has undergone minor modifications to ensure a better alignment between the musical arrangement and the lyrics (poem).

The military lives a life of enjoying life today, similar to the expression of the music, therefore the author incorporates this poem into that renowned musical composition.

## 2.16.1 Sheet music

$1 = C \quad \frac{4}{4}$

$\dot{2}\ ^\flat 2\ ^\sharp \dot{1}\cdot\ \underline{\dot{1}}\ |\ 7\cdot\ ^\flat \underline{7}\ 6\ 6\ |\ ^\sharp 5\ 5\ \underline{4\ 3}\ 4\ |\ 5\ 4\ 3-|$
葡 萄 美 酒 夜 光 杯， 欲 饮 琵 琶 马 上 催.

$\dot{2}\ ^\flat 2\ \dot{1}\cdot\ \underline{\dot{1}}\ |\ 7\cdot\ ^\flat \underline{7}\ 6\ 6\ |\ 5\ 4\ \underline{3\ 2}\ 3\ |\ 4\ 3\ 2-|$
葡 萄 美 酒 夜 光 杯， 欲 饮 琵 琶 马 上 催.

$2\ 3\ 4\cdot\ \underline{6}\ |\ 4\ 3\ 2\ 3\ |\ 4\ 5\ \underline{6\ 6}\ 0\ |\ 7\ 6\ 5-|$
醉 卧 沙 场 君 莫 笑， 古 来 征 战 几 人 回.

$3\ ^\sharp 4\ 5\cdot\ \underline{7}\ |\ 5\ ^\sharp 4\ 3\ 0\ |\ ^\sharp 4\ 5\ \underline{6\ 7}\ 0\ |\ ^\sharp \dot{1}\ 7\ 6-|$
醉 卧 沙 场 君 莫 笑， 古 来 征 战 几 人 回.

$\dot{2}\ \dot{3}\ \underline{\dot{4}\ \dot{5}}\ 0\ |\ 7\ 5\ \dot{1}\ |\ \dot{1}\ |\ \dot{1}$
古 来 征 战 几 人 回

## 2.16.2 Sheet music with Lyrics marked in Chinese pinyin without tones

```
2̇  ♭2̇  *1̇·  1̇ | 7·  ♭7  6   6 |*5   5   4·  3 | 5   4   3  - |
pu  tao  mei  jiu  ye  guang bei    yu  yin  pi  pa   ma  shang cui
葡  萄   美   酒   夜  光   杯,    欲  饮  琵  琶   马  上   催.

2̇  ♭2̇  1̇·   1̇ | 7·  ♭7  6   6 | 5   4   3·  2 | 4   3   2  - |
pu  tao  mei  jiu  ye  guang bei    yu  yin  pi  pa   ma  shang cui
葡  萄   美   酒   夜  光   杯,    欲  饮  琵  琶   马  上   催.

2   3   4·   6 | 4   3   2   3 | 4   5   6   6  0 | 7   6   5  - |
zui wo  sha  chang jun mo  xiao   gu  lai zheng zhan   ji  ren hui
醉  卧  沙   场   君  莫  笑,    古  来  征   战       几  人  回.

3  *4  5·   7 | 5  *4  3   0 |*4   5   6   7  0 |*1̇  7   6  - |
zui wo  sha  chang jun mo  xiao   gu  lai zheng zhan   ji  ren hui
醉  卧  沙   场   君  莫  笑,    古  来  征   战       几  人  回.

2̇  3̇  4̇   5̇ | 0   7̇  5̇ | 1̇ | 1̇  1̇
          gu  lai zheng zhan    ji  ren hui
          古  来  征   战       几  人  回.
```

### 2.16.3 Text of the lyrics

葡萄美酒夜光杯，欲饮琵琶马上催.
醉卧沙场君莫笑，古来征战几人回.

### 2.16.4 Text of the lyrics marked with tones in Chinese pinyin

pú táo měi jiǔ yè guāng bēi yù yǐn pí pá mǎ shàng cuī
葡 萄 美 酒 夜 光 杯，欲饮 琵琶 马 上 催.
zuì wò shā chǎng jun mò xiào   gǔ lái zhēng zhàn jǐ rén huí
醉 卧沙 场 君 莫 笑，古来 征 战 几 人 回.

### 2.16.5 Literal translation of the lyrics

The fine wine of grapes in the night light cup, ready to drink the pipa at once, the general is urged to get on the horse. If one drunkily lying on the battlefield, do not laugh; how many have returned from ancient battles?

### 2.16.6 A more polished and stylistically enhanced translation of the lyrics

The goblet sparkles with fine wine, and the pipa's melody beckons to drink, the general is urged to mount his warhorse. Do not mock those who lie drunken on the battlefield; how many have truly returned from ancient wars?

### 2.16.7 Translation sentence by sentence

葡萄美酒夜光杯，
The goblet sparkles with fine wine,
欲饮琵琶马上催.
And the pipa's melody beckons to drink, the general is urged to mount his warhorse.
醉卧沙场君莫笑，
Do not mock those who lie drunken on the battlefield,
古来征战几人回.

how many have truly returned from ancient wars.

## 2.16.8 Brief introduction of the author of the poem (lyrics)

王翰（公元 687 年 - 726 年），字子羽，并州晋阳人，唐代边塞诗人.与王昌龄同时期，其诗载于《全唐诗》仅 14 首.登进士第.

Wang Han (687 - 726 AD), styled Ziyu, was a native of Jinyang, Bingzhou. He was a frontier poet of the Tang Dynasty. During the same period as Wang Changling, only 14 of his poems were recorded in the Complete Tang Poems. He passed the imperial examination.

# 2.17 Song No.17, A Mountain Abode on a Clear Autumn Evening

山居秋暝　唐　王维

**Title of the poem: A Mountain Abode on a Clear Autumn Evening**
**Author of the poem (lyrics), Tang Dynasty, Wang Wei**

**2.17.0 About the score and lyrics (poem)**

This score (sheet music) is derived (excerpted) from the (pieces) of My Sun. O Sole Mio is one of the most well-known songs to emerge from Italy. It was written in 1898 by Giovanni Capurro and Eduardo di Capua. It has be undergone minor modifications to ensure a better alignment between the musical arrangement and the lyrics (poem).

Both poetry and music express the love for the wonderful scenery of nature, describe, praise and extol it. The music and the lyrics (the poem, original text and its translation see the following sections) are very similar in this meaning, so the author rewrites the poem (lyrics) for the song.

## 2.17.1 Sheet music

$1 = C \quad \frac{2}{4}$

| 5 0 | 4 3 2 | 1 0 | 1 2 3 | 1 7 | 6 6 7 | 1 2 |
空　　山 新 雨 后，　天 气 晚 来 秋.　　明 月 松 间

| 7 6 | 6 6 7 | 1 2 | 6 5 | 5 5 5 | 4 3 | 2 | 1 0 |
照，　　清 泉 石 上 流.　　竹 喧 归　浣 女

| 1 2 3 | 1 | 7 6 | 6 4 | 3 2 | 5 3 | 2 1 | 2 3 |
莲 动 下　渔 舟. 随 意　　春 芳 歇，　王 孙

| 2 3 2 | 1 7 6 |
自　　可　留.

## 2.17.2 Sheet music with Lyrics marked in Chinese pinyin without tones

| 5 0 | 4 3 2 | 1 0 | 1 2 3 | 1 7 | 6 6 7 | 1 2 |
kong　shan xin yu hou　tian qi wan lai qiu　ming yue song jian
空　　山 新 雨 后，　天 气 晚 来 秋.　　明 月 松 间

| 7 6 | 6 6 7 | 1 2 | 6 5 | 5 5 | 4 3 | 2 | 1 0 |
zhao　　qing quan shi shang liu　　zhu xuan　gui huan　nv
照，　　清 泉 石 上 流.　　　竹 喧　归 浣　女，

| 1 2 3 | 1 | 7 6 | 6 4 | 3 2 | 5 3 | 2 1 | 2 3 |
lian dong xia yu zhou　　sui yi　　chun fang xie　wang sun
莲 动 下 渔 舟.　　随 意　　春 芳 歇，　王 孙

| 2 3 2 | 1 7 6 |
zi　　　ke　liu
自　　　可　留.

### 2.17.3 Text of the lyrics

空山新雨后，天气晚来秋.明月松间照，清泉石上流.
竹喧归浣女，莲动下渔舟.随意春芳歇，王孙自可留.

### 2.17.4 Text of the lyrics marked with tones in Chinese pinyin

kōng shān xīn yǔ hòu tiān qì wǎn lái qiū míng yuè sōng jiān zhào
　空　山　新　雨　后,天　气　晚　来　秋.明　月　松　间　照,
qīng quán shí shàng liú zhú xuān guī huàn nǚ　lián dòng xià yú zhōu
　清　泉　石　上　流.竹　喧　归　浣　女,　莲　动　下　渔　舟.
suí yì chūn fāng xiē　wáng sūn zì kě liú
　随　意　春　芳　歇,　王　孙　自　可　留.

### 2.17.5 Literal translation of the lyrics

After a fresh rain on the empty mountain, the weather is like autumn during evening. The bright moon shines among the pines, and the clear spring flows over the rocks. The bamboo rustles as the washing girl returns, and the lotus blossoms sway as the fishing boat descends. Care about the spring flowers and accompany withit, even if one lives the life of a prince, one is reluctant to leave.

### 2.17.6 A more polished and stylistically enhanced translation of the lyrics

After a refreshing rain on the deserted mountain, the weather is similar to the arrival of autumn during evning. The bright moon shines through the pine trees, while a clear spring trickles over the rocks. The rustling bamboo announces the return of the laundry girl, and the swaying lotus blossoms signal the passage of a fishing boat downstream. Care about the spring flowers and accompany withit, one would be reluctant to leave even if offered the life of a prince.

## 2.17.7 Translation sentence by sentence

空山新雨后，
After a refreshing rain on the deserted mountain,
天气晚来秋.
the weather is similar to the arrival of late autumn during evning.
明月松间照，
The bright moon shines through the pine trees,
清泉石上流.
while a clear spring trickles over the rocks.
竹喧归浣女，
The rustling bamboo announces the return of the laundry girl,
莲动下渔舟.
and the swaying lotus blossoms signal the passage of a fishing boat downstream.
随意春芳歇，
Care about the spring flowers and accompany withit,
王孙自可留.
one would be reluctant to leave even if offered the life of a prince.

## 2.17.8 Brief introduction of the author of the poem (lyrics)

王维，公元701-761，字摩诘，山西蒲州（今永济）人.唐代诗人，画家.

Wang Wei, 701-761 AD, styled Mojie, was from Puzhou, Shanxi Province (now Yongji). Poet and painter of the Tang Dynasty.

# 2.18 Song No.18, Untitled

无题　唐　李商隐

**Title of the poem: Untitled**
**Author of the poem (lyrics), Tang Dynasty, Li Shang Yin**

**2.18.0 About the score and lyrics (poem)**

This score (sheet music) is derived (excerpted) from the (pieces) of Mozart's Serenade and has undergone minor modifications to ensure a better alignment between the musical arrangement and the lyrics (poem).

The author rewrites the poem (lyrics) for the song (the sheet music).

## 2.18.1 Sheet music (a)

1 = C  4/4

i· 5  i· 5 | i 5  i 3  5 - | 4· 2  4· 2 | 4 2  7 2
昨 夜 星 辰 昨  夜  风, 画 楼 西 畔 桂  堂

5 - | i  i  0  3 | 2  i  7  7 | 7 2  4 7  2  i
东. 身 无    彩 凤 双 飞 翼, 心 有 灵 犀 一 点 通.

i 7  6 7  i  i  3 2 | i 2  3 7  2  i  0 |
隔 座 送 钩 春 酒 暖,  分 曹 射 覆 蜡 灯 红.

5 -  6 - | 5  4  4 3  3 | 3 3  2  2  i 7  6 7
嗟 余 听 鼓   应 官 去, 应 官 去, 走 马 兰 台

i -  2 -  3 - | 5 -  6 - | 5  4  4 3  3 | 3 3  2  2 2
类 转 蓬, 嗟 余 听 鼓  应 官  去,

i 7 | 6 7  i -  2 -  i - |
走 马 兰 台 类  转  蓬.

## 2.18.2 Sheet music with Lyrics (a) marked in Chinese pinyin without tones

```
1· 5   1· 5 | 1  5   1  3   5 — | 4·  2   4·  2 | 4   2   7   2
zuo ye xing chen zuo     ye     feng  hua lou  xi  pan gui     tang
昨  夜  星  辰  昨      夜      风，  画  楼  西  畔  桂     堂

5 —  | 1   1   0   3 | 2   1   1   7   7 | 7   2   4   7   2   1   1
dong  shen wu            cai feng shuang fei yi  xin you ling xi  yi dian tong
东    身  无            彩  凤  双   飞  翼，心  有  灵  犀  一  点  通。

1   7   6   7   1   1   3   2 | 1   2   3   7   2   1   1   0 |
ge zuo song gou chun jiu nuan   fen cao she  fu  la  ju hong
隔  座  送  钩  春  酒  暖，    分  曹  射  覆  蜡  炬  红。

5 —   6 — | 5   4   4   4   3 | 3   3   2   2   2   1   7 | 6   7
jie   yu    ting gu ying guan qu       ying guan  qu  zou ma  lan tai
嗟    余   听  鼓  应  官  去，       应  官   去， 走  马  兰  台

1 —  2 —  3 — | 5 —  6 — | 5   4   4   4   3 | 3   3   2   2   2
lei  zhuan peng  jie   yu    ting gu ying          ying guan     qu
类  转  蓬。 嗟   余   听  鼓              应  官        去，

1   7 | 6   7   1 —  2 —  1 — |
zou ma  lan tai lei  zhuan peng
走  马  兰  台  类  转  蓬。
```

## 2.18.3 Sheet music (b)

$1 = C \quad \frac{4}{4}$

```
i· 5  i· 5 | i 5  i 3  5 - | 4· 2  4· 2 | 4 2  7 2
相 见 时 难 别    亦    难，东 风 无 力 百     花

5 - | i  i  0 3 | 2  i  i 7  7 | 7 2  4 7  2 i  i
残.  春 蚕     到 死 丝 方 尽，蜡 炬 成 灰 泪 始 干.

i 7  6 7  i i  3 2 | i 2  3 7  2 i  i 0 |
晓 镜 但 愁 云 鬓 改， 夜 吟 应 觉 月 光 寒.

5 -  6 - | 5 4  4 3  3 3  2 2  i 7  6 7
蓬 山   此 去   无 多 路，青 鸟 殷 勤 为 探 看.

i -  2 -  3 - | 5 -  6 - | 5 4  4 4  4 3 | 3 3  2 2  2 2
为 探 看， 蓬 山    此 去   无 多   路，

i 7 | 6 7  i -  2 -  i - |
青 鸟 殷 勤 为  探  看.
```

### 2.18.4 Text of the lyrics (a)

昨夜星辰昨夜风，画楼西畔桂堂东.身无彩凤双飞翼，心有灵犀一点通.
隔座送钩春酒暖，分曹射覆蜡灯红.嗟余听鼓应官去，走马兰台类转蓬.

### 2.18.5 Text of the lyrics (a) marked with tones in Chinese pinyin

zuó yè xīng chén zuó yè fēng　　huà lóu xī pàn guì tang dōng
昨　夜　星　辰　昨　夜　风，画　楼　西　畔　桂　堂　东.
shēn wú cǎi fèng shuāng fēi yì　　xīn yǒu ling xī yì diǎn tōng
身　无　彩　凤　双　　飞　翼，心　有　　灵犀　一　点　通.
gé zuò song gōu chūn jiǔ nuǎn　　fēn cáo shè fù là　jù hóng
隔　座　送　钩　春　酒　暖，　分　曹　射　覆蜡　炬　红.
jiē yú tīng gǔ yīng guān qù　　zǒu mǎ lán tái lèi zhuǎn péng
嗟余　听　鼓　应　官　去，走　马　兰　台　类　转　　蓬.

### 2.18.6 Literal translation of the lyrics (a)

Last night's stars shone and last night's wind blew. To the west of the painted building was the osmanthus hall to the east. The body is like a phoenix with two flying wings, but the heart is in perfect harmony. From another seat, the spring wine is sent off, warming the warmth; at the parting, the wax is shot again, the lamp is red. With a sigh, I listened to the drumbeat and left for the official position, walking around the Malantai and turning the tent.

### 2.18.7 A more polished and stylistically enhanced translation of the lyrics (a)

The stars shone brightly and the wind blew gently last night. To the west of the painted building stood the osmanthus hall, with the eastern wing extending in elegant symmetry. The structure resembles a phoenix in flight, its wings outstretched, while the interior embodies a harmonious balance. From an adjacent pavilion, spring wine was served, radiating warmth; at the moment of farewell, candles were lit once more, casting a soft red glow over the scene. With a wistful sigh, I listened to the distant drumbeats before departing for official duties, passing by the Malantai Pavilion and weaving through the tents.

### 2.18.8 Translation sentence by sentence of the lyrics (a)

昨夜星辰昨夜风,
The stars shone brightly and the wind blew gently last night.
画楼西畔桂堂东.
To the west of the painted building stood the osmanthus hall, with the eastern wing extending in elegant symmetry.
身无彩凤双飞翼,
The structure resembles a phoenix in flight, its wings outstretched,
心有灵犀一点通.
while the interior embodies a harmonious balance.
隔座送钩春酒暖,
From an adjacent pavilion, spring wine was served, radiating warmth,
分曹射覆蜡灯红.
at the moment of farewell, candles were lit once more, casting a soft red glow over the scene.
嗟余听鼓应官去,
With a wistful sigh, I listened to the distant drumbeats before departing for official duties,
走马兰台类转蓬.
passing by the Malantai Pavilion and weaving through the tents.

### 2.18.9 Text of the lyrics (b)

相见时难别亦难, 东风无力百花残.
春蚕到死丝方尽, 蜡炬成灰泪始干.
晓镜但愁云鬓改, 夜吟应觉月光寒.
蓬山此去无多路, 青鸟殷勤为探看.

### 2.18.10 Text of the lyrics (b) marked with tones in Chinese pinyin

xiāng jiàn shí nán bié yì nán dōng fēng wú lì bǎi huā cán
相 见 时 难 别 亦难，东 风 无 力百 花 残.
chūn cán dào sǐ sī fāng jǐn    là jù chéng huī lèi shǐ gàn
春 蚕 到 死丝 方 尽，蜡炬 成 灰泪 始 干.
xiǎo jìng dàn chóu yún bìn gǎi    yè yín yīng jué yuè guāng hán
晓 镜但 愁 云 鬓 改，夜 吟 应 觉 月 光 寒.
péng shān cǐ qù wú duō lù qīng niǎo yīn qín wèi tàn kàn
蓬 山 此去 无 多路，青 鸟 殷 勤 为 探 看.

### 2.18.11 Literal translation of the lyrics (b)

When we meet, it's hard to part. The east wind is weak, flowers wither, and the silkworm spins silk until it dies. When the candle burns to ashes, tears dry up. Get up in the morning, get dressed, and look in the mirror, sorrow for the hair color fades; at night, I sing; I should feel the coldness of the moonlight. There are no many bluebirds on the way to Peng Mountain who are eager to explore.

### 2.18.12 A more polished and stylistically enhanced translation of the lyrics (b)

When we meet, parting becomes exceedingly difficult; the east wind is faint, the flowers begin to wither, and the silkworm continues to spin silk until its death. When the candle has burned completely to ash, its tears finally cease. Rise in the morning, get dressed, and look in the mirror, sorrow for the color of hair gradually fades. Even in the quiet of night, I sing alone, sensing the chill of the moonlight. Along the distant path to Pengshan, few bluebirds remain to accompany or guide the way.

### 2.18.13 Translation sentence by sentence of the lyrics (b)

相见时难别亦难，
When we meet, parting becomes exceedingly difficult,
东风无力百花残.
the east wind is faint, the flowers begin to wither.

春蚕到死丝方尽,
and the silkworm continues to spin silk until its death,
蜡炬成灰泪始干.
When the candle has burned completely to ash, its tears finally cease.
晓镜但愁云鬓改,
Rise in the morning, get dressed, and look in the mirror, sorrow for the color of hair gradually fades,
夜吟应觉月光寒.
Even in the quiet of night, I sing alone, sensing the chill of the moonlight.
蓬山此去无多路,
Along the distant path to Pengshan,
青鸟殷勤为探看.
few bluebirds remain to accompany or guide the way.

### 2.18.14 Brief introduction of the author of the poem (lyrics)

李商隐（公元 813 年 - 858 年），晚唐著名诗人，字义山，原籍怀州河内. 837 年，李商隐登进士第，曾任秘书省校书郎等职.李商隐是晚唐乃至整个唐代，为数不多的刻意追求诗美的诗人.他擅长诗歌写作，骈文文学价值也很高，和杜牧合称"小李杜".其诗构思新奇，风格秾丽，优美动人，广为传诵.

Li Shangyin (813 - 858 AD), a renowned poet of the late Tang Dynasty, was known by his courtesy name Yishan and was originally from Henei, Huaizhou. In 837, Li Shangyin passed the imperial examination and held positions such as the Secretary of the Secretariat. Li Shangyin was one of the few poets in the late Tang Dynasty and even the entire Tang Dynasty who deliberately pursued the beauty of poetry. He was skilled in poetry writing and his parallel prose was also of high literary value. Together with Du Mu, they were known as "Little Li and Du". His poems are novel in conception, beautiful in style , beautiful and charming, widely recited.

# 2.19 Song No.19, Phoenix Hairpin

钗头凤　　南宋　　陆游　　唐婉

**Tune of the poem: Phoenix Hairpin.**
**Author of the poem (lyrics), Southern Song Dynasty, Lu You and his ex-wife Tang Wan**

**2.19.0 About the score and lyrics (poem)**

　　This score (sheet music) is derived (excerpted) from the (pieces) of Wolfgang Amadeus Mozart's You, who knows. From The Marriage of Figaro, (Voi, chesapete from Le nozze di Figaro), and has undergone minor modifications to ensure a better alignment between the musical arrangement and the lyrics (poem).

　　The author rewrites the poem (lyrics) for the song.

## 2.19.1 Sheet music (a)

$1 = C$  $\frac{4}{4}$

| $\dot{1}$ - 5 5 | $\dot{2}$ - 5 - | $\dot{3}$ - $\dot{1}\cdot\underline{\dot{2}}$ | $\dot{3}\cdot\underline{\dot{4}}$ $\dot{2}$ - | $\dot{3}$ - $\dot{4}$ #$\dot{4}$ |
红　酥　手，黄　　藤酒，满城　春色　宫墙柳，东　风恶，

$\dot{5}\cdot\underline{\dot{3}}$ $\dot{1}$ - | $\dot{2}$ - #$\underline{\dot{2}}$ $\dot{3}$ | $\dot{4}$ - $\dot{5}$ $\dot{3}$ | $\dot{5}$ $\dot{3}$ $\dot{2}$ $\dot{4}$ | $\dot{2}$ $\dot{4}$
东　风恶，欢　　情薄，一怀　愁绪，几年　离索，

$\dot{1}$ - | $\dot{5}\cdot\underline{\dot{5}}$ $\dot{3}$ - | $\dot{5}$ $\dot{3}$ $\dot{5}$ $\dot{3}$ | $\dot{2}$ $\dot{4}$ $\dot{2}$ $\dot{4}$ | $\dot{1}$ - 7$\cdot\underline{\dot{1}}$
错，　错，　　错．一怀　愁绪，几年　离索，错，　错，

$\dot{2}\cdot\underline{\dot{3}}$ | $\dot{1}$ -
错，错，错．

| $\dot{1}$ - 5 5 | $\dot{2}$ - 5 - | $\dot{3}$ - $\dot{1}\cdot\underline{\dot{2}}$ | $\dot{3}\cdot\underline{\dot{4}}$ $\dot{2}$ - | $\dot{3}$ - $\dot{4}$ #$\dot{4}$ |
春　如旧，人　　空瘦，泪痕　红浥　鲛绡透，桃　花落，

$\dot{5}\cdot\underline{\dot{3}}$ $\dot{1}$ - | $\dot{2}$ - #$\underline{\dot{2}}$ $\dot{3}$ | $\dot{4}$ - $\dot{5}$ $\dot{3}$ | $\dot{5}$ $\dot{3}$ $\dot{2}$ $\dot{4}$ | $\dot{2}$ $\dot{4}$
闲　池阁，闲　　池阁，山盟　虽在，锦书　难托，

$\dot{1}$ - | $\dot{5}\cdot\underline{\dot{5}}$ $\dot{3}$ - | $\dot{5}$ $\dot{3}$ $\dot{5}$ $\dot{3}$ | $\dot{2}$ $\dot{4}$ $\dot{2}$ $\dot{4}$ | $\dot{1}$ - 7$\cdot\underline{\dot{1}}$
莫，　莫，　　莫．山盟　虽在，锦书　难托，莫，　莫，

$\dot{2}\cdot\underline{\dot{3}}$ | $\dot{1}$ -
莫，莫，莫．

## 2.19.2 Sheet music with Lyrics marked in Chinese pinyin without tones

### (a)

| 1- | 5 | 5 | 2- | 5- | 3- | 1· 2 | 3· 4 | 2- | 3- | 4 #4 |
|---|---|---|---|---|---|---|---|---|---|---|
| hong | su | shou | huang | teng | jiu | man cheng | chun se | gong qiang | liu | dong feng e |
| 红 | 酥 | 手, | 黄 | 藤 | 酒. | 满 城 | 春 色 | 宫 墙 | 柳, | 东 风 恶, |

| 5· 3 | 1- | 2- | #2 | 3 | 4- | 5 3 | 5 | 3 | 2 | 4 | 2 | 4 |
|---|---|---|---|---|---|---|---|---|---|---|---|---|
| huan qing bao | | huan | | qing | bao | yi huai | chou | xu | ji | nian | li | suo |
| 欢 情 薄, | | 欢 | | 情 | 薄, | 一 怀 | 愁 | 绪, | 几 | 年 | 离 | 索, |

| 1- | 5· 5 | 3- | 5 | 3 | 5 | 3 | 2 | 4 | 2 | 4 | 1- | 7· 1 |
|---|---|---|---|---|---|---|---|---|---|---|---|---|
| cuo | cuo | cuo | yi | huai | chou | xu | ji | nian | li | suo | cuo | cuo |
| 错, | 错, | 错. | 一 | 怀 | 愁 | 绪, | 几 | 年 | 离 | 索, | 错, | 错, |

| 2· 3 | 1- |
|---|---|
| cuo | cuo |
| 错, | 错. |

| 1- | 5 | 5 | 2- | 5- | 3- | 1· 2 | 3· 4 | 2- | 3- | 4 #4 |
|---|---|---|---|---|---|---|---|---|---|---|
| chun | ru | jiu | ren | kong shou | lei hen | hong yi | jiao xiao | tou | tao | hua luo |
| 春 | 如 | 旧, | 人 | 空 瘦. | 泪 痕 | 红 浥 | 鲛 绡 | 透, | 桃 | 花 落, |

| 5· 3 | 1- | 2- | #2 | 3 | 4- | 5 3 | 5 | 3 | 2 | 4 | 2 | 4 |
|---|---|---|---|---|---|---|---|---|---|---|---|---|
| tao hua luo | | xian | | chi | ge | shan meng | sui | zai | jin | shu | nan | tuo |
| 桃 花 落, | | 闲 | | 池 | 阁, | 山 盟 | 虽 | 在, | 锦 | 书 | 难 | 托, |

| 1- | 5· 5 | 3- | 5 | 3 | 5 | 3 | 2 | 4 | 2 | 4 | 1- | 7· 1 |
|---|---|---|---|---|---|---|---|---|---|---|---|---|
| mo | mo | mo | shan meng | sui | zai | jin | shu | nan | tuo | mo | mo |
| 莫, | 莫, | 莫. | 山 盟 | 虽 | 在, | 锦 | 书 | 难 | 托, | 莫, | 莫, |

| 2· 3 | 1- |
|---|---|
| mo mo | mo |
| 莫, 莫, | 莫. |

### 2.19.3 Text of the lyrics (a)

红酥手，黄藤酒.满城春色宫墙柳.东风恶，
欢情薄，一怀愁绪，几年离索，错，错，错.
春如旧，人空瘦.泪痕红浥鲛绡透；桃花落，
闲池阁，山盟虽在，锦书难托，莫，莫，莫.

### 2.19.4 Text of the lyrics marked with tones in Chinese pinyin (a)

hóng sū shǒu huáng téng jiǔ mǎn chéng chūn sè gōng qiáng liǔ dōng fēng è
红 酥 手， 黄 藤 酒.满 城 春 色宫 墙 柳.东 风 恶，

huān qíng bo yī huái chóu xù jǐ nián lí suǒ cuò cuò cuò
欢 情 薄， 一 怀 愁 绪， 几 年 离 索， 错， 错， 错.

chūn rú jiù rén kōng shòu lèi hén hóng yì jiāo xiāo tòu táo huā luò
春 如旧， 人 空 瘦.泪 痕 红 浥 鲛 绡 透.桃 花 落，

xián chí gé shān méng suī zài jǐn shū nán tuō mò mò mò
闲 池 阁， 山 盟 虽 在，锦 书 难 托，莫， 莫， 莫.

### 2.19.5 Literal translation of the lyrics (a)

Red crispy hands, yellow vine wine. The city is filled with the beauty of spring, with willows along the palace walls. The east wind is harsh, joy is thin, a heart full of sorrow, years of separation, wrong, wrong, wrong. Spring remains the same, but people are thin and empty. The tear stains are soaked through silk kerchief. The peach blossoms have fallen, at the Xianchi Pavilion. Though the mountain vows remain, the brocade letters are hard to send. No, no, no.

### 2.19.6 A more polished and stylistically enhanced translation of the lyrics (a)

Crimson hands, yellow vine wine—spring beautifies the city, with willows lining palace walls. The east wind is cruel, joy fleeting, hearts burdened with sorrow, years of separation—wrong, wrong, wrong. Spring remains unchanged, yet people grow thin and hollow. Tears soak through delicate silk handkerchiefs; peach blossoms fall at Xianchi Pavilion. Though vows remain firm as mountains, love letters are difficult to transfer. No, no, no.

### 2.19.7 Translation sentence by sentence of the lyrics (a)

红酥手，黄藤酒.
Crimson hands, yellow vine wine,
满城春色宫墙柳.
spring beautifies the city, with willows lining palace walls.
东风恶，欢情薄，
The east wind is cruel, joy fleeting,
一怀愁绪，几年离索，
hearts burdened with sorrow, years of separation
错，错，错.
wrong, wrong, wrong.
春如旧，人空瘦
Spring remains unchanged, yet people grow thin and hollow.
泪痕红浥鲛绡透.
Tears soak through delicate silk handkerchiefs;
桃花落，闲池阁，
peach blossoms fall at Xianchi Pavilion.
山盟虽在，锦书难托.
Though vows remain firm as mountains, love letters are difficult to transfer.
莫，莫，莫.
No, no, no.

### 2.19.8 Brief introduction of the author of the poem (lyrics) (a)

陆游（公元 1125—1210），字务观，号放翁.
Lu You (1125–1210 AD), styled Wuguan, with the pseudonym Fangweng,

For details, please refer to section 2.09.7 of this book, we do not repeat here.

## 2.19.9 Sheet music (b)

```
|1̇ -  5  5 |2̇ -  5 - |3̇ -  1̇· 2̇ |3̇·  4̇  2̇ - |3̇ -  4̇ #4̇|
  世   情  薄，人  情   恶，而 送 黄 昏  花  易 落． 晓     风 干，

 5·  3  1̇ - |2̇ -  #2̇  3̇ |4̇ -  5̇  3̇ |5̇  3̇  2̇  4̇ |2̇  4̇
 泪  痕 残．  泪      痕  残． 欲 笺 心 事， 独 语 斜 阑．

|1̇ - |5·  5  3̇ - |5̇  3̇  5̇  3̇ |2̇  4̇  2̇  4̇ |1̇ -  7  1̇
 难，   难      难． 欲 笺 心 事， 独 语 斜 阑． 难， 难，

 2̇·  3̇ |1̇ -
 难， 难 难．


|1̇ -  5  5 |2̇ -  5 - |3̇ -  1̇· 2̇ |3̇·  4̇  2̇ - |3̇ -  4̇ #4̇|
  人   成  各，今  非   昨，病 魂 常 似  秋  千 索． 角     声 寒，

 5·  3  1̇ - |2̇ -  #2̇  3̇ |4̇ -  5̇  3̇ |5̇  3̇  2̇  4̇ |2̇  4̇
 角  声 寒 夜       阑 珊． 怕 人 寻 问， 掩 泪 装 欢．

|1̇ - |5·  5  3̇ - |5̇  3̇  5̇  3̇ |2̇  4̇  2̇  4̇ |1̇ -  7· 1̇
 瞒  瞒      瞒   怕 人 寻 问， 掩 泪 装 欢． 瞒， 瞒，

 2̇·  3̇ |1̇ -
 瞒， 瞒， 瞒．
```

## 2.19.10 Sheet music with Lyrics marked in Chinese pinyin without tones

### (b)

```
|1̇ -   5   5 |2̇ -   5 - |3̇ -   1̇· 2̇|3̇·  4̇   2̇ - |3̇ -   4̇ #4̇|
 shi qing bao ren qing  e    yu song huang hun hua yi luo   xiao feng gan
 世   情   薄， 人   情   恶，  而  送   黄    昏   花  易 落.    晓   风   干，

 5·  3   1̇ - |2̇ - #2̇   3̇|4̇ -   5̇   3̇|5̇   3̇   2̇|4̇   2̇   4̇
 lei hen can  lei       hen can     yu jian xin shi du  yu xie lan
 泪   痕   残. 泪        痕   残.    欲   笺   心   事， 独 语 斜 阑.

 1̇ - |5·  5   3̇ - |5̇   3̇   5̇   3̇|2̇   4̇   2̇   4̇|1̇ -   7· 1̇
 nan   nan  nan    yu jian xin shi du  yu xie lan nan    nan
 难，   难， 难.    欲   笺   心  事   独 语 斜 阑.  难，   难，

 2̇·  3̇ |1̇ -
 nan nan nan
 难， 难  难.


|1̇ -   5   5 |2̇ -   5 - |3̇ -   1̇· 2̇|3̇·  4̇   2̇ - |3̇ -   4̇ #4̇|
 ren cheng ge jin fei zuo bing hun chang si   qiu qian suo jiao sheng han
 人   成    各， 今 非 昨， 病   魂   常    似   秋   千    索.  角    声    寒，

 5·  3   1̇ - |2̇ - #2̇   3̇|4̇ -   5̇   3̇|5̇   3̇   2̇|4̇   2̇   4̇
 jiao sheng han  ye       lan shan   pa ren xun wen yan lei zhuang huan
 角   声    寒， 夜        阑   珊.    怕 人  寻  问，  掩  泪   装    欢.

 1̇ - |5·  5   3̇ - |5̇   3̇   5̇   3̇|2̇   4̇   2̇   4̇|1̇ -   7· 1̇
 man   man  man    pa ren xun wen yan lei zhuang huan man    man
 瞒，   瞒， 瞒.    怕 人  寻  问，  掩  泪   装      欢.  瞒，   瞒，

 2̇·  3̇ |1̇ -
 man man man
 瞒  瞒  瞒.
```

## 2.19.11 Text of the lyrics (b)

世情薄，人情恶，雨送黄昏花易落.晓风干，泪痕残.
欲笺心事，独语斜阑.难，难，难.
人成各，今非昨，病魂常似秋千索.角声寒，夜阑珊.
怕人寻问，咽泪装欢.瞒，瞒，瞒.

## 2.19.12 Text of the lyrics marked with tones in Chinese pinyin (b)

shì qíng bo rén qíng è　yǔ song huáng hūn huā yì luò xiǎo fēng gān
世　情　薄,人　情　恶 雨 送　黄　昏　花 易 落. 晓　风　干,
lèi hén cán yù jiān xīn shì　dú yǔ xié lán nán　nán　nán
泪 痕 残. 欲 笺 心 事, 独 语 斜 阑. 难, 难, 难.
rén chéng gè　jīn fēi zuó bìng hún cháng sì qiū qiān suǒ jiǎo shēng hán
人　成　各,　今 非 昨, 病　魂　常　似 秋 千　索. 角　声　寒,
yè lán shān pà rén xún wèn　yàn lèi zhuāng huān　mán mán mán
夜 阑 珊. 怕 人 寻　问,　咽 泪 装　欢.　瞒, 瞒, 瞒.

## 2.19.13 Literal translation of the lyrics (b)

The world is thin, human feelings are evil, and the rain brings the flowers to dusk, making them fall easily. The morning wind is dry, and the tear stains remain. To write down to express my thoughts, I speak alone in the slanting railing. Difficult, difficult, difficult! When people come together, today is no longer yesterday; the sick soul is always like a swing on a rope. The sound of the horn is cold, and the night is dim. Afraid of being questioned, they swallow their tears and pretend to be happy. Hide, hide, hide!

## 2.19.14 A more polished and stylistically enhanced translation of the lyrics (b)

The world grows shallow, human feelings turn cold; rain brings flowers to wilt at dusk, falling easily. Morning winds are dry, yet tear stains persist. To express my thoughts in letters, I speak alone by the slanting railing:

difficult, difficult, difficult. Human bonds today differ from yesterday; the tormented soul swings endlessly. The horn sounds cold, the night dim. Afraid of being questioned, I swallow tears and feign happiness: hide, hide, hide.

### 2.19.15 Translation sentence by sentence of the lyrics (b)

世情薄，人情恶，
The world grows shallow, human feelings turn cold,
雨送黄昏花易落.
rain brings flowers to wilt at dusk,
晓风干，泪痕残.
falling easily. Morning winds are dry, yet tear stains persist.
欲笺心事，独语斜阑.
To express my thoughts in letters, I speak alone by the slanting railing:
难，难，难.
difficult, difficult, difficult.
人成各，今非昨，
Human bonds today differ from yesterday;
病魂常似秋千索.
the tormented soul swings endlessly.
角声寒，夜阑珊.怕人寻问，
The horn sounds cold, the night dim. Afraid of being questioned,
咽泪装欢.瞒，瞒，瞒.
I swallow tears and feign happiness: hide, hide, hide.

### 2.19.16 Brief introduction of the author of the poem (lyrics) (b)

南宋唐婉，字蕙仙，（大约）（公元1126年-1268年）.陆游的表妹，陆游母舅唐诚女儿，自幼文静灵秀，才华横溢.她也是陆游的第一任妻子，后因陆母偏见而被拆散.后两人在亲友的私家花园《沈园》不期而遇，彼此写下此传世情愁诗词共四阕.古代中国版的罗密欧与朱丽叶

Tang Wan (c. 1126–1268 AD), styled Huixian, was a quiet, refined, and talented woman of the Southern Song Dynasty. As the daughter of Tang Cheng, Lu You's maternal uncle, she was also Lu You's first wife (ex-wife).

However, their marriage ended due to the disapproval of Lu You's mother. Years later, the two unexpectedly met again in a private garden known as "Shenyuan," which belonged to a mutual friend or relative.

There, each one composed two poems expressing love and sorrow, the works that have been cherished and passed down through generations. The real Chinese version of Romeo and Juliet

# 2.20 Song No.20, Go Hunting in Mi Zhou

## 江城子　密州出猎　北宋　苏轼

**Tune of the poem: Guys of Riverside Town.**
**Title of the poem: Go Hunting in Mi Zhou**
**Author of the poem (lyrics), Northern Song Dynasty, Su Shi**

### 2.20.0 About the score and lyrics (poem)

This score (sheet music) is derived (excerpted) from the (pieces) of Brahms's Hungarian Dance, and has undergone minor modifications to ensure a better alignment between the musical arrangement and the lyrics (poem).

Su Shi aspired to serve in the military on the northwest frontier, and this poem conveys his lofty ambitions through the theme of hunting. This musical composition exhibits a strong, martial character reminiscent of a traditional march. And this piece of music also has strong singability.

Thus the music and the poem (lyrics) manifest match each other obviously. Therefore the author incorporates this poem into that renowned musical composition.

## 2.20.1 Sheet music

$1 = C \quad \frac{2}{4}$

| 3· 6 i· 6 | #5· 6 7 | 6 - | 4· 5 6 | 3 - | 2 1 1 7 |
老夫聊发少年　　狂，左牵　黄，右

7· 3 | 6 - | 3· 6 1 | 3· 1 | 7· 1 2 | 1 - | 3 3 | 4· 3 |
擎　苍，锦帽　貂裘，千骑卷平冈。为报倾城

0 2 #1 2 | 3 2 #1 3 | 2 - | 2 2 | 3· 2 | 0 1 7 1 |
　随太守，亲　射　虎，亲　射虎　看孙郎．

2 1 7 2 | 1 - | 7 7 2 | 1 7 | 7 6 #5 6 |
看孙　郎．酒酣胸胆尚开张，

7 6 #5 7 | 6 - | 3· 3 | #4 #5 | 6 6 #5 6 | 7 6 #5 7 |
尚　开　张，鬓微霜，又何　妨．又　何

6 - | 6 3 3 3 | 3 2 1 2 | 3 3 | 6 3 3 3 | 3 2 |
妨　持节云中，何日遣冯唐．持节云中，何日

1 7 | 6 6 | 1 2 | 1 7 | 1 1 | 2 2 | 3 6 3 | 1 2 |
遣冯唐．会挽雕弓雕弓　如满月，西北

3 3 | 3 2 | 1 7 | 6 6 | 6 - |
望，射　天狼．射天狼．

## 2.20.2 Sheet music with Lyrics marked in Chinese pinyin without tones

```
|3·  6 | 1·  6 #5·  6  7 | 6 - | 4·  5  6 | 3 - | 2  1  1  7 |
 lao  fu  liao fa  shao nian  kuang  zuo qian  huang    you
 老   夫  聊   发  少   年,   狂,   左  牵   黄,     右

 7·  3 | 6 - | 3·  6 | 1  3·  1 | 7·  1  2 | 1 - | 3  3 | 4·  3 |
 qing    cang   jin mao  diao qiu qian qi juan ping gang  wei bao qing cheng
 擎      苍,   锦 帽   貂  裘, 千  骑 卷  平   冈.   为  报 倾   城

 0  2 #1  2 | 3  2  1 #3 | 2 - | 2  2 | 3·  2 | 0  1  7  1 |
    sui tai shou qin   she   hu   kan   sun lang   qin she hu
    随 太   守, 亲   射    虎,  看   孙 郎.   亲 射 虎,

 2  1  7  2 | 1 - | 7  7 | 2  1  7 | 7  6 #5  6 |
 kan  sun  lang   jiu han  xiong dan  shang kai zhang
 看   孙  郎.   酒 酣  胸  胆  尚   开  张,

 7  6 #5  7 | 6 - | 3·  3 #4 #5 | 6  6 #5  6 | 7  6 #5  7 |
 shang kai  zhang  bin wei shuang you  he  fang      you   he
 尚   开   张,   鬓  微  霜,   又  何  妨         又   何

 6 - | 6  3 | 3  3 | 3  2 | 1  2 | 3  3 | 6  3 | 3  3 | 3  2 |
 fang   chi jie  yun zhong he  ri  qian feng tang  chi jie yun zhong he ri
 妨,   持  节 云   中, 何  日  遣  冯   唐.   持  节 云   中, 何 日

 1  7 | 6  6 | 1  2 | 1  7 | 1  1 | 2  2 | 3  6 | 3 | 1  2 |
 qian feng tang  hui wan diao gong  diao     gong   ru man yue  xi  bei
 遣   冯  唐.   会  挽  雕  弓   雕        弓    如 满 月,   西  北

 3  3 | 3  2 | 1  7 | 6  6 | 6 - |
 wang   she  tian lang  she tian lang
 望,   射  天  狼. 射  天 狼.
```

### 2.20.3 Text of the lyrics

老夫聊发少年狂,左牵黄,右擎苍,帽貂裘,千骑卷平冈.
为报倾城随太守,亲射虎,看孙郎.酒酣胸胆尚开张,鬓微霜,又何妨.
持节云中,何日遣冯唐?会挽雕弓如满月,西北望,射天狼.

### 2.20.4 Text of the lyrics marked with tones in Chinese pinyin

lǎo fū liáo fā shǎo nián kuáng zuǒ qiān huáng yòu qíng cāng
老 夫聊 发 少年 狂,左 牵 黄,右 擎 苍,
jǐn mào diāo qiú    qiān qí juàn píng gāng wéi bào qīng chéng suí tài shǒu
锦 帽 貂 裘, 千 骑 卷 平 冈. 为 报 倾 城 随 太 守,
qīn shè hǔ    kàn sūn láng    jiǔ hān xiōng dǎn shàng kāi zhāng
亲 射虎, 看 孙 郎. 酒 酣 胸 胆 尚 开 张,
bìn wēi shuāng yòu hé fang    chí jiē yún zhōng hé rì qiǎn féng táng
鬓 微 霜, 又 何 妨. 持节 云 中,何 日 遣 冯 唐.
huì wǎn diāo gōng rú mǎn yuè    xī běi wàng shè tiān láng
会 挽 雕 弓 如 满 月, 西北 望, 射 天 狼.

### 2.20.5 Literal translation of the lyrics

The old man is full of youthful vigor, holding yellow dog in his left hand and blue hawk in his right, wearing a brocade hat and a mink coat, with a thousand riders rolling around the plain hill. To repay the fall of the city, I followed the governor, shot the tiger in person and watched over Sun Lang. When you are drunk and your chest is still open. The color of my temples has turned a little white like frost, what does it matter? When will Feng Tang be dispatched to the frontier city. It will draw its carved bow like a full moon, look northwest and shoot the celestial Wolf.

### 2.20.6 A more polished and stylistically enhanced translation of the lyrics

The old man brims with youthful vigor, holding a yellow hound in his left hand and a falcon in his right. Clad in a brocade hat and mink coat, he leads a thousand horsemen rolling across the plains and hills. To repay the people's enthusiasm of accompanying the governor, I shoot the tiger with my own hands personally emulating Emperor Sun Lang.

When drunk, my chest remains open with passion; even if my temples has slightly turned white color like frost, what does it matter? When will Feng Tang be sent to the Yun zhou city? He shall draw his carved bow like a full moon, gaze northwestward, and shoot down the celestial wolf.

## 2.20.7 Translation sentence by sentence

老夫聊发少年狂，
The old man brims with youthful vigor,
左牵黄，右擎苍，帽貂裘，
holding a yellow hound in his left hand and a falcon in his right. Clad in a brocade hat and mink coat,
千骑卷平冈.
he leads a thousand horsemen rolling across the plains and hills.
为报倾城随太守，
To repay the people's enthusiasm of accompanying the governor,
亲射虎，看孙郎.
I shoot the tiger with my own hands personally emulating Emperor Sun Lang.
酒酣胸胆尚开张，
When drunk, my chest remains open with passion,
鬓微霜，又何妨.
even if my temples hasslightly turned white color like frost, what does it matter.
持节云中，何日遣冯唐.
When will Feng Tang be sent to the Yun zhong city.
会挽雕弓如满月，
He shall draw his carved bow like a full moon,
西北望，射天狼.
gaze northwestward, and shoot down the celestial wolf.

## 2.20.8 Brief introduction of the author of the poem (lyrics)

苏轼（公元 1037—1101）宋代文学家，书画家.字子瞻，号东坡，世称苏东坡.四川眉州眉山人.嘉祐二年（公元 1057）参加礼部考试，中第二名.仁宗殿试时，与其弟苏辙同科进士及第.公元 1071 起，先后任杭州通判，密州等州知州.元丰公元 1079，以谤讪新政的罪名逮捕入狱.5 个月后被贬黄州为团练副使.苏轼是北宋中期的文坛领袖，文学巨匠，唐宋八大家之一.词开豪放一派，与辛弃疾并称苏辛.创作诗歌 2700 余首.

Su Shi (1037-1101 AD) was a literary figure and painter of the Song Dynasty. His courtesy name was Zizhan and his pseudonym was Dongpo. He was known as Su Dongpo in the world. From Meishan, Meizhou, Sichuan Province. In the second year of the Jiayou reign (1057 AD), he took the examination of the Ministry of Rites and ranked second. During the palace examination of Emperor Renzong, he and his younger brother Su Zhe passed the imperial examination as jinshi. From 1071 AD, he successively held the positions of Judge of Hangzhou and Governor of Mizhou and other states. In the 1079 AD of the Yuanfeng era, he was arrested and imprisoned on the charge of slandering the New Policies. Five months later, he was demoted to Huangzhou and appointed as the deputy commander of the militia. Su Shi was a literary leader and giant in the middle of the Northern Song Dynasty, and one of the Eight Great Prose Masters of the Tang and Song Dynasties. His lyrics are bold and unrestrained, and he is known as Su and Xin together with Xin Qiji. He Composed more than 2,700 poems.

# 2.21 Song No.21, Farewell at Jin Ling Tavern

### 金陵酒肆留别　唐　李白

### Title of the poem: Farewell at Jin Ling Tavern
### Author of the poem (lyrics), Tang Dynasty, Li Bai

### 2.21.0 About the score and lyrics (poem)

This score (sheet music) is derived from the of Dvořák 's Hymn of Love and has undergone minor modifications to ensure a better alignment between the musical arrangement and the lyrics (poem).

This piece of music seems also very appropriate to express the friendship between close friends. The poem is quite match to the music, therefore the author rewrites the poem (lyrics) for the song.

### 2.21.1 Sheet music

$1 = C \quad \frac{4}{4}$

| 3· 5  5  3· 2  1 | 2· 3  5· 3  2 — | 3· 5  5  3· 2  1 |
|---|---|---|
| 风 吹 柳 花 满 店 香, 吴 姬 压 酒 |

| 2  3  2· 1  1 — | 6· 1  1  7  5  6 | 6  1  7  5  6 — |
| 劝 客 尝. 金 陵 子 弟 来 相 送, |

| 6· 1  1  7  5  6 | 6  1  7  5  6 — | 3· 5  5  3· 2  1 |
| 欲 行 不 行 各 尽 觞. 请 君 试 问 |

| 2· 3  5· 3  2 — | 3· 5  5  1· 2  3 | 2· 1  2  6  1 — |
| 东 流 水, 别 意 与 之 谁 短 长. |

### 2.21.2 Sheet music with Lyrics marked in Chinese pinyin without tones

| 3· 5  5  3· 2  1 | 2· 3  5· 3  2 — | 3· 5  5  3· 2  1 |
|---|---|---|
| feng chui liu hua man dian xiang wu ji ya jiu |
| 风 吹 柳 花 满 店 香, 吴 姬 压 酒 |

| 2  3  2· 1  1 — | 6· 1  1  7  5  6 | 6  1  7  5  6 — |
| quan ke chang jin ling zi di lai xiang song |
| 劝 客 尝. 金 陵 子 弟 来 相 送, |

| 6· 1  1  7  5  6 | 6  1  7  5  6 — | 3· 5  5  3· 2  1 |
| yu xing bu xing ge jin shang qing jun shi wen |
| 欲 行 不 行 各 尽 觞. 请 君 试 问 |

| 2· 3  5· 3  2 — | 3· 5  5  1· 2  3 | 2· 1  2  6  1 — |
| dong liu shui bie yi yu zhi shui duan chang |
| 东 流 水, 别 意 与 之 谁 短 长. |

### 2.21.3 Text of the lyrics

风吹柳花满店香，吴姬压酒劝客尝.
金陵子弟来相送，欲行不行各尽觞.
请君试问东流水，别意与之谁短长.

### 2.21.4 Text of the lyrics marked with tones in Chinese pinyin

fēng chuī liǔ huā mǎn diàn xiāng wú jī　yā jiǔ quàn kè cháng
　风　吹　柳　花　满　店　　香，吴　姬　压酒　　劝　客　尝.
jīn líng zǐ dì lái xiāng song　　yù xíng bù xíng gè jǐn shāng
　金　陵　子弟来　相　　送，欲　行　不　行　各　尽　　觞.
qǐng jūn shì wèn dōng liú shuǐ　bié yì yǔ zhī shuí duǎn cháng
　请　君　试问　东　流　水，别　意　与　之　谁　短　　长.

### 2.21.5 Literal translation of the lyrics

The wind blows and the willow flowers fill the shop with their fragrance. A waitress from the Wu region presses wine and invites customers to taste it. The guys of Jinling came to see me off. Both those who were leaving and those who were hosting, they all get beastly drunk. Please ask the flowing water of the east, with whom does my heart contend?

### 2.21.6 A more polished and stylistically enhanced translation of the lyrics

The breeze blows gently, and the willow blossoms fill the tavern with their fragrance. Wu Ji pours wine and warmly invites guests to sample it. The people of Jinling have come to bid them farewell. Both hosts and guests, they all equally get beastly drunk. Please ask the flowing waters of the east: with whom does my sorrow linger?

### 2.21.7 Translation sentence by sentence

风吹柳花满店香，
The breeze blows gently, and the willow blossoms fill the tavern with their

fragrance.
吴姬压酒劝客尝.
Wu Ji pours wine and warmly invites guests to sample it.
金陵子弟来相送,
The people of Jinling have come to bid them farewell.
欲行不行各尽觞.
Both hosts and guests, they all equally get beastly drunk.
请君试问东流水,
Please ask the flowing waters of the east:
别意与之谁短长.
with whom does my sorrow linger?

## 2.21.8 Brief introduction of the author of the poem (lyrics)

For details, please refer to section 2.03.7 of this book, we do not repeat here.

# 2.22 Song No.22, Plum Blossoms and Willow Leaves

## 生查子　唐　牛希济

**Tune of the poem: Plum Blossoms and Willow Leaves**
**Author of the poem (lyrics), Tang Dynasty, Niu Xi Ji**

### 2.22.0 About the score and lyrics (poem)

This score (sheet music) is derived (excerpted) from the (pieces) of a Russian Folk Song: Night Song, and has undergone minor modifications to ensure a better alignment between the musical arrangement and the lyrics (poem).

The depictions and expressions of nightlife scenes through poetry and music are largely comparable and similar. Therefore the author rewrites the poem (lyrics) for the song.

## 2.22.1 Sheet music

$1 = C \quad \frac{4}{4} \frac{5}{4} \frac{3}{4}$

$\underline{1\ 3}\ \underline{3\ 1}\ 4\ 3 | 2\ \underline{\dot{6}\ \dot{5}}\ 2\ 1\ \dot{5} - | \underline{\dot{5}\ 3}\ \dot{6}\ 3$
春 山 烟 欲 收， 天 淡 稀 星 少. 残 月 脸 边

$2 | \underline{2\ 3}\ \underline{\dot{7}\ \dot{6}}\ \dot{5} - | \underline{1\ 3}\ \underline{3\ 1}\ 4\ 3 | 2\ \underline{\dot{6}\ \dot{5}}$
明， 别 泪 临 清 晓. 语 已 多， 情

$2\ 1\ \dot{5} - | \underline{\dot{5}\ 3}\ \dot{6}\ 3\ 2 | \underline{2\ 3}\ \underline{\dot{7}\ \dot{6}}\ \dot{5} - | 2\ 5$
未 了， 回 首 犹 重 道. 回 首 犹 重 道. 记 得

$\underline{5\ 1}\ 4\ 3\ 2 | \underline{3\ 1}\ 2\ 1\ \dot{5}\ 0 | \underline{3\ 6}\ \underline{6\ 2}\ 5\ 4$
绣 罗 裙， 处 处 怜 芳 草. 语 已 多，

$3 | \underline{\dot{7}\ \dot{6}}\ 3\ 2\ 6 - | \underline{\dot{5}\ 3}\ \dot{6} | 3\ 2 | 2 | \underline{2\ 3}\ \underline{\dot{7}\ \dot{6}}\ \dot{5} - |$
情 未 了， 回 首 犹 重 道. 处 处 怜 芳 草.

## 2.22.2 Sheet music with Lyrics marked in Chinese pinyin without tones

```
1   3    3   1   4   3 | 2    6  5   2   1   5 - | 5  3   6   3
chun shan yan yu  shou         tian dan xi xing shao can yue lian bian
春   山   烟  欲  收,           天   淡  稀  星   少.  残  月  脸   边

2 | 2    3   7  6   5 - | 1   3    3   1   4   3 | 2   6   5
ming bie  lei lin qing xiao       yu       yi        duo       qing
明,  别   泪  临  清   晓.   语       已        多,         情

2   1    5 - | 5  3   6   3   2 | 2   3   7  6   5 - | 2   5
wei      liao   hui shou you zhong dao  hui shou you zhong dao   ji  de
未       了,    回  首  犹  重   道.  回  首  犹  重   道.  记  得

5   1   4   3   2 | 3   1   2   1   5   0 | 3   6   6   2   5   4
xiu luo qun         chu chu lian fang cao       yu      yi        duo
绣  罗  裙,         处  处  怜  芳   草.       语      已        多,

3 | 7   6    3   2   6 - | 5  3   6   3   2   2 | 3   7   6   5 -
qing      wei      liao    hui shou you zhong dao chu chu lian fang cao
情        未       了,     回  首  犹  重   道.  处  处  怜  芳   草.
```

### 2.22.3 Text of the lyrics

春山烟欲收，天淡稀星少. 残月脸边明，别泪临清晓.
语已多，情未了，回首犹重道，记得绿罗裙，处处怜芳草.

### 2.22.4 Text of the lyrics marked with tones in Chinese pinyin

chūn shān yān yù shōu　　tiān dàn xī xīng shǎo cán yuè liǎn biān míng
春　山　烟　欲　收，天　淡　稀　星　少. 残月　脸　边　明，
bié lèi lín qīng xiǎo　　yǔ yǐ duō qíng wèi liǎo　　huí shǒu yóu chòng dào
别　泪　临　清　晓. 语已多，情　未了，回　首　犹　重　道，
jì de　 lǜ luó qún chǔ chù lián fāng cǎo
记得　绿 罗 裙，处 处　怜　芳 草.

### 2.22.5 Literal translation of the lyrics

The spring mountain smoke is about to clear, the sky with a little cloud has fewer stars. The waning moon's face is bright by the side, parting tears face the clear dawn. Words have gone by, but the affection remains. Looking back, I still recall: I remember the green silk dress, everywhere I cherished the fragrant grass.

### 2.22.6 A more polished and stylistically enhanced translation of the lyrics

The mountain mist begins to clear in spring, the sky, adorned with only a few clouds, reveals fewer stars. The waning moon shines brightly oneside of her face, and as dawn breaks, tears fall in farewell. Words may fade, but affection endures. Looking back, I still remember: the green silk dress, and cherish the fragrance of grass wherever I went.

### 2.22.7 Translation sentence by sentence

春山烟欲收，
The spring mountain mist begins to clear,
天淡稀星少.

the sky, adorned with only a few clouds, reveals fewer stars.
残月脸边明,
The waning moon shines brightly oneside of her face,
别泪临清晓.
and as dawn breaks, tears fall in farewell.
语已多, 情未了, 回首犹重道,
Words may fade, but affection endures. Looking back,
记得绿罗裙,
I still remember the green silk dress,
处处怜芳草.
and cherish the fragrance of grass wherever I went.

### 2.22.8 Brief introduction of the author of the poem (lyrics)

牛希济, 五代词人.公元 925 在世.陇西人.词人牛峤之侄.为前蜀主王建所赏识, 任起居郎.前蜀后主王衍时, 累官翰林学士, 御史中丞.公元 925, 随前蜀主降于后唐, 明宗时拜雍州节度副使.

Niu Xiji was a lyricist of the Five Dynasties. He was alive in 925 AD. A native of Longxi and is the nephew of the poet Niu Qiao. He was recognized by the former Shu King Wang Jian and appointed as a living attendant. During the reign of Wang Yan, the last emperor of the Former Shu, he held positions such as Hanlin Scholar and Imperial Censor. In 925 AD, he surrendered to the Later Tang Dynasty along with the Lord of the Former Shu. During the reign of Emperor Mingzong, he was appointed as the deputy governor of Yongzhou.

# 2.23 Song No.23, Chinese Marseillaise

唐　李贺　明　顾炎武　清　秋瑾

Tune of the poem: Seven-character Regulated verse
Title of the poem:
The actions of the governor of Yan Men city.
Responding to the second rhymes of the hermit Fu.
On a Yellow Sea ship, Japanese people asked for a sentence and saw a map of the war between Japan and Russia
Author of the poem (lyrics):
Tang Dynasty Li He, Ming Dynasty Gu Yan Wu and Qing Dynasty Qiu Jin

## 2.23.0 About the score and lyrics (poem)

This score (sheet music) is derived (excerpted) from the (pieces) of Marseille (Marseillaise，La Marseillaise), the French national anthem composed in 1792 during the French Revolution，and has undergone minor modifications to ensure a better alignment between the musical arrangement and the lyrics (poem).

This Marseillaise is appropriate globally for all humankind in inspiring people to fight for freedom and democracy, national liberation and for a just cause. The author of this book likes this piece of music very much.

The three poems are all full of the fighting spirit of sacrificing one's life for the country with loyalty, which perfectly aligns with the fighting spirit of the Marseillaise, therefore the author rewrites the poems (lyrics) for the song.

## 2.23.1 Sheet music (a)

$1 = C \quad \frac{4}{4}$

```
5  5·  5  | 1  1  2  2 | 5· 3  1· 1 | 3· 1 | 6  4  -
黑 云    压     城  城  欲  摧,  甲  光  向  日

2· 7 | 1  -  0  1· 2 | 3· 3  3  3  4· 3 | 3  2  0
金 鳞   开.        角  声  满  天      秋  色  里,

2· 3 | 4· 4  4  5· 4 | 3  -  0  5· 5 | 5  3· 1
塞 上   燕  脂  凝  夜  紫,    半  卷  红  旗

5  3· 1 | 5  -  0  5  5· 7 | 2  -  4  2· 7  7 | 2  1
临 易 水,   临  易    水,  霜  重  鼓  寒  声 不

7  -  | 6  1· 1  7· 1 | 2  -  0  7 | 1· 1  1  2· 3 |
起.    角 声 满 天 秋 色 里,      塞  上 燕 脂 凝 夜

7  -  0  1· 7 | 6· 6  6  1  7· 6 | 6  5  0  0  5  5 |
紫.    半 卷 红   旗  临  易  水,  霜     重

5  -  5· 5  3· 1 | 2  -  -  0  5  5 | 5  -  5· 5  3· 1 |
鼓  寒   声 不 起.        报  君  黄  金  台  上

2  -  -  5 | 1  -  -  2 | 3  -  -  0 | 4  -  5  6 | 2  -  -  6 | 5  -
意,    提 携    玉 龙     为    国    死.   提  携

0  3  4· 2 | 1  -  1· 0 |
玉 龙 为  国 死.
```

## 2.23.2 Sheet music (a) with Lyrics marked in Chinese pinyin without tones

```
5  5·  5  | 1   1   2   2 | 5·  3   1·  1 | 3·  1  | 6   4  —
hei    yun     ya          cheng   cheng yu  cui    jia   guang xiang ri
黑     云      压          城      城    欲   摧,    甲    光    向     日

2·  7  | 1  —   0   1·  2 | 3·  3   3   3 | 4·  3  | 3   2   0
jin lin kai         jiao sheng man tian         qiu  se  li
金  鳞  开,         角   声    满   天         秋   色  里,

2·  3  | 4·  4   4   5·  4 | 3  —   0   5·  5 | 5   3·  1
sai shang yan zhi       ning ye  zi.         ban juan     hong qi
塞  上   燕    脂        凝   夜  紫.          半   卷     红   旗

5   3·  1 | 5  —   0   5   5·  7 | 2  —   4   2·  7   7 | 2   1
lin yi    shui     lin yi       shui shuang zhong gu han      sheng bu
临  易    水,      临  易       水,  霜    重    鼓  寒       声   不

7  —   | 6   1·  1   1   7·  1 | 2  —   0   7 | 1·  1   1   1   2·  3
qi.         jiao sheng man tian qiu  se         li  sai shang yan zhi ning ye
起.        角   声    满   天   秋   色         里, 塞  上    燕   脂  凝   夜

7  —   0   1·  7 | 6·  6   6   1   7·  6 | 6   5   0   0   5   5
zi.         ban juan hong     qi      lin yi  shui         shuang zhong
紫.        半   卷   红       旗      临   易  水,         霜     重

5  —   5·  5   3·  1 | 2  —  —   0   5   5 | 5  —   5·  5   3·  1
gu  han     sheng bu  qi           bao jun     huang jin    tai shang
鼓  寒      声   不   起.          报  君      黄    金     台   上

2  —  —   5 | 1  —  —   2 | 3  —  —   0 | 4  —   5   6 | 2  —  —   6 | 5  —
yi,        ti  xie         yu  long             wei guo         si          ti  xie
意,        提  携          玉  龙             为  国          死.          提  携

3  —   4·  2 | 1  —   1·  0 |
yu  long wei guo   si
玉  龙  为  国   死.
```

## 2.23.3 Sheet music (b)

$\underline{5}$ $\underline{\dot5\cdot}$ $\underline{\dot5}$ | 1  1  2  2 | 5· $\underline{3}$  $\underline{1\cdot\ 1}$  $\underline{3\cdot\ 1}$ | 6  4 −
愁 听　　关　塞　遍 吹 笳,　不 见 中 原

$\underline{2\cdot\ \dot7}$ | 1 −  0  $\underline{1\cdot\ 2}$ | 3·  $\underline{3}$  3  $\underline{3}$  $\underline{4\cdot\ 3}$ | 3  2  0
有　战　车.　三　户　已　亡　　　熊　绎　国,

$\underline{2\cdot\ 3}$ | 4·  $\underline{4}$  4  $\underline{5\cdot\ 4}$ | 3 − 0  $\underline{5\cdot\ 5}$ | 5  $\underline{3\cdot\ 1}$
一 成 犹 启　少 康 家.　　苍 龙　日 暮

5  $\underline{3\cdot\ 1}$ | 5 − 0 $\underline{5}$  $\underline{5\cdot\ \dot7}$ | 2 − 4  $\underline{2\cdot\ \dot7}$  $\underline{\dot7}$ | 2  1
还 行　雨,　还 行　　雨,老 树 春 深 更 著

$\dot7$ − | 6  $\underline{\dot1\cdot\ \dot1}$  $\underline{\dot1}$  $\underline{\dot7\cdot\ \dot1}$ | 2 − 0  $\dot7$ | 1·  $\underline{1}$  1  $\underline{1}$  $\underline{2\cdot\ 3}$ |
花.　三 户 已 亡 熊 绎　国,一 成 犹 启 少 康

$\dot7$ − 0  $\underline{1\cdot\ \dot7}$ | 6·  $\underline{6}$  6  $\underline{1}$  $\underline{\dot7\cdot\ 6}$ | 6  5  0  $\underline{0\ 5}$ |
家.　苍 龙 日　暮　　还 行 雨,　　老 树

5 −  $\underline{5\cdot\ 5}$  $\underline{3\cdot\ 1}$ | 2 − − 0  $\underline{5}$ | 5 −  $\underline{5\cdot\ 5}$  $\underline{3\cdot\ 1}$ |
春 深　更 著 花.　　　待 得　汉 庭 明 诏

2 − − 5 | 1 − − 2 | 3 − − 0 | 4 − 5  6 | 2 − − 6 | 5 −
近,　五 湖　同 觅　　钓　鱼 樵.　五 湖

$\underline{0\ 3}$  $\underline{4\cdot\ 2}$ | 1 − 1·  0 |
同 觅 钓 鱼 樵.

## 2.23.4 Sheet music (b) with Lyrics marked in Chinese pinyin without tones

```
5  5·  5 | 1   1   2   2 | 5·  3   1·  1 | 3·  1 | 6   4  —
chou ting   guan    sai     bian chui   jia    bu  jian zhong yuan
愁   听    关    塞    遍  吹  笳,    不  见  中   原

2·  7 | 1 —  0   1·  2 | 3·  3   3   3   4·  3 | 3   2   0
you zhan che     san hu  yi  wang        xiong yi guo
有  战  车,    三  户  已  亡         熊   绎  国,

2·  3 | 4·  4   4   5·  4 | 3 — 0   5·  5 | 5   3·  1
yi  cheng you qi    shao kang jia    cang long   ri  mu
一   成   犹  启    少   康   家.    苍   龙    日  暮

5   3·  1 | 5 —  0   5   5·  7 | 2 — 4   2·  7   7 | 2   1
hai xing    yu        hai xing    yu  lao shu chun shen geng zhu
还   行    雨,       还   行    雨,  老 树  春   深   更   著

7 — | 6   1·  1   1   7·  1 | 2 — 0   7 | 1·  1   1   1   2·  3 |
hua.   san hu  yi  wang xiong yi     guo  yi  cheng you qi  shao kang
花.   三  户  已  亡   熊   绎     国,  一  成   犹  启  少   康

7 — 0   1·  7 | 6·  6   6   1   7·  6 | 6   5   0   0   5   5 |
jia.     cang long ri    mu      hai xing yu      lao shu
家.     苍   龙   日   暮     还  行   雨,      老  树

5 — 5·  5   3·  1 | 2 — —  0   5   5 | 5 — 5·  5   3·  1
chun shen geng zhu hua.      dai de     han ting ming zhao
春   深   更   著  花.      待  得    汉  庭   明   诏

2 — —  5 | 1 — —  2 | 3 — —  0 | 4 — 5   6 | 2 — —  6 | 5 —
jin     wu hu    tong mi    diao yu  cha    wu  hu
近,    五 湖   同   觅    钓  鱼  楼.    五  湖

3 —  4·  2 | 1 — 1·  0 |
tong mi  diao yu  cha.
同   觅  钓  鱼  楼.
```

## 2.23.5 Sheet music (c)

```
5  5·  5 | 1   1   2   2 | 5·  3   1·  1 | 3·  1 | 6   4 —
万 里  乘  风           去  复  来,   只  身  东  海

2·  7 | 1 — 0   1·  2 | 3·  3   3   3   4·  3 | 3   2   0
挟 春 雷.    忍 看  图  画     移  颜      色,

2·  3 | 4·  4   5·  4 | 3 — 0   5·  5 | 5   3·  1
肯 使  江  山   付 劫 灰.   浊  酒  不  销

5   3·  1 | 5 — 0   5   5·  7 | 2 — 4   2·  7   7 | 2   1
忧 国    泪,    忧  国   泪, 救 时 应 仗  出  群

7 — | 6   1·  1   1   7·  1 | 2 — 0   7 | 1·  1   1   1   2·  3 |
才.   忍 看 图 画  移 颜    色, 肯 使 江 山 付 劫

7 — 0   1·  7 | 6·  6   6   1   7·  6 | 6   5   0   0   5   5 |
灰.   浊 酒 不   销     忧  国  泪,   救  时

5 — 5·  5   3·  1 | 2 — — 0   5   5 | 5 — 5·  5   3·  1 |
应 仗   出  群 才.     拼  将  十 万 头 颅

2 — — 5 | 1 — — 2 | 3 — — 0 | 4 — 5   6 | 2 — — 6 | 5 —
血,   须 把   乾 坤     力 挽    回.   须 把

0   3   4·  2 | 1 — 1·  0 |
乾 坤 力  挽  回.
```

## 2.23.6 Sheet music (c) with Lyrics marked in Chinese pinyin without tones

```
5  5·  5 | 1   1   2   2 | 5·  3   1·  1 | 3·  1 | 6   4 —
wan li cheng     feng    qu  fu  lai    zhi shen dong hai
万  里  乘       风      去  复  来,    只  身  东   海

2·  7 | 1 — 0   1·  2 | 3·  3   3   3 | 4·  3 | 3   2   0
xie chun lei     ren kan tu  hua       yi  yan se
挟  春  雷,      忍  看  图  画        移  颜  色,

2·  3 | 4·  4   4   5·  4 | 3 — 0   5·  5 | 5   3·  1
ken shi jiang shan   fu  jie hui      zhuo jiu   bu xiao
肯  使  江   山      付  劫  灰.      浊   酒    不 销

5   3·  1 | 5 — 0   5   5·  7 | 2 — 4   2·  7   7 | 2   1
you guo  lei    you guo  lei   jiu shi ying zhang chu qun
忧  国   泪,    忧  国   泪,   救  时  应   仗    出  群

7 — | 6   1·  1   1   7·  1 | 2 — 0   7 | 1·  1   1   1   2·  3 |
cai     ren kan tu  hua yi yan      se    ken shi jiang shan fu jie
才      忍  看  图  画  移 颜       色,   肯  使  江   山   付  劫

7 — 0   1·  7 | 6·  6   6   1   7·  6 | 6   5   0   0   5   5 |
hui    zhuo jiu   bu       xiao you guo lei         jiu shi
灰.    浊   酒    不        销  忧  国  泪,         救  时

5 — 5·  5   3·  1 | 2 — — 0   5   5 | 5 — 5·  5   3·  1
ying zhang chu qun cai         pin     jiang shi wan tou lu
应   仗    出  群  才,         拼      将   十  万   头  颅

2 — — 5 | 1 — — 2 | 3 — — 0 | 4 — 5   6 | 2 — — 6 | 5 —
xue     xu ba     qian kun       li  wan hui     xu ba
血,     须 把     乾   坤        力  挽  回.     须 把

3·  — 4·  2 | 1 — 1·  0 |
qian kun  li wan hui
乾   坤   力 挽  回.
```

## 2.23.7 Texts of the lyrics

### (a)

### 雁门太守行唐李贺

黑云压城城欲摧，甲光向日金鳞开.角声满天秋色里，塞上燕脂凝夜紫.
半卷红旗临易水，霜重鼓寒声不起.报君黄金台上意，提携玉龙为君死.

### (b)

### 又酬傅处士次韵明顾炎武

愁听关塞遍吹笳，不见中原有战车.三户已亡熊绎国，一成犹启少康家.
苍龙日暮还行雨，老树春深更著花.待得汉庭明诏近，五湖同觅钓鱼槎.

### (c)

### 黄海舟中日人索句并见日俄战争地图清秋瑾

万里乘风去复来，只身东海挟春雷.忍看图画移颜色，肯使江山付劫灰.
浊酒不销忧国泪，救时应仗出群才.拼将十万头颅血，须把乾坤力挽回.

## 2.23.8 Texts of the lyrics marked with tones in Chinese pinyin

### Poem (a)

hēi yún yā chéng chéng yù cuī jiǎ guāng xiàng rì jīn lín kāi
黑 云 压 城   城 欲 摧，甲 光   向 日 金 鳞 开.
jiǎo shēng mǎn tiān qiū sè lǐ   sāi shàng yàn zhī níng yè zǐ
角   声   满   天   秋 色 里，塞   上     燕 脂   凝   夜 紫.
bàn juǎn hóng qí lín yì shuǐ shuāng zhòng gǔ hán shēng bù qǐ
半   卷   红   旗 临 易 水，霜       重     鼓 寒   声     不 起.
bào jūn huáng jīn tái shàng yì   tí xié yù long wèi guó sǐ
报   君   黄     金 台 上     意, 提 携 玉 龙   为   国 死.

### Poem (b)

chóu tīng guān sài biàn chuī jiā   bú jiàn zhōng yuán yǒu zhàn chē
愁     听   关     塞   遍     吹   笳，不 见     中     原     有   战   车.

sān hù yǐ wáng xióng yì guó   yī chéng yóu qǐ shào kāng jiā
三户已亡熊绎国，一成犹启少康家.
cāng long rì mù hái xíng yǔ   lǎo shù chūn shēn gēng zhu huā
苍龙日暮还行雨，老树春深更著花.
dài de hàn tíng míng zhào jìn   wǔ hú tong mì diào yú chá
待得汉庭明诏近，五湖同觅钓鱼槎.

### Poem (c)

wàn lǐ chéng fēng qù fù lái   zhī shēn dōng hǎi xia chūn léi
万里乘风去复来，只身东海挟春雷.
rěn kàn tú huà yí yán sè   kěn shǐ jiāng shān fù jié huī
忍看图画移颜色，肯使江山付劫灰.
zhuó jiǔ bù xiāo yōu guó lèi jiù shí yīng zhàng chū qún cái
浊酒不销忧国泪，救时应仗出群才.
pīn jiāng shí wàn tóu   lú xuè   xū bǎ qián kūn lì wǎn huí
拼将十万头颅血，须把乾坤力挽回.

### 2.23.9 Literal translations of the lyrics

**Lyrics (poem a)**

Dark clouds are pressing down on the city as if it were about to collapse, and the armor light is shining towards the sun, with golden scales spreading out. The sound of horns fills the autumn sky, and the makeup grease color clouds are in a deep purple at night.. Half a roll of red flag stands by the Yi River; the frost is heavy and the cold sound rises. The oath of repaying the king to the Heavenly Court is: holding a sword of jade dragon and die for the country.

**Lyrics (poem b)**

I'm sad to hear the sound of a reed pipe playing all over the pass, but I never see any chariots in the Central Plains. Even if the State of Chu had been reduced to only three households, it was certain to bring about the downfall of the State of Qin. Despite possessing merely one-tenth of the territory, Emperor Shao Kang successfully restored the rule of the Xia

Dynasty. Even at dusk, the dragon still rains; even in late spring, the old tree blossoms. When the imperial edict of the Han court approaches, people from all over the continent were simultaneously seeking weapons to kill the enemy.

### Lyrics (poem c)

Traveling thousands of miles with the wind, I return again; alone in the East sea, I carry the spring thunder. I can't bear to watch a picture change its color; I'm not willing to let the country turn to ashes. The turbid wine cannot quench the tears of sorrow for the country; to save the current crisis, it is necessary to rely on cultivating a large number of talents. With the blood of a hundred thousand heads, we must restore the power of the universe.

## 2.23.10 A more polished and stylistically enhanced translation of the lyrics:

### Lyrics (poem a)

Dark clouds loom over the city as if threatening its collapse, while armor gleams under the sunlight, scattering golden reflections. The horn's call echoes through the autumn sky, and the makeup grease color clouds of frontier appear in a deep purple shade at night. Half a red flag flutters beside the Yi River, where frost lies thick and the drumbeat is muted by the cold. The solemn oath sworn before the Heavenly Court to repay the king's favor states: holding the Jade Dragon Sword and sacrificing my life for the country.

### Lyrics (poem b)

In deep sorrow, I hear music echoing across the borders, yet see no chariots advancing from the Central Plains. Even if the State of Chu had been reduced to only three households, it was certain to bring about the downfall of the State of Qin, despite possessing merely one-tenth of the territory, Emperor Shao Kang successfully restored the rule of the Xia Dynasty. The azure dragon continues to bring rain at dusk, and ancient trees blossom even more vibrantly in the depth of spring. When the imperial decree from the Han court draws near, people from all corners of the country simultaneously sought arms to confront the enemy.

### Lyrics (poem c)

Riding the wind for thousands of miles, I return once again; alone across the East Sea, I carry the thunder of spring. I can't endure the sight of colors fading in portraits and unwillingly allow the land to be reduced to ashes. Turbid wine cannot wash away the tears of national concern; to resolve the present crisis, it is imperative to cultivate a great number of capable talents. It is necessary to sacrifice countless lives and rivers of blood to restore cosmic order.

### 2.23.11 Translation sentence by sentence of the lyrics

### The lyrics (a)

黑云压城城欲摧,
Dark clouds loom over the city as if threatening its collapse,
甲光向日金鳞开.
while armor gleams under the sunlight, scattering golden reflections.
角声满天秋色里,
The horn's call echoes through the autumn sky,
塞上燕脂凝夜紫.
and the makeup grease color clouds of frontier appear in a deep purple shade at night.
半卷红旗临易水,
Half a red flag flutters beside the Yi River,
霜重鼓寒声不起.
where frost lies thick and the drumbeat is muted by the cold.
报君黄金台上意,
The solemn oath sworn before the Heavenly Court to repay the king's favor states:
提携玉龙为君死.
holding the Jade Dragon Sword and sacrificing my life for the country.

### The lyrics (b)

愁听关塞遍吹笳，
In deep sorrow, I hear music echoing across the borders,
不见中原有战车.
yet see no chariots advancing from the Central Plains.
三户已亡熊绎国，
Even if the State of Chu had been reduced to only three households, it was certain to bring about the downfall of the State of Qin.
一成犹启少康家.
Despite possessing merely one-tenth of the territory, Emperor Shao Kang successfully restored the rule of the Xia Dynasty.
苍龙日暮还行雨，
The azure dragon continues to bring rain at dusk,
老树春深更著花.
and ancient trees blossom even more vibrantly in the depth of spring.
待得汉庭明诏近，
When the imperial decree from the Han court draws near,
五湖同觅钓鱼槎.
people from all corners of the country simultaneously sought arms to confront the enemy.

### The lyrics (c)

万里乘风去复来，
Riding the wind for thousands of miles, I return once again,
只身东海挟春雷.
alone across the East Sea, I carry the thunder of spring.
忍看图画移颜色，
I can't endure the sight of colors fading in portraits,
肯使江山付劫灰.
and unwillingly allow the land to be reduced to ashes.
浊酒不销忧国泪，
Turbid wine cannot wash away the tears of national concern,
救时应仗出群才.
to resolve the present crisis, it is imperative to cultivate a great number of capable talents.

拼将十万头颅血,

It is necessary to sacrifice countless lives and rivers of blood,

须把乾坤力挽回.

to restore cosmic order.

### 2.23.12 Brief introduction of the authors of the poems (lyrics)

#### The author (a)

李贺（公元791年-817年），字长吉，汉族，河南福昌人，家居福昌昌谷，后世称李昌谷，是唐宗室郑王李亮后裔.有"诗鬼"之称.

Li He (791 AD - 817 AD), styled Changji, was of Han ethnicity and from Fuchang, Henan Province. His home was in Changgu, Fuchang. Later generations called him Li Changgu. He was a descendant of Li Liang, the King of Zheng of the Tang Dynasty. He is known as the "Poet Ghost".

#### The author (b)

顾炎武（公元1613-1682），汉族，江苏苏州府昆山人，明末清初的杰出的思想家、经学家、史地学家和音韵学家，与黄宗羲、王夫之并称为明末清初"三大儒".其主要作品有《日知录》、《天下郡国利病书》、《肇域志》等

Gu Yanwu (1613-1682 AD), was from Kunshan, Suzhou Prefecture, Jiangsu Province. He was an outstanding thinker, Confucian scholar, historian, geographer and phonologist in the late Ming and early Qing dynasties. He was known as one of the "Three Great Scholars" of the late Ming and early Qing Dynasties along with Huang Zongxi and Wang Fuzhi. His major works include "Daily Knowledge Record", "Book on the Benefits and Illnesses of All Prefectures and Kingdoms", "Zhaoyu Zhi", etc

#### The author (c)

秋瑾（公元1875年－1907年），女，中国女权和女学思想的倡导者，近代民主革命志士.第一批为推翻满清政权和数千年封建统治而牺牲的革命先驱，为辛亥革命做出了巨大贡献.

Qiu Jin (1875 -1907 AD), female, was an advocate of women's rights and women's studies in China and a modern democratic revolutionary activist. The first batch of revolutionary pioneers who sacrificed their lives to overthrow the Qing regime and the feudal rule that lasted for thousands of years made tremendous contributions to the Xinhai Revolution.

# 2.24 Song No.24, Spring night brings joyous rain

春夜喜雨　唐　杜甫

**Title of the poem: Spring night brings joyous rain**
**Author of the poem (lyrics), Tang Dynasty Du Bu**

**2.24.0 About the score and lyrics (poem)**

This score (sheet music) is derived (excerpted) from the (pieces) of Russian composer Rubinstein's Spring Song, and has undergone minor modifications to ensure a better alignment between the musical arrangement and the lyrics (poem).

The most beloved spring is the spring rain. As the saying goes, spring rain is more precious than oil. According to the author's understanding, Rubinstein's "Spring Song" describes the singing of a hundred birds and the blooming of flowers after the spring rain. Therefore needless to say more, the author rewrites the poem (lyrics) for the song.

## 2.24.1 Sheet music

$1 = C \quad \frac{2}{4}$

| 5 #4 5 | 5 #4 5 | 1 7 1 | 5 - | 4 - | 3· 2 | 3· 2 |
好雨　　知时节，当春乃发　生．随风潜入

1 7 6 | 7 6 5 | 5 #4 5 | 5 #4 5 | 1 7 1 | 6 5 |
夜，润物细无声．野径　云俱黑，江船　火独

4 #1 2 | 3 2 | 1 - | 1 0 | 7 #4 3 | 2 6 7 | 1 |
明．江船火独明．　　晓看　红湿　处，

1 2 3 #4 | 5 5 | 7 2 #4 3 | 2 6 7 | 1 2 3 #4 |
花重锦官城．好雨　知时节，当春乃发生．

5 0 5 | 5 7 ♭6 | 5 0 5 | 5 7 6 | 5 0 | 5 4 5 |
晓　看红湿处，花重锦官城．锦官城．

## 2.24.2 Sheet music with Lyrics marked in Chinese pinyin without tones

```
| 5  #4  5 | 5  #4  5 | 1  7  1 | 5 - | 4 - | 3·  2 | 3·  2 |
  hao     yu    zhi shi    jie dang chun  nai     fa     sheng    sui feng   qian ru
  好       雨    知  时     节  当   春    乃      发     生.      随  风     潜   入

| 1  7  6 | 7  6  5 | 5  #4  5 | 5  #4  5 | 1  7  1 | 6  5 |
  ye run wu   xi wu sheng   ye  jing       yun    ju hei    jiang chuan   huo  du
  夜,润 物   细 无 声.      野  径        云     俱 黑,    江    船       火   独

| 4  #1  2 | 3  2 | 1 - | 1  0 | 7  #4  3 | 2  6  7 | 1 |
  ming xiao kan  hong shi  chu    hua      zhong jin guan cheng  hao        yu
  明.  晓  看    红  湿    处,    花       重   锦   官   城.   好         雨

| 1  2  3  #4 | 5  5 | 7  2  #4  3 | 2  6  7 | 1  2  3  #4 |
  zhi shi jie  dang chun nai      fa    sheng dang chun  nai  fa sheng
  知  时 节,   当  春   乃       发    生.   当   春    乃   发 生.

| 5  0  5 | ♭5  7  ♭6 | 5  0  5 | 5  7  6 | 5  0 | 5  4  5 |
  xiao       kan hong shi chu         hua zhong  jin guan cheng     jin guan cheng
  晓          看  红  湿  处,         花  重    锦  官   城.       锦  官  城.
```

### 2.24.3 Text of the lyrics

好雨知时节，当春乃发生.随风潜入夜，润物细无声.
野径云俱黑，江船火独明.晓看红湿处，花重锦官城.

### 2.24.4 Text of the lyrics marked with tones in Chinese pinyin

hǎo yǔ zhī shí jié dāng chūn nǎi fā shēng suí fēng qián rù yè
好 雨 知 时 节， 当 春 乃 发 生. 随 风 潜 入 夜，
rùn wù xì wú shēng yě jìng yún jù hēi jiāng chuan huǒ dú míng
润 物 细 无 声. 野 径 云 俱 黑， 江 船 火 独 明.
xiǎo kàn hóng shī chù huā zhòng jǐn guān chéng
晓 看 红 湿 处，花 重 锦 官 城.

### 2.24.5 Literal translation of the lyrics

Good rain knows its time; it falls when spring arrives. It comes with the wind at night, moistening all things silently. The wild path is dark with clouds, but the river boat's fire shines brightly alone. In the morning, I look at the red and damp places; the flowers are heavy in the city of Jin Guan.

### 2.24.6 A more polished and stylistically enhanced translation of the lyrics

Rainfall is timely, occurring precisely at the arrival of spring. It falls quietly with the night wind, nourishing all things without making a sound. The rural paths are obscured by darkened clouds, yet the solitary light from a boat on the river glimmers brightly. In the morning, I observe the dew-covered, crimson-hued areas where flowers have absorbed the moisture; in Jin Guan City, blossoms bloom heavily.

### 2.24.7 Translation sentence by sentence

好雨知时节，当春乃发生.
Rainfall is timely, occurring precisely at the arrival of spring.
随风潜入夜，

It falls quietly with the night wind,
润物细无声.
nourishing all things without making a sound.
野径云俱黑,
The rural paths are obscured by darkened clouds,
江船火独明.
yet the solitary light from a boat on the river glimmers brightly.
晓看红湿处,
In the morning, I observe the dew-covered, crimson-hued areas where flowers have absorbed the moisture;
花重锦官城.
in Jin Guan City, blossoms bloom heavily.

## 2.24.8 Brief introduction of the author of the poem (lyrics)

杜甫（公元712-770），字子美，自号少陵野老，世称"杜工部"、"杜少陵"等，河南巩县人，唐代伟大的现实主义诗人，杜甫被世人尊为"诗圣"。

Du Fu (712-770 AD), styled Zimei, with the pseudonym Shaoling Yelao, and also known as Du Gongbu and Du Shaoling, was a native of Gong County, Henan Province. He was a prominent realist poet of the Tang Dynasty and is widely revered as the Poet Sage. Du Fu is widely regarded as one of the greatest poets in Chinese literary history.

# 2.25 Song No.25, Magnolia

木兰花　乙卯年吴兴寒食节　北宋　张先

**Tune of the poem: Magnolia.**
**Title of the poem: Yi Mao year's Wuxing Cold Food Festival day,**
**Author of the poem (lyrics), Northern Song Dynasty, Zhang Xian**

**2.25.0 About the score and lyrics (poem)**

This score (sheet music) is derived (excerpted) from the (pieces) of The Swallow which was composed by the French composer Agua, and has undergone minor modifications to ensure a better alignment between the musical arrangement and the lyrics (poem).

Swallows are flying freely in spring, that are so similar to the young men and women enjoying themselves on spring outings, the author incorporates this poem into that renowned musical composition.

## 2.25.1 Sheet music

$1 = C \quad \frac{2}{4}$

$\dot{1}$ 7 $\dot{1}$   7 6 7 | 6 3 3   3   4 3 4   2 4 6 |
龙　头　舴　　艋　吴　儿　竞，　笋　　柱　秋　　千

7 5 5 0 | 3 1 3   5 2 5 | $\dot{1}$ 6 $\dot{1}$   $\dot{3}$ | $\dot{2}$ 6 7
游 女 并.　芳　洲 拾　翠 暮　　忘　归, 秀　　野

$\dot{1}$ 7 6   7 6 5   5 | $\dot{1}$ 7 $\dot{1}$   7 6 7 | 5 3 3   3
踏　青 来　　不 定. 行　云 去　　后 逸 山 瞑，

0 | 4 3 4   2 3 6 | 7 5 5 0 | 3 1 3   5 2 5
　 已 　放 笙　歌 池 院 静.　中　 庭　月　色

$\dot{1}$ 6 $\dot{1}$   3 | $\dot{3}$ $\dot{5}$ $\dot{3}$   $\dot{2}$ $\dot{1}$ 6 | 5 3 2   1 0 0 |
正　清 明, 无　数 杨　花 过　　无　影.

## 2.25.2 Sheet music with Lyrics marked in Chinese pinyin without tones

```
1̇  7  1̇  7  6  7 | 6  3  3  3  4  3  4  2  4  6 |
long  tou  ze    meng wu er jing    sun    zhu  qiu    qian
龙    头   非    艋   吴  儿 竟,    笋    柱   秋     千

7  5  5  0 | 3  1  3  5  2  5  1̇  6  1̇  3  2̇  6  7
you nv bing    fang    zhou shi    cui mu   wang gui xiu    ye
游  女 并.     芳      洲   拾    翠   暮   忘   归, 秀    野

1̇  7  6  7  6  5  5 | 1̇  7  1̇  7  6  7 | 5  3  3  3
ta   qing lai   bu ding xing    yun qu    hou yao shan ming
踏   青   来    不 定.  行      云  去    后  遥  山   暝,

0 | 4  3  4  2  3  6 | 7  5  5  0 | 3  1  3  5  2  5
    yi   fang sheng   ge chi yuan jing    zhong    ting yue    se
    已   放   笙     歌 池  院   静.     中      庭   月    色

1̇  6  1̇  3 | 3  5  3  2  1̇  6 | 5  3  2  1  0  0 |
zheng qing ming wu    shu yang   hua guo    wu ying
正    清   明,  无    数  杨    花  过        无 影.
```

### 2.25.3 Text of the lyrics

龙头舴艋吴儿竞，笋柱秋千游女并.
芳洲拾翠暮忘归，秀野踏青来不定.
行云去后遥山暝，已放笙歌池院静.
中庭月色正清明，无数杨花过无影.

### 2.25.4 Text of the lyrics marked with tones in Chinese pinyin

lóng tóu zé měng wú ér jìng　　sǔn zhù qiū qiān yóu nǚ bìng
　龙　头　舴　艋　吴　儿　竞，　笋　柱　秋　千　游　女　并.
fāng zhōu shí cuì mù wàng guī　　xiù yě　tà qīng lái bù dìng
　芳　洲　拾　翠　暮　忘　归，　秀　野　踏　青　来　不　定.
xíng yún qù hòu yáo shān míng　　yǐ fang shēng gē chí yuàn jìng
　行　云　去　后　遥　山　暝，　已　放　笙　歌　池　院　静.
zhōng tíng yuè sè zhèng qīng míng wú shù yang huā guò wú yǐng
　中　庭　月　色　正　清　明，无　数　杨　花　过　无　影.

### 2.25.5 Literal translation of the lyrics

Dragon Head Rowing, the young men from the Wu region are competing. The young women on the bamboo column swing are playing together. They forget to return at dusk when they pick up the greenery on FangzhouIsland, and come to the beautiful fields for a leisurely walk. After the drifting clouds have passed, the distant mountains are dark; the music and songs have been played, and the courtyard is quiet. The moonlight in the courtyard was clear and bright, and countless willow catkins passed by without a trace.

### 2.25.6 A more polished and stylistically enhanced translation of the lyrics

Dragon Boat Racing, young men from Wu race eagerly, while doubles young women gather joyfully in playing on a swing made of bamboo pillar. At dusk, they forget to return after gathering greenery on FangzhouIsland,

and stroll leisurely through the beautiful fields. After drifting clouds have passed, distant mountains grow dark; songs and music fade, leaving the courtyard still. The moonlight shone clearly in the courtyard, and countless willow catkins drifted silently by, leaving no trace.

### 2.25.7 Translation sentence by sentence

龙头舴艋吴儿竞,
Dragon Boat Racing, young men from Wu race eagerly,
笋柱秋千游女并.
While doubles young women gather joyfully in playing on a swing made of bamboo pillar.
芳洲拾翠暮忘归,
At dusk, they forget to return after gathering greenery on Fangzhou Island,
秀野踏青来不定.
and stroll leisurely through the beautiful fields.
行云去后遥山暝,
After drifting clouds have passed, distant mountains grow dark,
已放笙歌池院静.
Songs and music fade, leaving the courtyard calm down.
中庭月色正清明,
The moonlight shone clearly in the courtyard,
无数杨花过无影.
And countless willow catkins drifted silently by, leaving no trace.

### 2.25.8 Brief introduction of the author of the poem (lyrics)

张先（公元 990 -1078），字子野，浙江乌程人.北宋时期著名的词人，天圣八年进士，官至尚书都官郎中.晚年退居湖州与杭州之间.

Zhang Xian (990-1078 AD), styled Ziye, was from Wucheng, Zhejiang Province. A renowned lyricist during the Northern Song Dynasty, In the eighth year of the Tian Sheng era, he passed the imperial examination and rose to the position of Director of the Secretariat. In his later years, he retired between Lake and Hangzhou.

# 2.26 Song No.26, Longing for the imperial capital

思帝乡　唐　韦庄

**Tune of the poem: Longing for the imperial capital.
Author of the poem (lyrics), Tang Dynasty, Wei Zhuang**

### 2.26.0 About the score and lyrics (poem)

This score (sheet music) is derived (excerpted) from the (pieces) of Hungarian Folk Song: May, and has undergone minor modifications to ensure a better alignment between the musical arrangement and the lyrics (poem).

May is the season for young men and women to sing and dance and outing, both in ancient China and Hungary as well, the author rewrites the poem (lyrics) for the song.

### 2.26.1 Sheet music

$1 = C \quad \frac{4}{4}$

```
6̣ 7̣  1 2  3 6  3 | 1 2  1 7̣  6̣ 6̣ | 6̣ 7̣  1 2
春  日 游,   杏   花  吹    满    头.   陌 上  谁 家

3 6  3 | 1 2  1 7̣  6̣ 6̣ | 1 7̣  6̣ 5̣ | 1 2  3 0 |
年 少 足   风    流.   妾 拟   将 身  嫁    与

1 7̣  6̣ 5̣ | 1 2  3 0 | 6̣ 6̣  7̣ 6̣  3 0 | 6̣ 7̣
妾 拟   将 身  嫁   与      一   生   休.    纵

1 2  3 6  3 | 1 2  1 7̣  6̣ 6̣ |
被   无 情 弃, 不   能    羞.
```

### 2.26.2 Sheet music with Lyrics marked in Chinese pinyin without tones

```
6̣ 7̣   1 2   3 6   3 | 1 2   1 7̣   6̣ 6̣ | 6̣ 7̣   1 2
chun ri  you  xing    hua chui    man   tou    mo shang shui jia
春   日   游,   杏     花   吹      满    头.    陌   上   谁  家

3 6   3 | 1 2   1 7̣   6̣ 6̣ | 1 7̣   6̣ 5̣ | 1 2   3 0 |
nian  shao zu   feng    liu    qie ni  jiang shen jia  yu
年    少  足    风      流.   妾  拟    将    身   嫁    与

1 7̣   6̣ 5̣ | 1 2   3 0 | 6̣ 6̣   7̣ 6̣   3 0 | 6̣ 7̣
qie ni  jiang shen jia   yu       yi     sheng   xiu    zong
妾  拟   将   身   嫁    与       一     生      休.    纵

1 2   3 6   3 | 1 2   1 7̣   6̣ 6̣ |
bei   wu qing qi bu    neng   xiu
被    无 情 弃, 不    能      羞.
```

### 2.26.3 Text of the lyrics

春日游，杏花吹满头.陌上谁家年少足风流.
妾拟将身嫁与，一生休.纵被无情弃，不能羞.

### 2.26.4 Text of the lyrics marked with tones in Chinese pinyin

chūn rì yóu xìng huā chuī mǎn tóu mò shàng shuí jiā nián shào zú fēng liú
　春　日　游，杏　花　吹　满　头.陌　上　谁　家　年　少　足　风　流.
qiè nǐ jiāng shēn jià yǔ yī shēng xiū zòng bèi wú qíng qì　bù néng xiū
　妾　拟　将　身嫁　与　一　生　休.纵　被　无　情　弃,不　能　羞.

### 2.26.5 Literal translation of the lyrics

Spring outing, apricot blossoms are blowing all over girl's head. Which family's youth on the road is full of youthful charm. The girl (being me) intends to marry to the charming and handsome young man for her whole life. Even if abandoned by the heartless, one must not be ashamed.

### 2.26.6 A more polished and stylistically enhanced translation of the lyrics

On a spring outing, apricot blossoms fall gently upon my head. The youth being full of charming on the road belong to whose family.

The young girl (being me) desires to marry the charming and handsome young man to have the matter of life been settled; even if cruelly forsaken, one should not feel ashamed.

### 2.26.7 Translation sentence by sentence

春日游，杏花吹满头.
On a spring outing, apricot blossoms fall gently upon my head.
陌上谁家年少足风流.
The youth being full of charming on the road belong to whose family.
妾拟将身嫁与，一生休.
The young girl (being me) desires to marry the charming and handsome

young man to have the matter of life been settled;

纵被无情弃，不能羞.

even if cruelly forsaken, one should not feel ashamed.

### 2.26.8 Brief introduction of the author of the poem (lyrics)

韦庄（公元 836 年 - 910 年），字端己，长安杜陵人，晚唐诗人，词人，五代时前蜀宰相.公元 894 年，年近六十时方考取进士，任校书郎.公元 901 年，韦庄入蜀为王建掌书记，自此终身仕蜀.与温庭筠同为"花间派"代表作家.

Wei Zhuang (836 AD - 910 AD), styled Duanji, from Duling, Chang 'an. He was a poet and lyricist of the late Tang Dynasty and served as the prime minister of the former Shu during the Five Dynasties period. In 894 AD, when he was nearly sixty years old, he passed the imperial examination and was appointed as a librarian. In 901 AD, Wei Zhuang entered Sichuan and served as the secretary of Wang Jian's office. From then on, he spent his entire life serving in Sichuan. He is a representative writer of the "Living among Flowers School" along with Wen Tingyun.

# 2.27 Song No.27, Ferry to Jingmen for farewell

渡荆门送别　唐　李白

**Title of the poem: Ferry to Jingmen for farewell**
**Author of the poem (lyrics), Tang Dynasty Li Bai**

## 2.27.0 About the score and lyrics (poem)

This score (sheet music) is derived (excerpted) from the (pieces) of the Song Santa Lucia, which is a traditional Neapolitan song. It was transcribed by Teodoro Cottrau (1827 - 1879), and has undergone minor modifications to ensure a better alignment between the musical arrangement and the lyrics (poem).

The lyrics celebrate the picturesque district of Saint Lucia on the bay of Naples, and is sung by a boatman who invites the listener for a ride on his boat, to enjoy the breezy evening. How is similar of this to the artistic conception of Li Bai's poems, the author rewrites Li bai' poem (lyrics) for the song.

## 2.27.1 Sheet music

$1 = C \quad \dfrac{3}{8}$

| 5 | 5·  | $\dot{1}$ | $\dot{1}$ | 7 | 7 | 4 | 4· | 6 | 6 | 5 | 5 | 3 | 5 | 6 | 5  #4 |
|---|-----|-----------|-----------|---|---|---|----|---|---|---|---|---|---|---|-------|
| 渡 | | 远 | 荆 | 门 | 外， | 来 | | 从 | 楚 | 国 | 游， | 山 | 随 | 平 | 野 |

| 4 | 4 | 3 | 2 | 6 | 5 | $\dot{3}$ | $\dot{2}$ | $\dot{1}$ | 7 | 6 | $\dot{2}$ | $\dot{2}$ | $\dot{1}$ | 6  #4 | 5 |
|---|---|---|---|---|---|-----------|-----------|-----------|---|---|-----------|-----------|-----------|-------|---|
| 尽， | 江 | 入 | 大 | 荒 | 流. | 月 | 下 | 飞 | 天 | | 镜， | 云 | 生 | 结 | 海 |

| $\dot{1}$ | $\dot{3}$ | $\dot{1}$ | $\dot{1}$ | 5 | 5 | 3 | 4 | $\dot{2}$ | $\dot{2}$ | $\dot{2}$ | 6· | 7 | $\dot{2}$ | $\dot{1}$ | $\dot{2}$ |

楼. 仍　怜　　故　　乡　　水，万　里　送　行　舟. 万

$\dot{3}$· $\underline{\dot{2}}$ | $\underline{\dot{2}}$ $\dot{1}$ |

里　送　行　舟.

## 2.27.2 Sheet music with Lyrics marked in Chinese pinyin without tones

| 5 | 5· | $\dot{1}$ | $\dot{1}$ | 7 | 7 | 4 | 4· | 6 | 6 | 5 | 5 | 3 | 5 | 6 | 5  #4 |
|---|----|-----------|-----------|---|---|---|----|---|---|---|---|---|---|---|-------|
| du | | yuan | jing | men | wai | lai | | cong | chu | guo | you | | shan | sui | ping ye |
| 渡 | | 远 | 荆 | 门 | 外， | 来 | | 从 | 楚 | 国 | 游， | | 山 | 随 | 平 野 |

| 4 | 4 | 3 | 2 | 6 | 5 | $\dot{3}$ | $\dot{2}$ | $\dot{1}$ | 7 | 6 | $\dot{2}$ | $\dot{2}$ | $\dot{1}$ | 6  #4 | 5 |
|---|---|---|---|---|---|-----------|-----------|-----------|---|---|-----------|-----------|-----------|-------|---|
| jin | jiang | ru | da | huang | liu | yue | xia | fei | tian | | jing | yun | sheng | jie | hai |
| 尽， | 江 | 入 | 大 | 荒 | 流. | 月 | 下 | 飞 | 天 | | 镜， | 云 | 生 | 结 | 海 |

| $\dot{1}$ | $\dot{3}$ | $\dot{1}$ | $\dot{1}$ | 5 | 5 | 3 | 4 | $\dot{2}$ | $\dot{2}$ | $\dot{2}$ | 6· | 7 | $\dot{2}$ | $\dot{1}$ | $\dot{2}$ |
|---|---|---|---|---|---|---|---|---|---|---|---|---|---|---|---|
| lou | reng | | lian | | gu | | xiang | | shui | wan | li | song | xing | zhou | wan |
| 楼. | 仍 | | 怜 | | 故 | | 乡 | | 水， | 万 | 里 | 送 | 行 | 舟. | 万 |

$\dot{3}$· $\underline{\dot{2}}$ | $\underline{\dot{2}}$ $\dot{1}$ |

li　song　xing　zhou

里　送　行　舟.

### 2.27.3 Text of the lyrics

渡远荆门外，来从楚国游.山随平野尽，江入大荒流.
月下飞天镜，云生结海楼.仍怜故乡水，万里送行舟.

### 2.27.4 Text of the lyrics marked with tones in Chinese pinyin

dù yuǎn jīng mén wài lái cóng chǔ guó yóu
渡 远 荆 门 外，来 从 楚 国 游.
shān suí ping yě jìn jiāng rù dà huāng liú
山 随 平 野 尽，江 入 大 荒 流.
yuè xià fēi tiān jìng  yún shēng jié hǎi lóu
月 下 飞 天 镜，云 生 结 海 楼.
réng lián gù xiāng shuǐ  wàn lǐ song xíng zhōu
仍 怜 故 乡 水，万 里 送 行 舟.

### 2.27.5 Literal translation of the lyrics

Ferrying far beyond Jingmen, I came to travel from the State of Chu. The mountains follow the plain to the end, and the river flows into the vast wilderness. The setting moon just likes a Flying Mirror; clouds rise and form the sea tower. Still cherishing the water of my hometown, I see you off by boat for thousands of miles.

### 2.27.6 A more polished and stylistically enhanced translation of the lyrics

Ferrying far beyond Jingmen, I journey from the State of Chu. The mountains follow the plains until they vanish, and the river flows into the vast wilderness. The setting moon just like a celestial mirror seems to float; rising clouds form an illusory vision just like a mirages over the sea. Still cherishing the waters of my hometown, I watch you sail away for thousands of miles aboard a departing boat.

## 2.27.7 Translation sentence by sentence

渡远荆门外，
Ferrying far beyond Jingmen,
来从楚国游.
I journey from the State of Chu.
山随平野尽，
The mountains follow the plains until they vanish,
江入大荒流.
and the river flows into the vast wilderness.
月下飞天镜，
The setting moon just like a celestial mirror seems to float;
云生结海楼.
rising clouds form an illusory vision just like a mirages over the sea.
仍怜故乡水，
Still cherishing the waters of my hometown,
万里送行舟.
I watch you sail away for thousands of miles aboard a departing boat.

## 2.27.8 Brief introduction of the author of the poem (lyrics)

For details, please refer to section 2.03.7 of this book, we do not repeat here.

# 2.28 Song No.28, Song of a Wanderer

### 游子吟　唐　孟郊

**Title of the poem: Song of a Wanderer**
**Author of the poem (lyrics), Tang Dynasty Meng Jiao**

### 2.28.0 About the score and lyrics (poem)

This score (sheet music) is derived from the Song Home, Sweet Home, was written by American lyricist John Howard Payne and English composer Sir Henry Bishop for an opera that was first produced in London in 1823. It has been undergone minor modifications to ensure a better alignment between the musical arrangement and the lyrics (poem).

Just same as the original English lyrics say "I gaze on the moon as I tread the dear wild. And I feel that my mother now thinks her child…", how the poetry of Meng Jiao has a similar concept when you are read it, (the Meng Jiao's poem and its translation see the following sections). The author rewrites the poem (lyrics) for the song.

## 2.28.1 Sheet music

$1 = C \quad \frac{4}{4}$

| 1 2 | 3· 4 4 5 | 5· 3 3 5 | 4· 3 4 2 | 3 — 0 |

慈 母 手 中　　线，　游　　　子　　身 上 衣.

| 1 2 | 3· 4 4 5 | 5· 3 3 5 | 4· 3 4 2 | 1 — 0 |

临 行　　密 密 缝，　意　　　恐　　迟 迟 归.

| 5 5 | 1· 7 6 5 | 5 — 3 5 | 4· 3 4 2 | 3 — 0 |

谁　　言 寸 草 心，　报　　得　　三 春 晖.

| 5 5 | 1· 7 6 5 | 5 — 3 5 | 4· 3 4 2 | 1 — — 0 |

谁　　言 寸 草 心，　报　　得　　三 春 晖.

## 2.28.2 Sheet music with Lyrics marked in Chinese pinyin without tones

| 1 2 | 3· 4 4 5 | 5· 3 3 5 | 4· 3 4 2 | 3 — 0 |

ci mu　shou zhong　　xian　you　　　zi　　shen shang yi

慈 母 手 中　　线，　游　　　子　　身 上 衣.

| 1 2 | 3· 4 4 5 | 5· 3 3 5 | 4· 3 4 2 | 1 — 0 |

lin xing　　mi mi feng　yi　　　kong　chi chi gui

临 行　　密 密 缝　　意　　　恐　　迟 迟 归.

| 5 5 | 1· 7 6 5 | 5 — 3 5 | 4· 3 4 2 | 3 — 0 |

shui　　yan cun cao xin　bao　　de　　san chun hui

谁　　言 寸 草 心，　报　　得　　三 春 晖.

| 5 5 | 1· 7 6 5 | 5 — 3 5 | 4· 3 4 2 | 1 — — 0 |

shui　　yan cun cao xin　bao　　de　　san chun hui

谁　　言 寸 草 心，　报　　得　　三 春 晖.

### 2.28.3 Text of the lyrics

慈母手中线，游子身上衣.临行密密缝，
意恐迟迟归.谁言寸草心，报得三春晖.

### 2.28.4 Text of the lyrics marked with tones in Chinese pinyin

cí mǔ shǒu zhōng xiàn yóu zǐ shēn shàng yī　lín xíng mì mì féng
慈母　手　中　线，游子身　　上 衣. 临 行　密密　缝，
yì kǒng chí chí guī　shuí yán cùn cǎo xīn　bào dé sān chūn huī
意 恐　迟 迟 归. 谁　言　寸 草 心，报 得 三　春　晖.

### 2.28.5 Literal translation of the lyrics

The thread in the mother's hand, is the clothes of the son's wearing. Before leaving, there was a tight gap, fearing that I might return home later and later. Who can say that the tender grass can repay the warmth of the spring sun.

### 2.28.6 A more polished and stylistically enhanced translation of the lyrics

The thread held tightly in a mother's hand becomes the garment worn by her son. Before his departure, every seam is stitched with care, out of fear that he may back home later and later. Who could claim that even the humblest grass can repay the warmth of the spring sun.

### 2.28.7 Translation sentence by sentence

慈母手中线，游子身上衣.
The thread held tightly in a mother's hand becomes the garment worn by her son.
临行密密缝，
Before his departure, every seam is stitched with care,
意恐迟迟归.
out of fear that he may back home later and later.

谁言寸草心，报得三春晖.

Who could claim that even the humblest grass can repay the warmth of the spring sun.

### 2.28.8 Brief introduction of the author of the poem (lyrics)

孟郊，(公元 751 - 814)，唐代诗人.字东野.浙江湖州武康人.唐代著名诗人.现存诗歌 500 多首，以短篇的五言古诗最多.

Meng Jiao (751 - 814 AD), a poet of the Tang Dynasty. His courtesy name is Dongye. From Wukang, Huzhou, Zhejiang Province. A famous poet of the Tang Dynasty. There are over 500 existing poems, among which the short five-character ancient poems are the most numerous.

# 2.29 Song No.29, The Spring Scenery

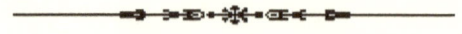

玉楼春　　北宋　　宋祁

**Tune of the poem: Enjoy the spring scenery on the Jade Tower**
**Title of the poem: The Spring Scenery**
**Author of the poem (lyrics), Northern Song Dynasty, Song Qi**

**2.29.0 About the score and lyrics (poem)**

This score (sheet music) is derived (excerpted) from the (pieces) of the song of Guno's Spring, and has undergone minor modifications to ensure a better alignment between the musical arrangement and the lyrics (poem).

The lyrics (the poem of Song Qi, and its translation see the following sections) describes the scenery of spring and poet's feelings in holiday in spring. The author rewrites the poem (lyrics) for the song.

## 2.29.1 Sheet music

$1 = C \quad \frac{2}{4}$

| 1 2 3 4 5 | 6 5 5 | 1 2 3 $\dot{1}$ | 6 6 5 5 |
|---|---|---|---|
| 东 城 渐　　觉 | 风 光 好, | 縠 皱 波　　纹 | 迎 客 棹. |

| 3 4 5 6 7 | $\dot{1}$ 7 $\dot{1}$ | $\dot{3}$ $\dot{2}$ $\dot{1}$ | 7 0 6 5 5 |
|---|---|---|---|
| 绿 杨 烟　　外 | 晓 寒 轻, | 红 杏 枝 头 | 春 意 闹. |

| 1 2 3 4 5 | 6 5 5 | 0 1 2 3 $\dot{1}$ | 6 6 5 5 |
|---|---|---|---|
| 浮 生 长　　恨 | 欢 娱 少, | 肯 爱 千 | 金 轻 一 笑. |

| 0 3 4 5 6 7 | $\dot{1}$ 7 $\dot{1}$ | $\dot{2}$ $\dot{3}$ $\dot{4}$ | $\dot{1}$ 7 $\dot{3}$ $\dot{2}$ $\dot{1}$ |
|---|---|---|---|
| 为 君 持　　酒 | 劝 斜 阳, | 且　　向 花 间 | 留 晚 照. |

$\dot{1}$ — |

## 2.29.2 Sheet music with Lyrics marked in Chinese pinyin without tones

| 1 2 3 4 5 | 6 5 5 | 1 2 3 $\dot{1}$ | 6 6 5 5 |
|---|---|---|---|
| dong cheng jian　　jue | feng guang hao, | hu zhou bo | wen ying ke zhao |
| 东 城 渐　　觉 | 风 光 好, | 縠 皱 波　　纹 | 迎 客 棹. |

| 3 4 5 6 7 | $\dot{1}$ 7 $\dot{1}$ | $\dot{3}$ $\dot{2}$ $\dot{1}$ | 7 0 6 5 5 |
|---|---|---|---|
| lv yang yan　　wai | xiao han qing | hong xing zhi tou | chun yi nao |
| 绿 杨 烟　　外 | 晓 寒 轻, | 红 杏 枝 头 | 春 意 闹. |

| 1 2 3 4 5 | 6 5 5 | 0 1 2 3 $\dot{1}$ | 6 6 5 5 |
|---|---|---|---|
| fu sheng chang　　hen | huan yu shao, | ken ai qian | jin qing yi xiao |
| 浮 生 长　　恨 | 欢 娱 少, | 肯 爱 千 | 金 轻 一 笑. |

| 0 3 4 5 6 7 | $\dot{1}$ 7 $\dot{1}$ | $\dot{2}$ $\dot{3}$ $\dot{4}$ | $\dot{1}$ 7 $\dot{3}$ $\dot{2}$ $\dot{1}$ |
|---|---|---|---|
| wei jun chi | jiu quan xie yang qie | xiang hua jian | liu wan zhao |
| 为 君 持　　酒 | 劝 斜 阳, | 且　　向 花 间 | 留 晚 照. |

$\dot{1}$ — |

### 2.29.3 Text of the lyrics

东城渐觉风光好，縠皱波纹迎客棹.
绿杨烟外晓寒轻，红杏枝头春意闹.
浮生长恨欢娱少，肯爱千金轻一笑.
为君持酒劝斜阳，且向花间留晚照.

### 2.29.4 Text of the lyrics marked with tones in Chinese pinyin

dōng chéng jiàn jué fēng guāng hǎo    hú zhòu bō wén yíng kè zhào
　东　　城　　渐 觉 风　　光　　好，縠 皱 波 纹 迎 客 棹.
lǜ yáng yān wài xiǎo hán qīng    hóng xìng zhī tóu chūn yì nào
绿 杨　 烟　外 晓　 寒　 轻，　红　　杏　枝 头　春　意 闹.
fú shēng cháng hèn huān yú shǎo kěn ài qiān jīn qīng yī xiào
浮　生　　 长　 恨 欢　　娱 少，肯 爱 千　 金　 轻　一 笑.
wèi jūn chí jiǔ quàn xié yang qiě xiàng huā jiān liú wǎn zhào
为　君 持 酒　劝 　斜 阳，且　 向　 花　间　留　晚　 照.

### 2.29.5 Literal translation of the lyrics

The scenery in the eastern part of the city gradually becomes more beautiful, with ripples on the rippling water welcoming the boats of visitors. The early morning chill is light outside the green poplar smoke, while the red apricot branches are brimming with the vitality of spring. Floating growth brings little sorrow and joy; willing to spend thousand pieces of gold to buy a young girl's a light smile. For you, I hold wine to soothe the setting sun and leave the evening glow among the flowers.

### 2.29.6 A more polished and stylistically enhanced translation of the lyrics

The landscape in the eastern part of the city gradually becomes more picturesque, with gentle ripples on the water welcoming visitors' boats. In the early morning, a light chill lingers outside the mist rising from the verdant poplar trees, while branches of red apricot burst with the vibrant energy of spring. The most regrettable thing in life is having too little joy and entertainment. One young girl's warm smile is worth more than a thousand golden coins. For your sake, I raise a cup of wine to bid farewell to the setting sun and linger in the evening glow amidst the blossoms.

## 2.29.7 Translation sentence by sentence

东城渐觉风光好,
The landscape in the eastern part of the city gradually becomes more picturesque,
縠皱波纹迎客棹.
with gentle ripples on the water welcoming visitors' boats.
绿杨烟外晓寒轻,
In the early morning, a light chill lingers outside the mist rising from the verdant poplar trees,
红杏枝头春意闹.
while branches of red apricot burst with the vibrant energy of spring.
浮生长恨欢娱少,
The most regrettable thing in life is having too little joy and entertainment.
肯爱千金轻一笑.
one young girl's warm smile is worth more than a thousand golden coins.
为君持酒劝斜阳,
For your sake, I raise a cup of wine to bid farewell to the setting sun
且向花间留晚照.
and linger in the evening glow amidst the blossoms.

## 2.29.8 Brief introduction of the author of the poem (lyrics)

宋祁（公元 998 - 1061）北宋文学家.字子京，湖北安州安陆人.天圣二年进士，官翰林学士，史馆修撰.与欧阳修等合修《新唐书》，书成，进工部尚书.

Song Qi (998 - 1061 AD) was a literary figure of the Northern Song Dynasty. Zi Jing, a native of Anlu, Anzhou, Hubei Province. In the second year of the Tian Sheng era, he passed the imperial examination and held the positions of Hanlin Scholar and Historian. He co-authored the New Book of

Tang with Ouyang Xiu and others. After the completion of the book, he was promoted to the position of Minister of Works.

# 2.30 Song No.30, The Long Song

## 长歌行　两汉　选自乐府民歌

**Tune of the poem: The Long Song,
Author of the poem (lyrics): excerpted from the folk songs of the official band, Han Dynasty**

### 2.30.0 About the score and lyrics (poem)

This score (sheet music) is derived (excerpted) from the (pieces) of Canadian Folk Songs: Drying Straw, and has undergone minor modifications to ensure a better alignment between the musical arrangement and the lyrics (poem). The author rewrites the poem (lyrics) for the song.

## 2.30.1 Sheet music

$1 = C \dfrac{2}{4}$

```
|5  1 3 |1 5 |1 3  1 1 |5 5  4 3 |2  5 |7 2
    青    青   园 中 葵，  朝 露  待 日   晞.    阳

 7 5 |7 2  7 5 |5 6  5 4 |3  5 |1 3  1 5 |
 春    布   德 泽，万 物  生 光   辉.    常    恐

 1 3  1 5 |5 5  4 3 |2  5 |1 3  1 1 |3 5
 秋 节 至，  焜 黄 华 叶 衰.  百    川    东 到

 3 5 |1 1  2 1 |6  1 1 6  6 1 |1 5  5 6 |
 海，  何 时 复 西  归.  少    壮    不    努 力，

 5  4  3  2 | 1
 老 大  徒 伤 悲.
```

## 2.30.2 Sheet music with Lyrics marked in Chinese pinyin without tones

```
|5   1 3   1 5 |1 3   1 1 |5 5   4 3 |2   5 |7 2
    qing  qing  yuan zhong kui  zhao lu  dai ri  xi      yang
     青    青    园  中  葵，  朝  露  待 日  晞.       阳

 7 5 |7 2   7 5 |5 6   5 4 |3   5 |1 3   1 5 |
 chun  bu   de  ze  wan wu sheng guang hui   chang     kong
 春    布    德  泽， 万 物  生  光   辉.   常         恐

 1 3   1 5 |5 5   4 3 |2   5 |1 3   1 1 |3   5
 qiu jie zhi  kun huang hua ye shuai  bai   chuan  dong dao
 秋 节 至，    焜 黄   华 叶 衰.   百     川     东 到

 3 5 |1 1   2 1 |6   1 1 6   6 1 |1 5   5 6 |
 hai   he shi fu  xi gui   shao  zhuang bu   nu  li
 海，  何 时 复 西  归.  少    壮    不    努 力，

 5   4   3   2 | 1
 lao da  tu shang bei
 老 大   徒 伤  悲.
```

### 2.30.3 Text of the lyrics

青青园中葵，朝露待日晞.阳春布德泽，万物生光辉.
常恐秋节至，焜黄华叶衰.百川东到海，何时复西归.
少壮不努力，老大徒伤悲.

### 2.30.4 Text of the lyrics marked with tones in Chinese pinyin

qīng qīng yuán zhōng kuí zhāo lù dài rì　xī yang chūn bù dé zé
　青　青　园　中　葵，朝　露　待 日 晞.阳　春　布 德泽，
wàn wù shēng guāng huī cháng kǒng qiū jié zhì　kūn huáng huá yè shuāi
　万 物　生　光　辉.常　恐　秋节至，焜　黄　华 叶 衰.
bǎi chuān dōng dào hǎi　hé shí fù xī guī shào zhuàng bù nǔ lì
 百　川　东　到 海，何 时 复 西 归. 少　壮　不努 力，
lǎo dà tú shāng bēi
 老 大 徒 伤　悲.

### 2.30.5 Literal translation of the lyrics

The sunflower in the garden is green, and the morning dew awaits the sun to dry. Spring bestows its blessings, and all things shine with radiance. It often fear that when autumn comes, the leaves will turn yellow and wither. All rivers flow eastward to the sea; when will they return westward again. If you don't work hard when you are young, you will only regret it when you are old!

### 2.30.6 A more polished and stylistically enhanced translation of the lyrics

The sunflower in the garden remains vibrant and green, while morning dew lingers, awaiting the warmth of the rising sun. Spring brings its blessings, and all living things bask in its radiant glow. Yet it often fear that with the arrival of autumn, leaves will yellow and wither away. Just like rivers flowing eastward to the sea, they shall never return westward. If one does not strive in youth, one can only lament in old age.

## 2.30.7 Translation sentence by sentence

青青园中葵,
The sunflower in the garden remains vibrant and green,
朝露待日晞.
while morning dew lingers, awaiting the warmth of the rising sun.
阳春布德泽,
Spring brings its blessings,
万物生光辉.
and all living things bask in its radiant glow.
常恐秋节至,
Yet it often fear that with the arrival of autumn,
焜黄华叶衰.
leaves will yellow and wither away.
百川东到海,
Just like rivers flowing eastward to the sea,
何时复西归.
they shall never return westward.
少壮不努力,
If one does not strive in youth,
老大徒伤悲.
one can only lament in old age.

# 2.31 Song No.31, Listen to the flute

闻笛  唐  赵碬

**Title of the poem: "Listen to the flute"**
**Author of the poem (lyrics), Tang Dynasty, Zhao Xia**

### 2.31.0 About the score and lyrics (poem)

This score (sheet music) is derived (excerpted) from the (pieces) of J. S. Bach (1685 – 1750) Johann Sebastian, Bach's Badinerie *Orchestral Suite No. 2* Suite No. 2 in B minor, and has undergone minor modifications to ensure a better alignment between the musical arrangement and the lyrics (poem).

This piece showcases the beautiful and melodious form of the flute and the player's proficient skills. This piece is also often played with Chinese bamboo flutes in Western bands. It can be seen that Chinese and Western artists have a very similar understanding and application of the flute.

The lyrics (the poem, and its translation see the following sections) describes the joy of hearing a flute, therefore it is very appropriate to combine the lyrics and the music. The author incorporates this poem into that renowned musical composition.

## 2.31.1 Sheet music

$1 = C \quad \frac{2}{4}$

$\underline{\dot{7}\cdot\ \dot{2}}\ \underline{7\ {}^\#\dot{4}\cdot}\ \underline{7\ {}^\#\dot{4}}\ |\ \underline{\dot{2}\cdot\ {}^\#\dot{4}}\ \underline{\dot{2}\ 7}\ |\ \underline{{}^\#\dot{4}\ 7}\ \underline{\dot{2}\ 7}\ \underline{{}^\#\dot{1}\ 7}$

谁家　吹笛　画楼　中,断　续　声

$\underline{\dot{1}\ 7}\ |\ \underline{6\ {}^\#\dot{1}}\ \underline{\dot{3}\ {}^\#\dot{1}}\ \underline{\dot{2}\ 7}\ |\ \underline{\dot{7}\cdot\ \dot{2}}\ \underline{7\ {}^\#\dot{4}\cdot}\ \underline{7\ {}^\#\dot{4}}\ |\ \underline{\dot{2}\cdot\ {}^\#\dot{4}}\ \underline{\dot{2}\ 2}$

随　断　续　风.　响　遏　行云　横碧

$7\ |\ \underline{\dot{2}\ \dot{1}}\ \underline{\dot{2}\ \dot{2}}\ |\ \underline{\dot{1}\ \dot{2}}\ |\ \underline{7\ \dot{2}}\ \underline{\dot{2}\ 1}\ |\ \underline{{}^\#\dot{4}\ 3}\ \underline{{}^\#\dot{4}\ {}^\#\dot{4}}\ \underline{3\ {}^\#\dot{4}}$

落,清　和冷　月　到　帘栊.清　和冷　月

$\underline{\dot{2}\ {}^\#\dot{4}}\ \underline{{}^\#\dot{4}\ 3}\ |\ \underline{{}^\#\dot{4}\cdot\ 6}\ \underline{{}^\#\dot{4}}\ \underline{1\cdot\ {}^\#\dot{4}}\ 1\ |\ \underline{6\cdot\ 1}\ \underline{6\ {}^\#\dot{4}}\ \underline{{}^\#\dot{1}\ 7}$

到　帘栊.兴来　三弄　有桓　子,赋就

$\underline{3\cdot\ 2}\ {}^\#\dot{4}\ |\ \underline{6\cdot\ 4}\ \underline{5\ 3}\ 0\ |\ \underline{5\cdot\ 7}\ \underline{5\ 3}\cdot\ \underline{5\ 3}\ |\ \underline{{}^\#\dot{1}\cdot\ 3}\ {}^\#\dot{1}$

一　篇怀　马融.　曲罢　不知　人在

$6\ |\ \underline{6\ \dot{2}}\ \underline{{}^\#\dot{4}\ 2}\ |\ \underline{3\ 2}\ \underline{3\ 2}\ |\ \underline{{}^\#\dot{1}\ 3}\ \underline{5\ 3}\ 0\ |\ \underline{{}^\#\dot{4}\ {}^\#\dot{4}}$

否,余　音嘹　亮尚　飘空.　兴来

$\underline{\dot{4}\ {}^\#\dot{4}}\ \underline{\dot{2}\ {}^\#\dot{4}}\ \underline{{}^\#\dot{4}\ \dot{3}}\ |\ 3\ 3\ \underline{3\ 3}\ |\ {}^\#\dot{1}\ \underline{3\ 3}\ \underline{3\ 2}\ |\ 6\ 4$

三弄有桓子,　赋就一　篇怀　马融.曲罢

$\underline{5\ 4}\ |\ \underline{7\ 6}\ \dot{1}\ \underline{3\cdot\ \dot{2}}\ {}^\#\dot{1}\ |\ 0\ 0\ |\ \underline{{}^\#\dot{4}\cdot\ \dot{2}}\ \underline{{}^\#\dot{4}\ 7}\ {}^\#\dot{4}\ |$

不知人在否,人在否,　　余　音嘹亮

$\underline{\dot{3}\ \dot{2}}\ \underline{{}^\#\dot{1}\ \dot{2}}\ 7\ |$

尚　飘　空.

## 2.31.2 Sheet music with Lyrics marked in Chinese pinyin without tones

```
7·  2   7  #4·  7  #4 | 2·  #4   2   7 |#4   7   2   7 |#1   7
shui jia   chui di   hua lou    zhong duan    xu     sheng
谁   家    吹   笛    画    楼    中   断      续      声

1   7  6  #1   3  #1 | 2   7 | 7·  2   7  #4·  7  4 | 2·  #4   2
sui    duan   xu     feng    xiang e    xing yun    heng bi
随     断     续      风.    响    遏    行   云    横    碧

7  | 2  1   2   2   1 | 2   7   2   1 |#4   3  #4 | #4   3  #4
luo  qing  he leng   yue  dao  lian long qing  he leng    yue
落,  清    和  冷     月   到   帘   栊. 清    和  冷     月

2  #4  #4   3  #4·  6  #4 | 1·  #4   1 | 6·   1   6  #4 | #1   7
dao   lian long xing lai   san nong   you huan   zi fu   jiu
到    帘   栊. 兴  来      三  弄     有 桓     子 赋    就

3·  2  #4 | 6·  4   5   3   0 | 5·  7   5   3·  5   3 | 1·  3  #1
yi   pian huai  ma rong       qu   ba   bu  zhi  ren zai
一   篇   怀    马 融.        曲   罢   不   知   人 在

6   6   2  #4   2 | 3   2   3   2 |#1   3   5   3   0 |#4  #4
fou yu  yin    liao liang shang  piao kong    xing lai
否, 余  音    嘹    亮    尚     飘   空.      兴  来

4  #4 | 2  #4  #4   3 | 3   3   3   3 |#1   3   3   2 | 6   4
san nong you huan zi   fu  jiu  yi  pian huai   ma rong qu ba
三  弄  有 桓   子,  赋  就  一  篇  怀     马   融 曲 罢

5   4 | 7   6   1   3·  2  #1 | 0   0 |#4·  2  #4   7  #4
bu  zhi ren zai fou ren zai fou        yu    yin liao liang
不  知  人 在  否, 人 在  否,            余    音 嘹    亮

3   2  #1   2   7 |
shang piao kong
尚     飘   空.
```

### 2.31.3 Text of the lyrics

谁家吹笛画楼中，断续声随断续风.
响遏行云横碧落，清和冷月到帘栊.
兴来三弄有桓子，赋就一篇怀马融.
曲罢不知人在否，余音嘹亮尚飘空.

### 2.31.4 Text of the lyrics marked with tones in Chinese pinyin

shuí jiā chuī dí huà lóu zhōng   duàn xù shēng suí duàn xù fēng
　谁　家　吹　笛　画　楼　中，　断　续　声　随　断　续　风.
xiǎng è xíng yún héng bì luò   qīng hé lěng yuè dào lián lóng
　响　遏　行　云　横　碧　落，　清　和　冷　月　到　帘　栊.
xìng lái sān nòng yǒu huán zi   fù jiù yī piān huái mǎ róng
　兴　来　三　弄　有　桓　子，赋就　一　篇　怀　马　融.
qū bà bù zhī rén zài fǒu   yú yīn liáo liàng shàng piāo kōng
　曲罢　不　知人　在　否，余音　嘹　亮　尚　飘　空.

### 2.31.5 Literal translation of the lyrics

Who plays the flute in the painting tower house. Intermittent sounds follow intermittent winds. The sound stops the clouds from crossing the blue sky, and the clear and cold moon reaches the pillars of the corridor. In the mood, it is played the famous piece "Three Variations on Plum Blossoms" by Huan Yi, a general of the Eastern Jin Dynasty. It seems as if a prose piece by litterateur Ma Rong of the Han Dynasty, "Ode to the Flute", has been rewritten.

The melody has ended, and it's unknown if the person is there or not. The lingering sound is still resounding and floating in the air.

### 2.31.6 A more polished and stylistically enhanced translation of the lyrics

Who is playing the flute within the pavilion of a painting house. Intermittent melodies accompany the gusts of wind. The music seems to halt the clouds drifting across the azure sky, while the bright, cold moonlight reaches the pillars of the corridor. In this contemplative mood, it performed the renowned piece "Three Variations on Plum Blossoms," composed by Huan Yi, a general of the Eastern Jin Dynasty; It seemed as though the Eastern Han Dynasty litterateur Ma Rong's prose piece "Ode to the Flute" had been brought to life. Although the melody has ended, it is unknown whether the player is still there. But the lingering notes continue to echo and drift through the air.

### 2.31.7 Translation sentence by sentence

谁家吹笛画楼中，
Who is playing the flute within the pavilion of a painting house.
断续声随断续风.
Intermittent melodies accompany the gusts of wind.
响遏行云横碧落，
The music seems to halt the clouds drifting across the azure sky,
清和冷月到帘栊.
while the bright, cold moonlight reaches the pillars of the corridor.
兴来三弄有桓子，
In this contemplative mood, it performed the renowned piece "Three Variations on Plum Blossoms," composed by Huan Yi, a general of the Eastern Jin Dynasty;
赋就一篇怀马融.
It seemed as though the Eastern Han Dynasty litterateur Ma Rong's prose piece "Ode to the Flute" had been brought to life.
曲罢不知人在否，
Although the melody has ended, it is unknown whether the player is still there.
余音嘹亮尚飘空.
But the lingering notes continue to echo and drift through the air.

### 2.31.8 Brief introduction of the author of the poem (lyrics)

赵嘏（公元806年 - 853年），字承佑，楚州山阳人，唐代诗人.年轻时四处游历.会昌四年进士及第，一年后东归.入仕为渭南尉.

Zhao Xia (806 - 853 AD), styled Chengyou, was a native of Shanyang, Chuzhou. He was a poet of the Tang Dynasty. Travel around when young. In the fourth year of Huichang, he passed the imperial examination and returned eastward the following year. He was appointed as the magistrate of Weinan.

## 2.32 Song No.32, Moor at Guazhou city

南宋　郑会　唐　李白　宋　王安石

**Title of the poem:**

**(a)**

题邸间壁郑会

Write a poem for the next door of the residence, Zheng hui

**(b)**

早发白帝城李白

Bid farewell and Set off from the White Emperor City at dawn, Li Bai

**(c)**

泊船瓜州王安石

Moor at Guazhou city, Wang An Shi

**Author of the poem (lyrics):**
Southern Song Dynasty，Zheng Hui,
Tang Dynasty Li Bai,
Northern Song Dynasty Wang An Shi

### 2.32.0 About the score and lyrics (poem)

This score (sheet music) is derived (excerpted) from the (pieces) of Dean Martin' Song of Come back to Sorrento, and has undergone minor modifications to ensure a better alignment between the musical arrangement and the lyrics (poem).

When he composed this song, Dean Martin gazing out at the sea whose beauty he was praising.

Revisiting an old place or returning to one's hometown, to a place familiar and beloved, the heart is filled with admiration and embrace for the scenery, and this is true for poets, musicians and other artists alike. The author rewrites the poems (lyrics) for the song.

## 2.32.1 Sheet music

$1 = C \quad \frac{3}{4}$

| $\underline{6 \cdot \ \ 7} \ \ \underline{1 \ \ 2} \ \ \underline{3 \ \ 1} \ | \ 3 \ \ 3 - \ | \ \underline{2 \ \ 3} \ \ \underline{4 \ \ 2} \ \ \underline{4 \ \ 2} \ | \ 6 \ \ 6 - \ |$

馀 酿 香 梦 怯 春 寒， 翠 掩 重 门 燕 子 闲．

$\underline{6 \ \ 7} \ \ \underline{\dot{1} \ \ 7} \ \ \underline{6 \ \ 7} \ | \ 3 \ \ 3 - \ | \ \underline{2 \ \ 3} \ \ \underline{2 \ \ 1} \ \ \underline{7 \cdot \ \ 1} \ | \ 6 - \quad |$

敲 断 玉 钗 红 烛 冷， 计 程 应 说 到 常 山．

$\underline{\dot{1} \ \ 7} \ \ \underline{5 \ \ 6} \ \ \underline{7 \ \ 5} \ | \ 6 \ \ 6 - \ | \ \underline{7 \ \ 6} \ \ \underline{5 \ \ 6} \ \ \underline{7 \ \ 5} \ | \ 6 \ \ 6 - \ |$

朝 辞 白 帝 彩 云 间， 千 里 江 陵 一 日 还．

$\underline{3 \ \ 4} \ \ \underline{5 \ \ 3} \ \ \underline{2 \ \ 1} \ | \ 4 \ \ 4 - \ | \ \underline{5 \ \ 6} \ \ \underline{7 \ \ 6} \ \ \underline{5 \ \ 7} \ | \ 3 - \quad |$

两 岸 猿 声 啼 不 住， 轻 舟 已 过 万 重 山．

$\underline{\dot{1} \ \ 7} \ \ \underline{5 \ \ 6} \ \ \underline{7 \ \ 5} \ | \ 6 \ \ 6 - \ | \ \underline{\dot{2} \ \ \dot{1}} \ \ \underline{7 \ \ \dot{1}} \ \ \underline{\dot{2} \ \ 7} \ | \ \dot{1} - \quad |$

京 口 瓜 洲 一 水 间， 钟 山 只 隔 数 重 山．

$\underline{\dot{1} \ \ \dot{2}} \ \ \underline{\dot{3} \ \ \dot{2}} \ \ \underline{\dot{1} \ \ \dot{2}} \ | \ 5 \ \ 5 - \ | \ \underline{4 \ \ 5} \ \ \underline{4 \ \ 3} \ \ \underline{2 \ \ 3} \ | \ 1 - \quad |$

春 风 又 绿 江 南 岸， 明 月 何 时 照 我 还．

## 2.32.2 Sheet music with Lyrics marked in Chinese pinyin without tones

| 6 7 1 2 3 1 | 3 3 - | 2 3 4 2 | 4 2 | 6 6 - |
tu mi xiang meng qie chun han　　cui yan zhong men　yan zi　xian
酴 醾 香 梦 怯 春 寒，　　　翠 掩 重 门　燕 子　闲。

| 6 7 1 7 6 7 | 3 3 - | 2 3 2 1 | 7 1 | 6 - |
qiao duan yu chai hong zhu leng　　ji cheng ying shuo　dao chang shan
敲 断 玉 钗 红 烛 冷，　　　计 程 应 说　到 常 山。

| 1 7 5 6 7 5 | 6 6 - | 7 6 5 6 | 7 5 | 6 6 - |
chao ci bai di cai yun jian　　qian li jiang ling　yi ri huan
朝 辞 白 帝 彩 云 间，　　千 里 江 陵　一 日 还。

| 3 4 5 3 2 1 | 4 4 - | 5 6 7 6 | 5 7 | 3 - |
liang an yuan sheng ti bu zhu　　qing zhou yi guo wan chong shan.
两 岸 猿 声 啼 不 住，　　轻 舟 已 过 万 重 山。

| 1 7 5 6 7 5 | 6 6 - | 2 1 7 1 | 2 7 | 1 - |
jing kou gua zhou yi shui jian　　zhong shan zhi ge shu chong shan
京 口 瓜 洲 一 水 间，　　钟 山 只 隔 数 重 山。

| 1 2 3 2 1 2 | 5 5 - | 4 5 4 3 | 2 3 | 1 - |
chun feng you lv jiang nan an　　ming yue he shi zhao wo huan
春 风 又 绿 江 南 岸，　　明 月 何 时 照 我 还。

### 2.32.3 Text of the lyrics (a)

### 题邸间壁宋郑会

酴醾香梦怯春寒，翠掩重门燕子闲.
敲断玉钗红烛冷，计程应说到常山.

### 2.32.4 Text of the lyrics (a) marked with tones in Chinese pinyin

tú mí xiāng mèng qiè chūn hán　　cuì yǎn chòng mén yàn zi xián
酴 醾 香 梦 怯 春 寒, 翠 掩 重 门 燕 子 闲.
qiāo duàn yù chāi hóng zhú lěng　　jì chéng yīng shuō dào cháng shān
敲 断 玉 钗 红 烛 冷, 计 程 应 说 到 常 山.

### 2.32.5 Literal translation of the lyrics (a)

Dream accompanied by the aroma of fine wine is intimidated by the cold of spring; green leaves cover the heavy door and swallows are leisurely. The jade hairpin was broken and the red candle was cold. Calculating the distance of the journey; it could say that he is arriving Changshan town.

### 2.32.6 A more polished and stylistically enhanced translation of the lyrics (a)

Dream accompanied by the fragrance of wine is intimidated by the chill of spring; green leaves cover the heavy gate as swallows rest leisurely. The jade hairpin lies broken, and the red candle has gone cold. Counting the journey I should say he arriveChangshan.

### 2.31.7 Translation sentence by sentence of the lyrics (a)

酴醾香梦怯春寒,
Dream accompanied by the fragrance of wine is intimidated by the chill of spring,
翠掩重门燕子闲.
Green leaves cover the heavy gate as swallows rest leisurely.

敲断玉钗红烛冷,
The jade hairpin lies broken, and the red candle has gone cold.
计程应说到常山.
Counting the journey I should say he arriveChangshan.

### 2.32.8 Brief introduction of the author of the poem (lyrics-a)

郑会, 字文谦, 号亦山, 江西贵溪人.少游学朱熹, 陆九渊之门.公元 1211 年进士.十年, 擢礼部侍郎.公元 1225 引疾归里.卒年八十二.

Zheng Hui, styled Wenqian and with the pseudonym Yishan, was from Guixi, Jiangxi Province. Study in the schools of Zhu Xi and Lu Jiuyuan at a young age. He passed the imperial examination in 1211 AD. After ten years, he was promoted to the position of Vice Minister of Rites. In 1225 AD, he dueto his illness back to his hometown. He died at the age of eighty-two.

### 2.32.9 Text of the lyrics (b)

### 早发白帝城唐李白

朝辞白帝彩云间, 千里江陵一日还.两岸猿声啼不住, 轻舟已过万重山.

### 2.32.10 Text of the lyrics(b) marked with tones in Chinese pinyin

cháo cí bái dì cǎi yún jiān qiān lǐ jiāng líng　yī rì huán
　朝　辞 白 帝 彩　云 间, 千 里 江　陵　一 日 还.
liǎng àn yuán shēng tí bú zhù　qīng zhōu yǐ guò wàn chóng shān
　两　岸　猿　声　啼 不　住, 轻　舟 已 过 万　重　山.

### 2.32.11 Literal translation of the lyrics (b)

I bid farewell to the White Emperor City in the colorful clouds in the morning and return to a thousand miles away Jiangling could be in one day. The cries of apes on both banks never cease, and the light boat has already crossed thousands of mountains.

## 2.32.12 A more polished and stylistically enhanced translation of the lyrics (b)

At dawn, I bid farewell to the White Emperor City amidst colorful clouds. A thousand miles to Jiangling can be traversed in a single day. The cries of apes echo on both banks without ceasing, while the light boat glides past countless mountains.

## 2.32.13 Translation sentence by sentence of the lyrics (b)

朝辞白帝彩云间，
At dawn, I bid farewell to the White Emperor City amidst colorful clouds.
千里江陵一日还.
A thousand miles to Jiangling can be traversed in a single day.
两岸猿声啼不住，
The cries of apes echo on both banks without ceasing,
轻舟已过万重山.
while the light boat glides past countless mountains.

## 2.32.14 Brief introduction of the author of the poem (b)

Refer to section 2.03.7 of this book.

## 2.32.15 Text of the lyrics (c)

**泊船瓜州宋王安石**

京口瓜洲一水间，钟山只隔数重山.春风又绿江南岸，明月何时照我还.

## 2.32.16 Text of the lyrics (c) marked with tones in Chinese pinyin

jīng kǒu guā zhōu yī shuǐ jiān  zhōng shān zhǐ gé shù chóng shān
 京  口  瓜  洲  一  水  间，  钟   山  只 隔 数   重   山.
chūn fēng yòu lǜ jiāng nán àn   míng yuè hé shí zhào wǒ huán
 春   风  又 绿  江   南  岸，  明   月  何 时  照   我  还.

### 2.32.17 Literal translation of the lyrics (c)

The Jingkou city and the Guazhou city is separated by a river, and Zhongshan Mountain is just a few mountains apart. The spring breeze has once again turned the south bank of the river green; when will the bright moon shine upon my return

### 2.32.18 A more polished and stylistically enhanced translation of the lyrics (c)

The Jingkousity and the Guazhou city lie across the river, and Zhongshan Mountain is just beyond a few hills. Once again, the spring breeze has turned the southern bank of the Yangtze green, but when will the bright moon illuminate my journey home.

### 2.32.19 Translation sentence by sentence of the lyrics (c)

京口瓜洲一水间，
The Jingkousity and the Guazhou city lie across the river,
钟山只隔数重山.
and Zhongshan Mountain is just beyond a few hills.
春风又绿江南岸，
Once again, the spring breeze has turned the southern bank of the Yangtze green,
明月何时照我还.
but when will the bright moon illuminate my journey home.

### 2.32.20 Brief introduction of the author of the poem (lyrics)

王安石（公元1021年-1086年），字介甫，号半山，封荆国公.世人称王荆公.抚州临川人，北宋著名政治家，文学家，改革家，唐宋八大家之一.

Wang Anshi (1021 - 1086 AD), styled Jiefu and with the pseudonym Half a Hill, was enfeoffed as the Duke of Jing. The world called him Wang Jinggong. He was from Linchuan, Fuzhou. He was a renowned, litateur and reformer of the Northern Song Dynasty and one of the Eight Great Prose Masters of the Tang and Song Dynasties.

# 2.33 Song No.33, New Year's Day

## 元日　北宋　王安石

**Title of the poem: "New Year's Day"**
**Author of the poem (lyrics): Northern Song Dynasty Wang An Shi**

### 2.33.0 About the score and lyrics (poem)

This score (sheet music) is derived (excerpted) from the British Christmas Song: We Wish You a Merry Christmas, and has undergone minor modifications to ensure a better alignment between the musical arrangement and the lyrics (poem).

The joy, cheerful and blessings of celebrating the New Year are the same throughout history and across the world. The author rewrites the poem (lyrics) for the song.

### 2.33.1 Sheet music

| 5 | i i̲ 2̲̇ i̲ 7̲ | 6 6 6 | 2 2̇ 3̇ 2̇ i̲ | 7 5 5 |

爆 竹 声 中 一 岁 除， 春 风 送 暖 入 屠 苏. 千

| 3 3̲ 4̲ 3̲ 2̲ | i 6 5̲ 5̲ | 6 2̇ 7 | i - 5 | i i |

门 万 户 瞳 瞳 日， 总 把 新 桃 换 旧 符. 千 门

| i | 7 - 7 | i 7 6 | 5 - 2̇ | 3̇ 2̇ i | 5̲ 5̲ 5̲ 5̲ |

万 户 瞳 瞳 日， 总 把 新 桃 换 旧

| 6 2̇ 7 | i - - |

符

### 2.33.2 Sheet music with Lyrics marked in Chinese pinyin without tones

| 5 | i i̲ 2̲̇ i̲ 7̲ | 6 6 6 | 2 2̇ 3̇ 2̇ i̲ | 7 5 5 |

bao zhu sheng zhong yi sui chu chun feng song nuan ru tu su qian

爆 竹 声 中 一 岁 除， 春 风 送 暖 入 屠 苏. 千

| 3 3̲ 4̲ 3̲ 2̲ | i 6 5̲ 5̲ | 6 2̇ 7 | i - 5 | i i |

men wan hu tong tong ri zong ba xin tao huan jiu fu qian jia

门 万 户 瞳 瞳 日， 总 把 新 桃 换 旧 符 千 家

| i | 7 - 7 | i 7 6 | 5 - 2̇ | 3̇ 2̇ i | 5̲ 5̲ 5̲ 5̲ |

wan hu tong tong ri zong ba xin tao huan jiu

万 户 瞳 瞳 日， 总 把 新 桃 换 旧

| 6 2̇ 7 | i - - |

fu

符

### 2.33.3 Text of the lyrics

爆竹声中一岁除，春风送暖入屠苏.
千门万户曈曈日，总把新桃换旧符.

### 2.33.4 Text of the lyrics marked with tones in Chinese pinyin

bào zhú shēng zhōng yī suì chú chūn fēng sòng nuǎn rù tú sū
爆 竹 声 中 一 岁 除，春 风 送 暖 入 屠苏.
qiān mén wàn hù tóng tóng rì　zǒng bǎ xīn táo huàn jiù fú
千 门 万 户 曈 曈 日，总 把 新 桃 换 旧符.

### 2.33.5 Literal translation of the lyrics

The sound of firecrackers marks the passing of a year, and the spring breeze brings the warm enter the Tusu wines. On a bright and auspicious day, every household always replaces the old talismans with new ones

### 2.33.6 A more polished and stylistically enhanced translation of the lyrics

The sound of firecrackers signifies the transition from one year to the next, while the gentle spring breeze brings warm air into the ceremonyTusu wine. On a bright and auspicious day, households traditionally replace old talismans with new ones.

### 2.33.7 Translation sentence by sentence

爆竹声中一岁除，
The sound of firecrackers signifies the transition from one year to the next,
春风送暖入屠苏.
while the gentle spring breeze brings warm air into the ceremony Tusu wine.
千门万户曈曈日，总把新桃换旧符.
On a bright and auspicious day, Tens of thousands households traditionally replace old talismans with new ones.

## 2.33.8 Brief introduction of the author of the poem (lyrics)

For details, please refer to section 2.32.16. of this book.

# 2.34 Song No.34, Autumn night

秋夕　唐　杜牧

**Title of the poem: Autumn night**
**New Author of the poem (lyrics), Tang Dynasty Du Mu**

### 2.34.0 About the score and lyrics (poem)

This score (sheet music) is derived from the of Twinkle Twinkle Little Star, a lullaby songs, traditional nursery rhymes is a lullaby and one of the most beloved nursery rhymes across the world. It has been undergone minor modifications to ensure a better alignment between the musical arrangement and the lyrics (poem).

The lyrics (the poem, original text and its translation see the following sections) describe childes lying on his or her back with a small fan on an autumn night, gazing at the night sky. It is quite appropriate for lyrics and music to match each other. The author rewrites the poem (lyrics) for the song.

### 2.34.1 Sheet music

$1 = C \quad \frac{2}{4}$

| 1 | 1 | 5 | 5 | 6 | 6 | 5 — | 4 | 4 | 3 | 3 | 2 | 2 | 1 — |
|---|---|---|---|---|---|---|---|---|---|---|---|---|---|
| 银 | 烛 | 秋 | 光 | 冷 | 画 | 屏， | 轻 | 罗 | 小 | 扇 | 扑 | 流 | 萤. |

| 5 | 5 | 4 | 4 | 3 | 3 | 2 — | 4 | 4 | 3 | 3 | 2 | 2 | 1 — |
|---|---|---|---|---|---|---|---|---|---|---|---|---|---|
| 天 | 阶 | 夜 | 色 | 凉 | 如 | 水， | 卧 | 看 | 牵 | 牛 | 织 | 女 | 星. |

| 1 | 1 | 5 | 5 | 6 | 6 | 5 — | 4 | 4 | 3 | 3 | 2 | 2 | 1 — |
|---|---|---|---|---|---|---|---|---|---|---|---|---|---|
| 银 | 烛 | 秋 | 光 | 冷 | 画 | 屏， | 卧 | 看 | 牵 | 牛 | 织 | 女 | 星. |

### 2.34.2 Sheet music with Lyrics marked in Chinese pinyin without tones

| 1 | 1 | 5 | 5 | 6 | 6 | 5 — | 4 | 4 | 3 | 3 | 2 | 2 | 1 — |
|---|---|---|---|---|---|---|---|---|---|---|---|---|---|
| yin | zhu | qiu | guang | leng | hua | ping | qing | luo | xiao | shan | pu | liu | ying |
| 银 | 烛 | 秋 | 光 | 冷 | 画 | 屏， | 轻 | 罗 | 小 | 扇 | 扑 | 流 | 萤. |

| 5 | 5 | 4 | 4 | 3 | 3 | 2 — | 4 | 4 | 3 | 3 | 2 | 2 | 1 — |
|---|---|---|---|---|---|---|---|---|---|---|---|---|---|
| tian | jie | ye | se | liang | ru | shui | wo | kan | qian | niu | zhi | nv | xing |
| 天 | 阶 | 夜 | 色 | 凉 | 如 | 水， | 卧 | 看 | 牵 | 牛 | 织 | 女 | 星. |

| 1 | 1 | 5 | 5 | 6 | 6 | 5 — | 4 | 4 | 3 | 3 | 2 | 2 | 1 — |
|---|---|---|---|---|---|---|---|---|---|---|---|---|---|
| yin | zhu | qiu | guang | leng | hua | ping | wo | kan | qian | niu | zhi | nv | xing |
| 银 | 烛 | 秋 | 光 | 冷 | 画 | 屏， | 卧 | 看 | 牵 | 牛 | 织 | 女 | 星. |

### 2.34.3 Text of the lyrics

银烛秋光冷画屏，轻罗小扇扑流萤．
天阶夜色凉如水，卧看牵牛织女星．

### 2.34.4 Text of the lyrics marked with tones in Chinese pinyin

yín zhú qiū guāng lěng huà píng qīng luó xiǎo shàn pū liú yíng
银 烛 秋 光 冷 画 屏，轻 罗 小 扇 扑 流 萤．
tiān jiē yè sè liáng rú shuǐ   wò kàn qiān niú zhī nǚ xīng
天 阶 夜色 凉 如 水， 卧 看 牵 牛 织 女 星．

### 2.34.5 Literal translation of the lyrics

The autumn light and the silver candle light shine on the painting screen looks cold, and using the light silk fan pounces the fireflies. The night on the court's steps is as cool as water. Lying down, she watch the stars Altair and Vega.

### 2.34.6 A more polished and stylistically enhanced translation of the lyrics

The silver candle's glow in the autumn light cools the painted screen, while using a delicate silk fan flutters amidst the fireflies. The night air on the stone steps feels as cool as water. Lying down, the little girl gazes at the stars Altair and Vega.

### 2.34.7 Translation sentence by sentence

银烛秋光冷画屏，
The silver candle's glow in the autumn light cools the painted screen,
轻罗小扇扑流萤．
while using a delicate silk fan flutters amidst the fireflies.
天阶夜色凉如水，
The night air on the stone steps feels as cool as water.
卧看牵牛织女星．

Lying down, the little girl gazes at the stars Altair and Vega.

**2.34.8 Brief introduction of the author of the poem (lyrics)**

杜牧（公元 803 - 852 年），字牧之，号樊川，京兆万年人，唐代诗人.

Du Mu (803 - 852 AD), styled Mu Zhi and with the pseudonym Fan Chuan, was from Wannian, Jingzhao. He was a poet of the Tang Dynasty.

# 2.35 Song No.35, Small Overlapping Mountain

## 小重山　南宋　岳飞

**Tune of the poem: Small Overlapping Hills.**
**Author of the poem (lyrics), Southern Song Dynasty, Yue Fei**

### 2.35.0 About the score and lyrics (poem)

This score (sheet music) is derived (excerpted) from the pieces of Tchaikovsky's The seasons June Barcarolle, and has undergone minor modifications to ensure a better alignment between the musical arrangement and the lyrics (poem).

Tchaikovsky's The seasons June Barcarolle gave the author aimpression of deep and sorrowful, Yue Fei's poem Small Overlapping Mountain expresses a very melancholy and sorrowful emotion, the music and the poem seems quite match. The author incorporates this poem into that renowned musical composition.

## 2.35.1 Sheet music

$1 = C \quad \dfrac{2}{4}$

$\underline{2\ 3\ {}^{\#}4}\ |\ \underline{5\ 6}\ \underline{{}^{\flat}7\ \dot{1}}\ |\ \underline{\dot{2}\ \dot{5}}\ \underline{{}^{\#}4\ 5}\ |\ \underline{2\ 2}\ \underline{6\ \dot{1}}\ |\ {}^{\flat}7$
昨 夜 寒 蛩 不 住 鸣 惊 回 千 里 梦 已 三 更

$\underline{7\ {}^{\#}4}\ \underline{6\ 5}\ |\ \underline{2\ 3}\ \underline{{}^{\#}4\ 5}\ |\ \underline{6\ 7}\ \underline{\dot{1}\ \dot{2}}\ |\ \underline{\dot{5}\ {}^{\#}4}\ \underline{5\ 2}\ |$
已 三 更 起 来 独 自 绕 阶 行 人 悄 悄

$\underline{\dot{4}\ {}^{\flat}\dot{3}}\ \underline{\dot{4}\ \dot{1}}\ |\ \underline{3\ 2}\ \underline{3\ 7}\ |\ \underline{\dot{2}\ \dot{1}}\ \dot{2}\ |\ \underline{\dot{1}\ 7}\ \underline{6\ 5}\ |\ \underline{7\cdot\ 6}\ |$
人 悄 悄 帘 外 月 胧 明 帘 外 月 胧

$\underline{5\ 2}\ \underline{3\ {}^{\#}4}\ |\ \underline{5\ 6}\ \underline{{}^{\flat}7\ \dot{1}}\ |\ \underline{\dot{2}\ \dot{5}}\ \underline{{}^{\#}4\ 5}\ |\ \underline{2\ 2}\ \underline{6\ \dot{1}}\ |\ {}^{\flat}7$
明 白 首 为 功 名 旧 山 松 竹 老 阻 归 程

$\underline{7\ {}^{\#}4}\ \underline{6\ 5}\ |\ \underline{2\ 3}\ \underline{{}^{\#}4\ 5}\ |\ \underline{6\ {}^{\flat}7}\ \dot{1}\ |\ \underline{\dot{2}\ \dot{5}}\ \underline{{}^{\#}4\ 5}\ |\ \dot{2}\ |$
阻 归 程 欲 将 心 事 付 瑶 琴 知 音 少

$\underline{\dot{4}\ {}^{\flat}\dot{3}}\ \underline{\dot{4}\ \dot{1}}\ |\ \underline{3\ 2}\ \underline{3\ 7}\ |\ \underline{\dot{2}\ \dot{1}}\ \dot{2}\ |\ \underline{\dot{1}\ {}^{\flat}7}\ \underline{6\ 5}\ |\ {}^{\flat}\underline{7\cdot\ 6}\ |$
弦 断 有 谁 听 知 音 少 弦 断 有 谁

$5\ -\ |$
听

## 2.35.2 Sheet music with Lyrics marked in Chinese pinyin without tones

```
2  3  #4 | 5  6  b7  1  2  5  #4  5 | 2  2  6  1  b7
zuo ye han qiong bu zhu ming jing hui qian li meng yi   san jing
昨  夜 寒  蛩  不 住  鸣  惊  回  千  里  梦  已      三  更

7  #4 6 | 5  2  3  #4 | 5  6  7  1  2  5  #4  5 | 2
yi    san jing qi lai du zi rao jie xing ren qiao     qiao
已    三   更  起 来 独 自 绕  阶  行  人  悄        悄

4  b3 4 | 1  3  2  3  7  2  1  2 | 1  7  6  5  7· 6
ren    qiao qiao lian  wai  yue long ming lian  wai yue long
人      悄   悄   帘    外    月  胧   明    帘    外  月  胧

5  2  3  #4 | 5  6  b7  1  2  5  #4  5 | 2  2  6  1  b7
ming bai shou wei  gong  ming jiu shan song zhu lao zu   gui cheng
明   白   首   为    功    名   旧   山   松   竹  老  阻   归   程

7  #4 6 | 5  2  3  #4 | 5  6  b7  1  2  5  #4  5 | 2
zu    gui cheng yu jiang xin shi fu yao qin zhi yin    shao
阻    归   程   欲 将   心  事  付 瑶  琴  知  音     少

4  b3 4 | 1  3  2  3  7  2  1  2  b7  6  5  b7· 6
xian  duan  you  shui ting zhi yin shao xian  duan  you shui
弦     断   有   谁   听   知  音  少   弦    断    有  谁

5  —
ting
听
```

### 2.35.3 Text of the lyrics

昨夜寒蛩不住鸣，惊回千里梦，已三更.
起来独自绕阶行，人悄悄，簾外月胧明.
白首为功名，旧山松竹老，阻归程.
欲将心事付瑶琴，知音少，弦断有谁听.

### 2.35.4 Text of the lyrics (a) marked with tones in Chinese pinyin

zuó yè hán qióng bú zhù míng jīng huí qiān lǐ mèng　yǐ sān jīng
　昨 夜 寒 蛩 不 住 鸣, 惊 回 千 里 梦, 已 三 更.
qǐ lái dú zì rào jiē xíng　rén qiāo qiāo　lián wài yuè long míng
起 来 独 自 绕 阶 行, 人 悄 悄, 簾 外 月 胧 明.
bái shǒu wèi gōng míng jiù shān sōng zhú lǎo zǔ guī chéng
白 首 为 功 名, 旧 山 松 竹 老, 阻 归 程.
yù jiāng xīn shì fù yáo qín　zhī yīn shǎo xián duàn yǒu shuí tīng
欲 将 心 事 付 瑶 琴, 知 音 少, 弦 断 有 谁 听.

### 2.35.5 Literal translation of the lyrics

Last night, the cold cicadas kept chirping, it woke me up from a distant dream that spanned a thousand miles. It was already zero o'clock in the morning. I got up and walked alone around the steps. People were quiet, and the moon was bright outside the curtain. From my youth to my age of white hair, I spent half of my life pursuing fame and fortune; old mountains and pines and bamboo grow old, blocking the way home. I wish to entrust my worries to the jade zither, but there are few kindred spirits. When the strings break, who will listen?

### 2.35.6 A more polished and stylistically enhanced translation of the lyrics

Last night, the cold cicadas continued chirping, it abruptly roused me from a distant dream that extended across a thousand miles. It was already midnight. I rose and walked alone near the steps. The surroundings were quiet, and the moonlight shone brightly beyond the curtains. From my early youth to the age of white hair, I have dedicated half of my life to the pursuit of fame and fortune; ancient mountains, pines, and bamboo grow old with time, obstructing the path homeward. I wish to confide my worries to the jade zither, yet kindred spirits are few. When the strings snap, who would like to truly listen?

### 2.35.7 Translation sentence by sentence

昨夜寒蛩不住鸣，
Last night, the cold cicadas continued chirping,
惊回千里梦，已三更.
it abruptly roused me from a distant dream that extended across a thousand miles. It was already midnight.
起来独自绕阶行，
I rose and walked alone near the steps.
人悄悄，簾外月胧明.
The surroundings were quiet, and the moonlight shone brightly beyond the curtains.
白首为功名，
From my early youth to the age of white hair, I have dedicated half of my life to the pursuit of fame and fortune.
旧山松竹老，阻归程.
ancient mountains, pines, and bamboo grow old with time, obstructing the path homeward.
欲将心事付瑶琴，
I wish to confide my worries to the jade zither, yet kindred spirits are few.
知音少，弦断有谁听.
When the strings snap, who would like to truly listen.

### 2.35.8 Brief introduction of the author of the poem

岳飞（公元 1103 年 - 1142 年），字鹏举，河南安阳汤阴县人，南宋抗金名将，中国历史上著名军事家，战略家，民族英雄，位列南宋中兴四将之一.

他于北宋末年投军，从 1128 年到 1141 年的十余年间，率领岳家军同金军进行了大小数百次战斗，所向披靡. 1140 年，完颜兀术毁盟攻宋，岳飞挥师北伐，先后收复郑州，洛阳等地，又于郾城，颍昌大败金军，进军朱仙镇. 宋朝皇帝赵构，以及宰相秦桧却一意投降，以十二道"金字牌"下令退兵，岳飞在孤立无援之下被迫班师. 在宋朝投降过程中，岳飞遭受秦桧、张俊等人的诬陷，被捕入狱. 1142 年 1 月，岳飞以"不必要证据"的"谋反"罪名，与长子岳云和部将张宪同被杀害. 后冤狱被平反，改葬于西湖畔栖霞岭. 追谥武穆，后又追谥忠武，鄂王.

Yue Fei (1103 - 1142 AD), styled Pengju, was born in Tangyin County, Anyang City, Henan Province. He was a celebrated general of the Southern Song Dynasty who resisted the Jin forces, and is regarded as a distinguished military strategist and national hero in Chinese history. Yue Fei was also one of the Four Generals of the Southern Song Dynasty's revival period. He enlisted in the army at the end of the Northern Song Dynasty. Between 1128 and 1141, over the course of more than a decade, he commanded the Yue Family Army in numerous battles against the Jin forces, achieving an undefeated record. In 1140, Wanyan Wushu violated the peace agreement and launched an invasion against the Song. Yue Fei led his troops northward and successfully recaptured Zhengzhou, Luoyang, and other strategic locations. He also defeated the Jin army in the battles of Yancheng and Yingchang, advancing as far as Zhuxian Town. However, Emperor Zhao Gou of the Song Dynasty and Chancellor Qin Hui pursued a policy of unilateral surrender and issued twelve imperial orders—delivered under the authority of golden plaques—to recall Yue Fei's forces. Left isolated and without reinforcements, Yue Fei was compelled to withdraw. During the surrender process, he was falsely accused by Qin Hui, Zhang Jun, and others and was subsequently imprisoned. In January 1142, Yue Fei was executed together with his eldest son Yue Yun and his subordinate Zhang Xiantong on fabricated charges of treason, supported by flimsy evidence. Later, his name was cleared posthumously, and his remains were reburied on Qixia Ridge near West Lake. He was posthumously honored with the title "Wumu" and later granted the additional honorific title "Zhongwu, the King of E."

# 2.36 Song No.36, The wine will be served

## 将进酒　唐　李白

**Title of the poem: The wine will be served**
**Author of the poem (lyrics), Tang Dynasty Li Bai**

### 2.36.0 About the score and lyrics (poem)

This score (sheet music) is derived (excerpted) from the (pieces) of Italian composer Verdi's Drinking Song, and has undergone minor modifications to ensure a better alignment between the musical arrangement and the lyrics (poem).

Drinking is primarily associated with the pursuit of pleasure. Toasts are frequently characterized by a lack of reason and are seldom grounded in rationality. This is a common phenomenon that has been being historically and globally. The author rewrites the poem (lyrics) for the song.

## 2.36.1 Sheet music

$1 = C \quad \dfrac{3}{8}$

| 5 | 3 | 3 | 5 | 3 | 3 | 5 | 3 | 2 | 3 | 5 | 5 | 4 | 3 | 2 | 2 | 1 |
|---|---|---|---|---|---|---|---|---|---|---|---|---|---|---|---|---|
| 君 | 不 | 见 | 君 | 不 | 见 | 黄 | 河 | 之 | 水 | 天 | | 上 | | 来， | | |

奔流到海不　复　回．君不见君不见，

高堂明镜悲　白　发，朝　如　青丝

暮成雪．人生得意须　尽　欢，莫使金樽

空　对月，空　对月．天生我材必　有

用，千金散尽还复　来．烹羊宰牛且为

乐，会须一饮三百杯．与君歌一曲，请君

为我　倾耳听．钟鼓馔玉不足贵，但愿

长醉　不复醒．古来圣贤皆寂　寞，

惟有饮者留其名．留其名．径须沽取对君

酌．　与尔同销万古愁．

## 2.36.2 Sheet music with Lyrics marked in Chinese pinyin without tones

```
5 | 3 | 3  5 | 3 | 3  5 | 3 | 2  3 | 5 | 5  4 | 3 | 2  2 | 1
jun  bu  jian  jun  bu  jian  huang he  zhi  shui tian        shang    lai
君   不   见   君   不   见   黄   河   之   水   天            上      来，

2 3 | 2  2 | 1  2 3 | 2  1 | 5  0 | 5 | 3 | 3  5 | 3 | 3
ben liu dao hai bu        fu       hui    jun bu jian jun bu jian
奔  流  到  海  不        复       回，   君  不  见  君  不  见

5  3 | 2  3 | 5·| 5  4  3 | 2  2 | 1  2 3 | 2  2 | 1
gao tang ming jing bei    bai  fa chao    ru      qing si
高   堂  明   镜   悲    白   发  朝    如      青  丝

2 3 | 1  0 | 1  4 | 4  4 | 3  4 | 5 | 4 | 3 | 3  5 | 2
mu cheng xue  ren sheng de yi   xu  jin     huan mo shi jin zun
暮  成   雪．  人  生   得 意   须 尽     欢，  莫 使  金  樽

2 | 2  2 | 1  2 3 | 2·| 1  0 | 1 | 4  4 | 4  4 | 3  4 | 5
kong    dui yue kong    dui yue    tian sheng wo  cai   bi      you
空      对  月．空      对  月．   天   生   我  材   必      有

4·| 3  5 | 7  7 | 7  7 6 | 7  1 | 7·| 7  2 | 5 | 3 | 3  5
yong qian jin san jin hai fu   lai      peng yang zai niu qie wei
用，千   金  散  尽  还  复   来．     烹   羊   宰  牛  且  为

3 | 3  5 | 3 | 3  2 | 3 | 6  0 | 6  5 | 4 | 3  3 2 | 3  4
le    hui xu  yi    yin san bai bei   yu  jun ge  yi   qu  qing jun
乐，  会  须  一    饮  三  百  杯，  与  君 歌  一   曲， 请  君

2 | 2 | 1  2 | 3 | 1  0 | 3 | 3  5 | 4 | 3  3 | 2 | 0 | 3  4
wei wo    qing er   ting    zhong gu zhuan yu bu zu    gui dan yuan
为  我    倾   耳   听．    钟   鼓 馔   玉 不 足    贵， 但 愿

2 | 2 | 1  2 | 3 | 1  0 | 1·| 4  4 | 4  4 | 3  4 | 5 | 4 | 0
chang zui   bu fu  xing    gu lai sheng xian  jie    ji      mo
长   醉    不 复   醒．    古 来 圣   贤   皆    寂      寞，

3  5 | 2  2 | 2  2 | 1  2 | 3 | 1  0 | 7  2 | 5 | 3·| 3  5
wei you yin zhe liu qi ming liu qi ming    jing xu  gu  qu dui jun
惟  有  饮  者  留 其 名，  留 其 名．    径   须 沽  取 对  君

3 | 0·| 3  5 | 3 | 3  2 | 3 | 5·|
zhuo     yu  er  tong xiao wan gu chou
酌．    与   尔  同  销  万  古 愁．
```

207

### 2.36.3 Text of the lyrics

君不见黄河之水天上来，奔流到海不复回.君不见高堂明镜悲白发，朝如青丝暮成雪.人生得意须尽欢，莫使金樽空对月.天生我材必有用，千金散尽还复来.烹羊宰牛且为乐，会须一饮三百杯.与君歌一曲，请君为我倾耳听.钟鼓馔玉不足贵，但愿长醉不复醒.古来圣贤皆寂寞，惟有饮者留其名.径须沽取对君酌.与尔同销万古愁.

### 2.36.4 Text of the lyrics marked with tones in Chinese pinyin

jūn bú jiàn huáng hé zhī shuǐ tiān shàng lái bēn liú dào hǎi bù fù huí
君 不 见 黄 河 之 水 天 上 来,奔 流 到 海 不 复 回.
jūn bú jiàn gāo tang míng jìng bēi bái fà  cháo rú qīng sī mù chéng xuě
君 不 见 高 堂 明 镜 悲 白发, 朝 如 青 丝 暮 成 雪.
rén shēng de yì xū jìn huān  mò shǐ jīn zūn kōng duì yuè
人 生 得意 须尽 欢, 莫 使 金 樽 空 对 月.
tiān shēng wǒ cái bì yǒu yòng qiān jīn sàn jìn hái fù lái
天 生 我 材必 有 用, 千 金散 尽 还 复来.
pēng yang zǎi niú qiě wéi lè  huì xū  yī yǐn sān bǎi bēi
烹 羊 宰 牛 且 为 乐, 会 须 一 饮 三 百 杯.
yǔ jūn gē yī qǔ  qǐng jūn wèi wǒ qīng ěr tīng
与 君 歌一 曲, 请 君 为 我 倾 耳 听.
zhōng gǔ zhuàn yù bù zú guì  dàn yuàn cháng zuì bù fù xǐng
钟 鼓 馔 玉 不足贵, 但 愿 长 醉 不 复 醒.
gǔ lái shèng xián jiē jì  mò  wéi yǒu yǐn zhě liú qí míng
古来 圣 贤 皆寂 寞, 惟 有 饮 者 留其名.
jìng xū gū qǔ duì jūn zhuó  yǔ ěr tong xiāo wàn gǔ chóu
径 须沽 取 对 君 酌. 与 尔 同 销 万 古 愁.

### 2.36.5 Literal translation of the lyrics

Have you not seen that the waters of the Yellow River come from the sky and rush to the sea, never to return? Have you not seen the high hall and the bright mirror grieve over the white hair? In the morning it like black silk, in the evening like snow. When life is going well, enjoy it to the fullest; don't let the golden cup face the moon in vain. Everyone has their own value. Even if all the gold is spent, it will come back. Cooking sheep and slaughtering cattle for pleasure would require drinking three hundred cups at a time. Sing a song with you Please listen attentively for me. Bells, drums, delicacies and jade are not precious; may I be drunk forever and never wake up. Since ancient times, sages and virtuous men have all been lonely. Only the drinker leaves his name. Just buy wine and drink with you. Let's dispel the eternal sorrows together.

### 2.36.6 A more polished and stylistically enhanced translation of the lyrics

Have you not noticed that the waters of the Yellow River originate from high in the heavens, rushing ceaselessly toward the sea without return? Have you not observed the sorrow reflected in the mirror within the grand hall over the aging white hair? In the morning, it is as dark as silk, by evening, it has turned to snow. When fortune smiles upon us, we ought to embrace life's pleasures fully; let us not allow the golden goblet to remain empty beneath the moonlight. Heaven bestows talents upon each individual for a purpose, and no one is without value. Even if a thousand gold coins are spent, more shall inevitably follow. For feasts of roasted lamb and oxen, joyous occasions call for drinking hundreds of cups at once. Allow me to sing a verse for you. Please listen attentively to me singing. The luxuries of bells, drums, delicacies, and jade pales are not precious, I would like to indulge in eternal intoxication, never to awaken.

Since antiquity, sages and virtuous individuals have often lived in obscurity; yet only those who indulge in drink have left their names behind. Just buy wine and offer you wine to share to dispel the eternal sorrows together.

### 2.36.7 Translation sentence by sentence

君不见黄河之水天上来，
Have you not noticed that the waters of the Yellow River originate from high in the heavens,

奔流到海不复回.
rushing ceaselessly toward the sea without return.
君不见高堂明镜悲白发,
Have you not observed the sorrow reflected in the mirror within the grand hall over the aging white hair.
朝如青丝暮成雪.
In the morning, it is as dark as silk; by evening, it has turned to snow.
人生得意须尽欢,
When fortune smiles upon us, we ought to embrace life's pleasures fully,
莫使金樽空对月.
let us not allow the golden goblet to remain empty beneath the moonlight.
天生我材必有用,
Heaven bestows talents upon each individual for a purpose, and no one is without value.
千金散尽还复来.
Even if a thousand gold coins are spent, more shall inevitably follow.
烹羊宰牛且为乐,
For feasts of roasted lamb and oxen,
会须一饮三百杯
joyous occasions call for drinking hundreds of cups at once.
与君歌一曲,
Allow me to sing a verse for you,
请君为我倾耳听.
Please listen attentively to me singing.
钟鼓馔玉不足贵,
The luxuries of bells, drums, delicacies, and jade pales are not precious,
但愿长醉不复醒.
I would like to indulge in eternal intoxication, never to awaken.
古来圣贤皆寂寞,
Since antiquity, sages and virtuous individuals have often lived in obscurity;
惟有饮者留其名.
yet only those who indulge in drink have left their names behind.
径须沽取对君酌.与尔同销万古愁.
Just buy wine and offer you wine to share to dispel the eternal sorrows

together.

**2.36.8 Brief introduction of the author of the poem (lyrics)**

Please refer to section 2.03.7, we do not repeat here.

## 2.37 Song No.37, The peach tree is in full bloom

---

### 桃夭  选自诗经  孔子

**Title of the poem: The peach tree is in full bloom**
**Author of the poem (lyrics), Spring and Autumn period, Confucius**

### 2.37.0 About the score and lyrics (poem)

This score (sheet music) is derived (excerpted) from the (pieces) of French Folk Song: Jacques Brothers, and has undergone minor modifications to ensure a better alignment between the musical arrangement and the lyrics (poem).

Frère Jacques is a French nursery rhyme and song. The English name for the song is Brother John. The song is about a French monk who has overslept and is called to wake up for the morning prayers. This is a song for kids and is often sung in rounds.

Are you sleeping? Are you sleeping? Morning bells are ringing! Morning bells are ringing! Ding, dang, dong. Ding, dang, dong.

The lyrics that the author of this book re-arranged for this song are about the most simple life lessons in daily life. The author rewrites the poem (lyrics) for the song.

## 2.37.1 Sheet music

$1 = C \quad \dfrac{3}{4}$

```
1  2  3  1 | 1  2  3  1 | 3  4  5 — | 3  4  5 — |
桃 之 夭 夭, 桃 之 夭 夭, 灼 灼 其 华. 灼 灼 其 华.

5̲6̲ 5̲4̲ 3  1 | 5̲6̲ 5̲4̲ 3  1 | 3  5̣  1 — | 3  5̣  1 — |
之  子  于 归, 之  子  于 归, 宜 其 室 家. 宜 其 室 家.

1  2  3  1 | 1  2  3  1 | 3  4  5 — | 3  4  5 — |
桃 之 夭 夭, 桃 之 夭 夭, 有 蕡 其 实. 有 蕡 其 实.

5̲6̲ 5̲4̲ 3  1 | 5̲6̲ 5̲4̲ 3  1 | 3  5̣  1 — | 3  5̣  1 — |
之  子  于 归, 之  子  于 归, 宜 其 家 室. 宜 其 家 室.

1  2  3  1 | 1  2  3  1 | 3  4  5 — | 3  4  5 — |
桃 之 夭 夭, 桃 之 夭 夭, 其 叶 蓁 蓁. 其 叶 蓁 蓁.

5̲6̲ 5̲4̲ 3  1 | 5̲6̲ 5̲4̲ 3  1 | 3  5̣  1 — | 3  5̣  1 — |
之  子  于 归, 之  子  于 归, 宜 其 家 人. 宜 其 家 人.
```

## 2.37.2 Sheet music with Lyrics marked in Chinese pinyin without tones

| 1 | 2 | 3 | 1 | 1 | 2 | 3 | 1 | 3 | 4 | 5 — | 3 | 4 | 5 — |
|---|---|---|---|---|---|---|---|---|---|---|---|---|---|
| tao | zhi | yao | yao | tao | zhi | yao | yao | zhuo | zhuo | qi hua | zhuo | zhuo | qi hua |
| 桃 | 之 | 夭 | 夭, | 桃 | 之 | 夭 | 夭, | 灼 | 灼 | 其华. | 灼 | 灼 | 其华. |

| 5 6 | 5 4 | 3 | 1 | 5 6 | 5 4 | 3 | 1 | 3 | 5 | 1 — | 3 | 5 | 1 — |
|---|---|---|---|---|---|---|---|---|---|---|---|---|---|
| zhi | zi | yu | gui | zhi | zi | yu | gui | yi qi | shi | jia | yi qi | shi | jia |
| 之 | 子 | 于 | 归, | 之 | 子 | 于 | 归, | 宜其 | 室 | 家. | 宜其 | 室 | 家. |

| 1 | 2 | 3 | 1 | 1 | 2 | 3 | 1 | 3 | 4 | 5 — | 3 | 4 | 5 — |
|---|---|---|---|---|---|---|---|---|---|---|---|---|---|
| tao | zhi | yao | yao | tao | zhi | yao | yao | you | fen | qi shi | you | fen | qi shi |
| 桃 | 之 | 夭 | 夭, | 桃 | 之 | 夭 | 夭, | 有 | 蕡 | 其实. | 有 | 蕡 | 其实. |

| 5 6 | 5 4 | 3 | 1 | 5 6 | 5 4 | 3 | 1 | 3 | 5 | 1 — | 3 | 5 | 1 — |
|---|---|---|---|---|---|---|---|---|---|---|---|---|---|
| zhi | zi | yu | gui | zhi | zi | yu | gui | yi qi | jia | shi | yi qi | jia | shi |
| 之 | 子 | 于 | 归, | 之 | 子 | 于 | 归, | 宜其 | 家 | 室. | 宜其 | 家 | 室. |

| 1 | 2 | 3 | 1 | 1 | 2 | 3 | 1 | 3 | 4 | 5 — | 3 | 4 | 5 — |
|---|---|---|---|---|---|---|---|---|---|---|---|---|---|
| tao | zhi | yao | yao | tao | zhi | yao | yao | qi | ye | zhen zhen | qi | ye | zhen zhen |
| 桃 | 之 | 夭 | 夭, | 桃 | 之 | 夭 | 夭, | 其 | 叶 | 蓁蓁. | 其 | 叶 | 蓁蓁. |

| 5 6 | 5 4 | 3 | 1 | 5 6 | 5 4 | 3 | 1 | 3 | 5 | 1 — | 3 | 5 | 1 — |
|---|---|---|---|---|---|---|---|---|---|---|---|---|---|
| zhi | zi | yu | gui | zhi | zi | yu | gui | yi qi | jia | ren | yi qi | jia | ren |
| 之 | 子 | 于 | 归, | 之 | 子 | 于 | 归, | 宜其 | 家 | 人. | 宜其 | 家 | 人. |

### 2.37.3 Text of the lyrics

桃之夭夭，灼灼其华.之子于归，宜其室家.
桃之夭夭，有蕡其实.之子于归，宜其家室.
桃之夭夭，其叶蓁蓁.之子于归，宜其家人.

### 2.37.4 Text of the lyrics marked with tones in Chinese pinyin

táo zhī yāo yāo zhuó zhuó qí huá zhī zǐ yú guī　yí qí shì jiā
桃　之　夭　夭，灼　　灼　　其华.之子于 归，宜其 室家.
táo zhī yāo yāo　yǒu fén qí shí zhī zǐ yú guī　yí qí jiā shì
桃　之 夭　夭，　有 蕡 其实.之 子于归，　宜其家 室.
táo zhī yāo yāo　qí yè zhēn zhēn zhī zǐ yú guī　yí qí jiā rén
桃　之 夭　夭，　其叶 蓁　　蓁.之 子于归，宜其 家 人.

### 2.37.5 Literal translation of the lyrics

The peach trees are full of buds on the branches, and the flowers are as brilliant as red clouds. The girl is about to get married and it will be a harmonious family between husband and wife. The peach trees are full of buds on the branches, and the fruits are abundant and hanging from the branches. The girl is about to get married and will be beneficial to the new big family. The peach trees are full of buds on the branches, and the peach leaves are thick and lush with a green color. The girl is about to get married and will be beneficial to the new family.

### 2.37.6 A more polished and stylistically enhanced translation of the lyrics

The peach trees are covered with buds on their branches, and the blossoms shine brilliantly like red clouds. My daughter is about to get married, which will contribute to a harmonious relationship between the couple.The peach trees are covered with buds on their branches, and the fruits are plentiful and hang heavily from the limbs. My daughter's marriage will bring blessings to the extended family.The peach trees are covered with buds on their branches, and the leaves are thick, lush, and vibrant green. My daughter's upcoming marriage is expected to bring positive benefits to the new family.

### 2.37.7 Translation sentence by sentence

桃之夭夭，灼灼其华.
The peach trees are covered with buds on their branches, and the blossoms shine brilliantly like red clouds.
之子于归，宜其室家.
My daughter is about to get married, which will contribute to a harmonious relationship between the couple.
桃之夭夭，有蕡其实.
The peach trees are covered with buds on their branches, and the fruits are plentiful and hang heavily from the limbs.
之子于归，宜其家室.
My daughter's marriage will bring blessings to the extended family.
桃之夭夭，其叶蓁蓁. The peach trees are covered with buds on their branches, and the leaves are thick, lush, and vibrant green.
之子于归，宜其家人.
My daughter's upcoming marriage is expected to bring positive benefits to the new family.

### 2.37.8 Brief introduction of the author of the poem (lyrics)

Confucius, for details, please refers to Section 2.14.7 of this book, we do not repeat here.

## 2.38 Song No.38, Broke the deadlock

破阵子　陈同甫赋壮词以寄之　南宋　辛弃疾

**Tune of the poem: Broke the deadlock**
**Title of the poem: Composing a grand poem for Chen Tongfu and sent it to him.**
**Author of the poem (lyrics): Southern Song Dynasty Xin Qi Ji**

### 2.38.0 About the score and lyrics (poem)

This score (sheet music) is derived (excerpted) from the (pieces) of The Bullfighter song (The Toreador Song) from the opera Carmen, by the French composer Bizet and has undergone minor modifications to ensure a better alignment between the musical arrangement and the lyrics (poem).

The entire piece is imbued with a profound sense of martial fervor. In this regard, Xin Qi Ji's poetic style exhibits resemblance to that of the aforementioned. The author rewrites the poem (lyrics) for the song.

## 2.38.1 Sheet music

$1 = C \quad \frac{4}{4}$

5 6· 5 3 0 3 | 3 2 3 4 3 0 | 4 2· 5 3 0 |
醉 里 挑 灯 看 剑， 梦 回 吹 角

1 6· 2 5 0 | 2 - 2 6 5 4 4 | 3 2 3 4 3 0
连 营． 八 百 里 分 麾 下 炙，

7· 3 3 5 2 4 | 7 - - - | 7 6 7 6 5 6 2 3
五 十 弦 翻 塞 外 声， 沙 场 秋 点

4 | 0 3 4 3 1 6 5 0 | 1 2 1 5· 4 3 2 1 |
兵． 沙 场 秋 点 兵． 沙 场 秋 点 兵．

0 5 6· 5 3· 0 3 | 3 2 3 4 3 0 | 4 2· 5 3
马 作 的 卢 飞 快， 弓 如 霹 雳

0 | 1 6· 2 5 0 | 2 - 2 6 5 4 4 | 3 2 3 4 3
弦 惊． 了 却 君 王 天 下 事，

0 | 7· 3 3 5 2 4 | 7 - - - | 7 6 7 6 5 6 2 3
赢 得 生 前 身 后 名． 赢 得 生 前 身 后

4 | 0 3 4 3 1 6 5 0 | 0 1 2 1 5· 4 3 2 |
名． 可 怜 白 发 生． 可 怜 白 发

1
生．

## 2.38.2 Sheet music with Lyrics marked in Chinese pinyin without tones

```
5   6· 5   3  0  3 | 3   2   3  4   3  0 | 4   2· 5   3  0 |
zui li     tiao deng kan     jian         meng hui chui jiao
醉  里     挑   灯  看        剑，         梦   回  吹   角

1   6  2   5   0 | 2 -   2  6   5  4  4 | 3   2   3  4   3  0
lian   ying    ba   bai li    fen      hui     xia    zhi
连     营．    八   百  里    分        麾     下    炙，

7   3   3  5   2  4 | 7 - - - | 7   6  7  6   5  6   2  3
wu  shi xian fan sai wai sheng    sha chang   qiu     dian
五  十  弦  翻  塞  外  声，     沙   场       秋      点

4   0   3  4  3   1  6   5  0 | 1   2   1   5  4   3  2   1 |
bing    sha chang  qiu dian bing    sha chang  qiu dian   bing
兵．    沙  场     秋   点  兵．   沙   场     秋  点     兵．

0   5   6· 5   3· 0   3 | 3   2   3  4   3  0 | 4   2· 5   3
    ma  zuo    di    lu fei       kua         gong ru  pi  li
    马  作     的    卢 飞，       快          弓   如  霹  雳

0 | 1   6· 2   5   0 | 2 -   2  6   5  4  4 | 3   2   3  4   3
    xian   jing     liao que   jun wang    tian    xia    shi
    弦     惊，     了  却    君   王       天      下    事，

0 | 7   3   3  5   2  4 | 7 - - - | 7   6  7  6   5  6   2  3
    ying de sheng qian shen hou ming    ying de   sheng qian shen hou
    赢   得  生   前   身   后  名．   赢   得    生    前    身   后

4   0   3  4  3   1  6   5   0 | 0   1   2   1   5  4   3  2 |
ming    ke hen    bai fa sheng       ke  hen    bai fa
名．    可 恨    白  发  生，       可  恨     白  发

1
sheng
生．
```

### 2.38.3 Text of the lyrics

醉里挑灯看剑,梦回吹角连营.八百里分麾下炙,
五十弦翻塞外声,沙场秋点兵.马作的卢飞快,
弓如霹雳弦惊.了却君王天下事,
赢得生前身后名.可怜白发生.

### 2.38.4 Text of the lyrics marked with tones in Chinese pinyin

zuì lǐ tiǎo dēng kàn jiàn mèng huí chuī jiǎo lián yíng bā bǎi lǐ fēn huī xià zhì
醉 里 挑 灯 看 剑, 梦 回 吹 角 连 营. 八 百 里 分 麾 下 炙,
wǔ shí xián fān sài wài shēng shā chǎng qiū diǎn bīng mǎ zuò dì  lú fēi kuài
五 十 弦 翻 塞 外 声, 沙 场 秋 点 兵. 马 作 的 卢 飞 快,
gōng rú  pī  lì xián jīng liǎo què jūn wáng tiān xià shì
弓 如 霹 雳 弦 惊. 了 却 君 王 天 下 事,
yíng de shēng qián shēn hòu míng   kě lián bái fà shēng
赢 得 生 前 身 后 名. 可 怜 白 发 生.

### 2.38.5 Literal translation of the lyrics

Drunk, I lean on the lamp to watch the sword; in my dreams, I blow the horn to the camp. Eight hundred miles under his command, fifty strings stirring the sounds of the frontier, the call every solders name of my troops on the battle fieldat autumn season. The horse's gallop was swift, and the bow was like thunderbolts, startling the strings. Settle the king's affairs of the country and earn a good reputation both in life and after death. Poor white hair has grown out.

### 2.38.6 A more polished and stylistically enhanced translation of the lyrics

Drunk, I light a lamp to gaze upon my sword; in my dreams, I hear the horns echoing through the military camp. Commanding eight hundred miles of land, fifty strings resonate with the sounds of the frontier in this autumn on the battlefield when calling every solder's name. The horse gallops swiftly, and the bowstring twangs like thunder, startling the enemy. Devoted to fulfilling the emperor's ambitions and securing both present and posthumous renown, I lament the arrival of white hair.

### 2.38.7 Translation sentence by sentence

醉里挑灯看剑,
Drunk, I light a lamp to gaze upon my sword,
梦回吹角连营.
in my dreams, I hear the horns echoing through the military camp.
八百里分麾下炙,
Commanding eight hundred miles of camps,
五十弦翻塞外声, 沙场秋点兵.
fifty strings resonate with the sounds of the frontier of calling every solders name of my troops on the battlefield in this autumn
马作的卢飞快, 弓如霹雳弦惊.
The horse gallops swiftly, and the bowstring twangs like thunder, startling the enemy.
了却君王天下事, 赢得生前身后名.
Devoted to fulfilling the emperor's ambitions and securing both present and posthumous renown,
可怜白发生.
I lament the arrival of white hair.

### 2.38.8 Brief introduction of the author of the poem (lyrics)

辛弃疾（公元 1140 - 1207）, 南宋爱国词人.字幼安, 别号稼轩, 历城人.出生时, 中原已为金兵所占.诗人 21 岁参加抗金义军, 不久归南宋. 历任江西, 和福建通判.

Xin Qiji (1140 - 1207 AD) was a patriotic poet of the Southern Song Dynasty. His courtesy name was You 'an, and his pseudonym was Jiaxuan. He was from Licheng. When he was born, the Central Plains had already been occupied by the Jin army. At the age of 21, the poet joined the Anti-Jin rebel army and soon returned to the Southern Song Dynasty. He has successively held the positions of assistant judge in Jiangxi, and Fujian.

# 2.39 Song No.39, Magpie Bridge Immortal

鹊桥仙　宋　秦观

**Tune of the poem: Magpie Bridge Immortal**
**Author of the poem (lyrics), Northern Song Dynasty Qing Guan**

### 2.39.0 About the score and lyrics (poem)

This score (sheet music) is derived (excerpted) from the (pieces) of English Folk Song: Green Sleeves, and has undergone minor modifications to ensure a better alignment between the musical arrangement and the lyrics (poem).

Green Sleeves is a famous traditional medieval English love song of the sixteenth century, dedicated to Lady Green Sleeves (a mysterious Lady with green sleeves).

There are various theories regarding the origin of the Greensleeves song. The song has been attributed to King Henry VIII. It has been said that the King either composed the tune or the lyrics of the song, or both.

Whatever, the song is gentle and elegant, is quite match to Qin Guan's poem which stands as the most tender, elegant, and beautiful love poem in the history of Chinese literature. The author rewrites the poem (lyrics) for the song.

## 2.39.1 Sheet music

1 = C  3/4

| 6 | 1 — 2 | 3 4 3 | 2 — 7 | 5· 6 7 | 1 — 6 | 6 5 |
纤 云 织 巧, 飞 星 传 憾, 银 汉 逗 逗 暗

| 6 | 7 — 5 | 3 — 6 | 1 — 2 | 3 4 3 | 2 — 7 | 5· 6 7 |
度. 暗 度. 金 风 玉 露 一 相 逢, 便 胜 却, 人

| 1 7 6 | 5· 4 5 | 6 — 6 | 5 — — | 5 4 3 | 2 — 7 |
间 无 数, 人 间 无 数. 柔 情 似 水, 佳

| 5· 6 7 | 1 — 6 | 6· 5 6 | 7 — 5 | 3 — — | 5 — — | 5 4 |
期 如 梦, 忍 顾 鹊 桥 归 路. 两 情 若 是

| 3 | 2 — 7 | 5· 6 7 | 1 7 6 | 5 4 5 | 6 — — | 6 — — |
久 长 时, 久 长 时, 又 岂 在, 朝 朝 暮 暮.

## 2.39.2 Sheet music with Lyrics marked in Chinese pinyin without tones

```
|6 | 1 -    2  | 3    4    3 | 2 -    7 | 5·  6    7 | 1 -    6 | 6    5
 xian yun      zhi  qiao  fei    xing chuan han    yin  han      tiao tiao an
 纤   云      织   巧    飞     星   传    憾,    银   汉      逗   逗  暗

 6 | 7 -   5 | 3 -    6 | 1 -    2 | 3    4    3 | 2 -    7 | 5·   6    7 |
     du        an   du      jin  feng    yu   lu   yi    xiang feng    bian sheng que  ren
     度       暗   度.     金   风      玉   露   一    相    逢,     便   胜    却,  人

 1    7    6 | 5·  4    5 | 6 -     6 | 5 - -    5    4    3 | 2 -    7 |
 jian wu  shu  ren jian wu shu        rou qing         si          shui   jia
 间   无  数. 人  间  无 数.       柔  情          似          水,   佳

 5·  6    7 | 1 -    6 | 6·  5    6 | 7 -    5    3 - -    5 - -    5    4
 qi       ru meng  ren gu  que      qiao  gui  lu       liang qing   ruo  shi
 期       如 梦,   忍 顾   鹊      桥    归   路.      两    情     若   是

 3 | 2 -   7 | 5·  6    7 | 1     7    6 | 5    4    5 | 6 - -    6 - - |
 jiu chang shi jiu chang      shi  you  qi  zai zhao       zhao mu      mu
 久 长    时 久 长           时, 又   岂  在, 朝          朝   暮     暮.
```

224

### 2.39.3 Text of the lyrics

纤云织巧，飞星传憾，银汉迢迢暗度.
金风玉露一相逢，便胜却，人间无数.
柔情似水，佳期如梦，忍顾鹊桥归路.
两情若是久长时，又岂在，朝朝暮暮.

### 2.39.4 Text of the lyrics marked with tones in Chinese pinyin

xiān yún zhī qiǎo fēi xīng chuan hàn yín hàn tiáo tiáo àn dù
　纤　云 织 巧，飞 星　传　　憾，银 汉 迢　迢 暗度.
jīn fēng yù lù yī xiāng féng biàn shèng què rén jiān wú shù
　金 风　玉露一　相　逢，便　胜　　却 人 间　无 数.
róu qíng sì shuǐ　jiā qī rú mèng rěn gù què qiáo guī lù
　柔　情 似 水,　佳期如 梦，忍　顾　鹊 桥　归 路.
liǎng qíng ruò shì jiǔ cháng shí　yòu qǐ zài zhāo zhāo mù mù
　两　　情 若是 久　长　时，又 岂 在 朝　朝　暮 暮.

### 2.39.5 Literal translation of the lyrics

The fine clouds are intricately woven, the flying stars carry the regrets, and the silver sky stretches far and wide in darkness. When the golden wind and jade dew meet, they surpass countless others in the world. Tender feelings flow like water, a fortunate date is like a dream, and they endure to look back on the way home from the magpie bridge. If love lasts for a long time, do not care about could it be being together a particular day and night.

### 2.39.6 A more polished and stylistically enhanced translation of the lyrics

The fine clouds weave ingeniously, and the flying stars convey regrets …the fleeting stars appear to carry messages, and the Milky Way stretches boundlessly through the night. When autumn winds meet dew-kissed moments, they transcend all worldly affairs. As tender as water, those fleeting moments pass like dreams, and they hesitate before turning back along the magpie bridge path. If love can endure, should not care one or two particular dating.

### 2.39.7 Translation sentence by sentence

纤云织巧，飞星传憾.
The fine clouds weave ingeniously, and the flying stars convey regrets.
银汉迢迢暗度.
the fleeting stars appear to carry messages, and the Milky Way stretches boundlessly through the night.
金风玉露一相逢，便胜却，人间无数.
When autumn winds meet dew-kissed moments, they transcend all worldly affairs.
柔情似水，佳期如梦，
As tender as water, those fleeting moments pass like dreams,
忍顾鹊桥归路.
and they hesitate before turning back along the magpie bridge path.
两情若是久长时，又岂在，朝朝暮暮.
If love can endure, should not care one or two particular dating.

### 2.39.8 Brief introduction of the author of the poem (lyrics)

秦观（公元 1049 - 1100），北宋词人，字少游.扬州高邮人.曾任国史院编修官等职.公元 1098 后贬谪.文辞为苏轼所赏识，为苏门四学士之一.词多写情爱，风格委婉含蓄，清丽雅淡.

Qin Guan (1049 - 1100 AD), a lyricist of the Northern Song Dynasty, was known by the courtesy name Shaoyou, was from Gaoyou, Yangzhou. He once held positions of the Secretariat and the editor of the National History Institute. He was demoted after 1098 AD. His literary style was highly appreciated by Su Shi, and he was one of the "Four Scholars of the Su School". The lyrics mostly depict love affairs, with a gentle and reserved style, elegant and refined.

# 2.40 Song No.40, Nostalgia for Red Cliff

念奴娇　赤壁怀古　宋　苏轼

**Tune of the poem: Charm of a maiden Singer.**
**Title of the poem: Nostalgia for Red Cliff.**
**Author of the poem (lyrics), Song Dynasty, Su Shi**

### 2.40.0 About the score and lyrics (poem)

The score of sheet music (a) is derived (excerpted) from the (pieces) of Romanian composer Ivanovicilon's Waves of The Danube (Donauwellen), and has undergone minor modifications to ensure a better alignment between the musical arrangement and the lyrics (poem).

The score of sheet music (b) is derived (excerpted) from the (pieces) of Austrian great composer J Strauss's Beautiful Blue Danube, and has undergone minor modifications to ensure a better alignment between the musical arrangement and the lyrics (poem).

While enjoying the scenery of the great rivers and streams, the artists (poets and composers as well) fall into reveries, their hearts are surging with emotions and many memories emerged.

The author incorporates this renowned poem into that two great wonderful musical composition.

## 2.40.1a Sheet music (a)

1 = C  $\frac{3}{4}$

| 3 - - | 3 #5 6 | 7 - - | 7 #5 3 | $\dot{1}$ - - | $\dot{1}$ 7 6 | $\dot{3}$ - -
　　　　大　江　东　去，　浪　淘　　尽，　千　古　风　流

$\dot{3}$ $\dot{4}$ - | $\dot{4}$ $\dot{3}\cdot$ $\dot{2}$ | $\dot{3}$ - - | 3 2 $\dot{1}$ | 7 - - | 7 $\dot{1}\cdot$ $\underline{7}$ | 6 - -
人　物．故　垒　西　边，　人　道　是，　人　道　是，

$\dot{6}\cdot$ $\underline{\dot{6}}$ $\dot{6}$ | $\dot{6}$ $\dot{6}$ 5 | 4 5 - | 4$\cdot$ $\underline{4}$ 4$\cdot$ $\underline{4}$ | 0 4 3 | $\dot{2}$
三　国　周　郎　赤　　壁．乱　石　穿　空，　惊　涛　拍

$\dot{3}$ - | $\dot{2}\cdot$ $\underline{\dot{2}}$ $\dot{2}$ | $\dot{2}$ $\dot{2}$ - | $\dot{2}$ $\dot{1}\cdot$ $\underline{7}$ | 6 0 6 | 4 $\dot{2}$ 7 | $\dot{1}$
岸，卷　起　千　堆　雪．江　山　如　画，　一　时　多　少　豪

7 6 - | 3 #5 6 | 7 - 7 | #5 3 $\dot{1}$ - | $\dot{1}$ 7 6 | $\dot{3}$ $\dot{4}$ - |
杰．遥　想　公　瑾　当　　年，小　乔　初　嫁　了，

4 3 $\dot{2}$ | $\dot{3}$ $\dot{3}$ $\dot{2}$ | $\dot{1}$ 7 - | 7 $\dot{1}$ 7 | 6 - 5 | $\dot{1}\cdot$ $\underline{\dot{3}}$ $\dot{5}$ |
雄　姿　英　发．羽　扇　纶　巾，雄　姿　英　发．谈　笑　　间，

- $\underline{\dot{6}\,\dot{5}}$ $\underline{\dot{4}\,\dot{3}}$ | $\dot{2}$ $\dot{1}$ $\dot{1}$ | 7 7 - | 5 7$\cdot$ $\underline{\dot{2}}$ | $\dot{4}$ - $\underline{7\,6}$ |
　　樯　橹　灰　飞　烟　　灭．　故　国　神　游，　多　情

$\dot{5}$ $\dot{4}$ $\dot{3}$ $\dot{2}$ | $\dot{2}$ $\dot{1}$ $\dot{1}$ | 5 $\dot{1}\cdot$ $\underline{\dot{3}}$ | $\dot{5}$ - | $\underline{\dot{6}\,\dot{5}}$ $\underline{\dot{4}\,\dot{3}}$ $\dot{2}$ $\dot{1}$ |
应　笑　我，早　生　华　发．人　生　如　梦，　一　尊　还　酹　江

$\dot{1}$ 7 7 | 5 7$\cdot$ $\underline{\dot{2}}$ | $\dot{4}$ - | $\underline{\dot{7}\,\dot{6}}$ 5 4 | $\underline{\dot{3}\,\dot{2}}$ | 2 $\dot{1}$ $\dot{1}$ |
月．江　山　如　画，　一　尊　还　酹　江　　月．

## 2.40.1b Sheet music (b)

```
1  3  5 | 5 - - | 5  0  1 | 1  3  5 | 5 - - | 5  0  7 | 7
大 江 东 去,       浪    淘 尽,            千    古

2  6  6 - - | 6  0  7 | 7  2  6 | 6 - - | 6  0  1 | 1  3
风 流 人 物.        故    垒 西 边,        人    道

5 | 1 - - | 1  0  1 | 3  3  5 | 1 - - | 1  0  2 | 2  4  6 |
是,  三    国 周 郎 赤 壁.        乱    石 穿 空,

6 - - | 6  4  5 | 3 - - | 3  1  3 | 3 - 2 | 6 - 5 | 1 - 0
      惊 涛 拍 岸,     卷 起 千       堆       雷.

0  1  7 | 7  6  6 | 0  6  5 | 5  6  6 | 0  2  2 | 3 - 2
 江 山 如 画,    一 时 多 少 豪 杰.    遥 想 公 瑾

0  2  2 | 6 - 5 | 0  1  7 | 7  6  6 | 0  6  7 | 2  1  1
 当 年,     小 乔 初 嫁 了,    雄 姿 英 发,

0  4  6 | 6 - 5 | 4 - 3 | 3  0  2 | 5  0  1 | 7  5  0
 羽 扇 纶 巾,  谈 笑    间,   羽 扇

5 | 4  0  5 | 4  0  5 | 3 - - | 3  2  5 | 1  2  3 | 5 - 4
纶 巾,  谈 笑    间,     樯    橹 灰       飞

3 - 2 | 1  0  5 | 3  0  1 | 3 - - | 3  4  3 | 2  1  7 |
烟 灭.  故 国   神 游,      多    情 应 笑

6 - 6 | 2  0  2 | 0  5  6 · 5 | 5 - 5 | 4 - 3 | 3 - 2 |
我,   早 生 华    发.  人 生 如       梦

3  2  5 | 1  2  3 | 5 - 4 | 3 - 2 | 1 - - |
一 尊 还   酹 江    月.
```

## 2.40.2 Sheet music (a) with Lyrics marked in Chinese pinyin without tones

```
|3 — — |3 #5 6 |7 — — |7 #5 3 |1· — — |1· 7 6 |3· — —
     da  jiang dong qu      lang tao       jin      qian gu feng liu
     大   江   东   去，   浪    淘     尽，    千   古  风   流

3· 4 — |4  3·#2 |3 — — |3  2  1 |7 — — |7  1· 7 |6 — —
ren wu    gu lei xi bian    ren dao      shi      ren dao   shi
人  物，  故  垒 西  边，  人  道     是，    人   道    是，

6· 6· 6 |6· 6· 5 |4· 5 — |4· 4· 4· 4· |0 4· 3 2
san guo zhou lang    chi      bi      luan shi chuan kong   jing tao pai
三   国   周   郎     赤     壁，   乱   石   穿    空，    惊   涛  拍

3 — |2·· 2 2 |2  2 — |2  1· 7 |6  0  6 |4  2  7 |1·
an     juan qi qian dui xue    jiang shan ru hua    yi    shi duo shao hao
岸，   卷   起  千  堆  雪，  江    山    如 画，   一     时  多  少  豪

7 6 — |3 #5 6 |7 — — |7 #5 3 |1· — |1· 7 6 |3· 4 —
jie    yao xiang gong jin    dang      nian    xiao qiao chu jia liao
杰，  遥   想   公   瑾      当       年，    小   乔    初  嫁  了，

4  3  2 |3  3  2 |1  7 — |7  1· 7 |6 — 5 |1·· 3  5
xiong zi ying fa yu shan guan jin    xiong zi ying fa    tan xiao    jian
雄   姿  英  发  羽  扇   纶   巾，  雄   姿  英   发.   谈  笑    间，

— 6· 5 |4· 3 2 |1  1 |7  7 — |5  7· 2 |4 — — |7· 6·
    qiang lu    hui fei yan     mie     gu guo shen you     duo qing
    樯     橹   灰  飞  烟     灭       故  国  神    游，    多   情

5· 4  3· 2 |2  1  1 |5  1· 3 |5 — |6· 5  4· 3 |2  1·
ying xiao wo zao sheng hua  fa ren sheng ru meng    yi  zun hai lei jiang
应   笑   我，早  生   华   发. 人   生    如  梦，  一   尊  还   酹  江

1·  7   7 |5  7· 2 |4 — |7· 6· 5  4 |3· 2  2 |1·  1·
         yue     jiang shan ru hua    yi zun hai lei jiang         yue
         月.    江    山  如  画，   一  尊 还   酹  江              月.
```

## 2.40.3 Text of the lyrics

大江东去，浪淘尽，千古风流人物.故垒西边，人道是，三国周郎赤壁.
乱石穿空，惊涛拍岸，卷起千堆雪.江山如画，一时多少豪杰.
遥想公瑾当年，小乔初嫁了，雄姿英发.羽扇纶巾，谈笑间，
樯橹灰飞烟灭.故国神游，多情应笑我，早生华发.
人生如梦，一尊还酹江月.

## 2.40.4 Text of the lyrics (a) marked with tones in Chinese pinyin

dà jiāng dōng qù làng táo jǐn qiān gǔ fēng liú rén wù   gù lěi xī biān
大  江   东   去,  浪  淘 尽, 千  古   风  流  人  物. 故 垒  西 边,
rén dào shi sān guó zhōu láng chì bì luàn shí chuān kōng
人  道  是, 三  国   周    郎   赤 壁. 乱   石   穿    空,
jīng tāo pāi àn juǎn qǐ qiān duī xuě jiāng shān rú huà yī shí duō shǎo háo jié
惊   涛  拍 岸  卷   起 千   堆  雪.  江    山   如 画, 一 时  多   少   豪  杰.
yáo xiǎng gōng jǐn dāng nián xiǎo qiáo chū jià le   xióng zī yīng fā
遥   想    公    瑾  当    年,  小   乔   初  嫁 了,  雄    姿 英  发.
yǔ shàn guān jīn tán xiào jiān qiáng lǔ huī fēi yān miè
羽  扇   纶    巾, 谈  笑  间,  樯    橹 灰  飞  烟  灭.
gù guó shén yóu   duō qíng yīng xiào wǒ   zǎo shēng huá fà
故 国   神    游,   多   情   应    笑   我,  早   生    华  发.
rén shēng rú mèng   yī zūn huán lèi jiāng yuè
人   生    如 梦,    一 尊   还  酹  江   月.

## 2.40.5 Literal translation of the lyrics

The great river flows eastward, washing away all the heroic figures of all eras. To the west of the old fortress, it is said that Zhou Lang of The Three Kingdoms was at Red Cliffs. Rocks Pierce through the sky, waves crash against the shore, and a thousand piles of snow are whipped up. The land is as beautiful as a painting, and how many heroes there were at that time. Looking back to the days of Gongjin, when Xiao Qiao lady first got married, the couple was full of vigor and vitality. Talking and laughing with a visiting military advisor scholar Zhuge, with feather fan and a silk scarf, in the blink of an eye, the warships were burnt and reduced to ashes. Wandering in my homeland, I am affectionate and should laugh at me, for I have grown grey hair early. Life is but a dream; I still pay tribute to the moon over the river.

## 2.40.6 A more polished and stylistically enhanced translation of the lyrics

The great river flows eastward, carrying away the heroic figures of bygone eras. To the west of the ancient fortress lies the Red Cliffs, where Zhou Yu of the Three Kingdoms once stood. Jagged rocks pierce the sky, waves crash violently against the shore, and surging foam rises like a thousand piles of snow. The landscape is as picturesque as a masterpiece, bearing witness to the countless heroes who once thrived in those tumultuous times. Recalling the days of Zhou Yu, full of vigor and vitality, when he married the beautiful Xiao Qiao lady, he commanded battles while engaging in conversation and laughter with the Visiting Military advisor Zhuge Scholar with a feather fan and a silk scarf, in an instant, enemy warships were reduced to ashes. As I wander through this historic land, I am filled with emotion and can only smile at my own sentimentality, for I have aged prematurely with grey hair. Life is but an ephemeral dream; still, I raise my cup in tribute to the moon shining over the river.

## 2.40.7 Translation sentence by sentence

大江东去，浪淘尽，千古风流人物.
The great river flows eastward, carrying away the heroic figures of bygone eras.
故垒西边，人道是，三国周郎赤壁.
To the west of the ancient fortress lies the Red Cliffs, where Zhou Yu of the Three Kingdoms once stood.
乱石穿空，惊涛拍岸，卷起千堆雪.
Jagged rocks pierce the sky, waves crash violently against the shore, and surging foam rises like a thousand piles of snow.
江山如画，一时多少豪杰.

The landscape is as picturesque as a masterpiece, bearing witness to the countless heroes who once thrived in those tumultuous times.

遥想公瑾当年，小乔初嫁了，

Recalling the days of Zhou Yu, full of vigor and vitality, when he married the beautiful Xiao Qiao lady,

雄姿英发.羽扇纶巾，

he commanded battles while engaging in conversation and laughter with the Visiting Military advisor Zhuge Scholar with a feather fan and a silk scarf,

谈笑间，强虏灰飞烟灭.

in an instant, enemy warships were reduced to ashes.

故国神游，多情应笑我，早生华发.

As I wander through this historic land, I am filled with emotion and can only smile at my own sentimentality, for I have aged prematurely with grey hair.

人生如梦，一尊还酹江月.

Life is but an ephemeral dream; still, I raise my cup in tribute to the moon shining over the river.

### 2.40.8 Brief introduction of the author of the poem (lyrics)

Su Shi (1037 – 1101 AD). For details, please refer to section 2.13.7 of this book, we do not repeat here.

## 2.41 Song No.41, The Bodhisattva minority

## 菩萨蛮  唐  韦庄

**Tune of the poem: The Bodhisattva minority.**
**Author of the poem (lyrics), Tang Dynasty Wei Zhuang**

### 2.41.0 About the score and lyrics (poem)

This score (sheet music) is derived (excerpted) from the (pieces) of Schumann's Robert Schumann's Childhood Dreams and has undergone minor modifications to ensure a better alignment between the musical arrangement and the lyrics (poem).

Sweet dreams can bring about the most wonderful memories of life. The author incorporates this poem into that renowned musical composition.

## 2.41.1 Sheet music

$1 = C \quad \frac{4}{4}$

5 | 1 -  1 7  1 3 | 5 1  1 -  7 6 | 5 1  2 3
人人　尽说　江南　好，　游人只合江南

4 6  1 2 | 3 5  2 -  5 | 1 -  1 7  1 3 | 5 3
老．只合江南老．春水　碧　于　　天，

3· 2  1 7 | 1 3  6 1  7·⁺6 | 6 7  5· 5 | 1 -
画船听　雨　眠．画船听雨眠．垆边

1 7  1 3 | 5 1  1 -  7 6 | 5 1  2 3  4 6
人　似　　月，皓腕　凝霜　雪．皓　腕

1 2 | 3 5  2 -  5 | 1 -  1 7  1 3 | 5 3  3· 2
凝　霜　雪．未老莫　还　　乡，还乡

1 7 | 1 3  6 1  7·⁺6 | 6 7  5· 5 | 1 -  1 7
须　断　肠．还乡须断肠．春水　碧于

1 3 | 5 6  6 -  6 5 | 4 6  2 3  4· 3 | 2· 6  6
天，　画船听雨眠．　画船听雨

0 1 |
眠．

## 2.41.2 Sheet music with Lyrics marked in Chinese pinyin without tones

```
5 | 1 -   1 7   1 3 | 5 1   1 -   7 6 | 5 1   2 3
  ren  ren    jin shuo  jiang nan   hao        you ren  zhi he   jiang nan
  人   人    尽  说    江   南     好,        游  人   只 合    江    南

4    6   1 2 | 3 5   2 -   5 | 1 -   1 7   1 3 | 5 3
lao      zhi he  jiang nan lao  chun shui     bi      yu          tian
老,      只 合   江   南   老,  春   水       碧      于          天,

3· 2   1 7 | 1   3   6 1   7· #6   6 7   5· 5 | 1 -
hua chuan ting   yu       mian    hua chuan ting  yu mian  lu bian
画  船  听      雨       眠,     画  船  听     雨 眠,   垆 边

1 7   1 3 | 5 1   1 -   7 6 | 5 1   2 3   4 6
ren   si        yue      hao wan  ning shuang xue   hao wan
人    似        月,      皓  腕   凝   霜    雪,   皓  腕

1 2 | 3 5   2 -   5 | 1 -   1 7   1 3 | 5 3   3· 2
ning shuang  xue  wei lao  mo       huan       xiang huan xiang
凝   霜     雪,  未 老   莫       还         乡,  还  乡

1 7 | 1 3   6 1   7· #6   6 7   5· 5 | 1 -   1 7
xu      duan    chang  huan xiang xu duan chang chun shui  bi  yu
须      断     肠,    还   乡   须 断   肠,    春   水     碧  于

1 3 | 5 6   6 -   6 5 | 4 6   2 3   4· 3 | 2· 6   6
         tian   hua chuan ting yu mian   hua chuan ting  yu
         天,    画  船  听     雨 眠,    画  船  听     雨

0   1 |
    mian
    眠.
```

### 2.41.3 Text of the lyrics

人人尽说江南好，游人只合江南老.
春水碧于天，画船听雨眠.
垆边人似月，皓腕凝霜雪.
未老莫还乡，还乡须断肠.

### 2.41.4 Text of the lyrics (a) marked with tones in Chinese pinyin

rén rén jǐn shuō jiāng nán hǎo　yóu rén zhǐ hé jiāng nán lǎo
人　人　尽　说　江　南　好，游　人　只　合　江　南　老.
chūn shuǐ bì yú tiān huà chuan tīng yǔ mián lú biān rén sì yuè
春　水　碧　于　天，画　船　听　雨　眠.垆　边　人　似　月，
hào wàn níng shuāng xuě wèi lǎo mò huán xiāng
皓　腕　凝　霜　雪.未　老　莫　还　乡，
huán xiāng xū duàn cháng
还　乡　须　断　肠.

### 2.41.5 Literal translation of the lyrics

Everyone says the lower reaches of the Yangtze River are wonderful, so the tourists only live in the south of the Yangtze River until get older. The spring water is greener than the sky; painting a boat and listening to the rain, I fall asleep. The people by the tavern are like the moon, their white wrists frozen with frost and snow. Don't return to your hometown before you are old; if you do, your heart will be broken.

### 2.41.6 A more polished and stylistically enhanced translation of the lyrics

It is often said that the lower reaches of the Yangtze River are breathtakingly beautiful. So, many tourists stay at the southern regions until they are older. The spring waters appear greener than the sky; drifting in a painted boat while listening to the gentle rain, one easily falls into a peaceful slumber. The fair-skinned women by the tavern shine like the moon, their delicate wrists pale as frost and snow. One should not return home before growing old; If go back home earlier, their hearts will break.

### 2.41.7 Translation sentence by sentence

人人尽说江南好，
It is often said that the lower reaches of the Yangtze River are breathtakingly beautiful.
游人只合江南老.
So, many tourists stay at the southern regions until they are older.
春水碧于天，
The spring waters appear greener than the sky，
画船听雨眠.
drifting in a painted boat while listening to the gentle rain, one easily falls into a peaceful slumber.
垆边人似月，
The fair-skinned women by the tavern shine like the moon,
皓腕凝霜雪.
Her delicate wrists pale as frost and snow.
未老莫还乡，
One should not return home before growing old;
还乡须断肠.
If go back home earlier, their hearts will break.

### 2.41.8 Brief introduction of the author of the poem

韦庄（公元836年-910年），字端己，杜陵人，词风清丽.曾任前蜀宰相，谥文靖.

Wei Zhuang (836 - 910 AD), styled Duanji, was from Duling. His lyrics were elegant and refined. He once served as the prime minister of the former Shu State and was posthumously titled Wenjing.

# 2.42 Song No.42, Written the ancient meadow to bid farewell

赋得古原草送别　唐　白居易

**Title of the poem: The ancient meadow grass was written to bid farewell
Author of the poem (lyrics), Tang Dynasty, Bai Ju Yi**

**2.42.0 About the score and lyrics (poem)**

This score (sheet music) is derived (excerpted) from the Finish Folk Song: The Flute Sound of the Pasture (or The Shepherd's Flute Sound) and has undergone minor modifications to ensure a better alignment between the musical arrangement and the lyrics (poem).

People's emotions towards the wild grass on the grassland are quite similar, the author rewrites the poem (lyrics) for the song.

## 2.42.1 Sheet music

$1 = C \quad \dfrac{4}{4}$

```
|5  |5  i  3  6|5  3  1  3|2  7  2  5|3  2  1  
    离 离 原 上 草， 一 岁 一 枯       荣， 野 火

3  3|2  2  3  4|5  6  7  5  5|i  6  i  6  7|
烧 不 尽，  春 风 吹 又   生，  春 风 吹 又

5 - - -|i - 5 -|6  5  4  5 -|5 - 3 -|2  3  2
生，    远 芳   侵 古 道 晴   翠  接 荒

1 -|i - 5 -|6  5  4  5 -|5 - 3 -|2  3  2  1 -|
城． 又 送   王 孙   去，  萋 萋 满 别   情．
```

## 2.42.2 Sheet music with Lyrics marked in Chinese pinyin without tones

```
|5  |5  i  3  6|5  3  1  3|2  7  2  5|3  2  1
    li  li yuan shang cao yi sui yi ku    rong ye huo
    离 离 原  上   草 一 岁 一 枯     荣 野 火

3  3|2  2  3  4|5  6  7  5  5|i  6  i  6  7|
shao bu jin   chun feng chui you sheng chun feng chui you
烧 不 尽，  春 风 吹 又   生，  春 风 吹 又

5 - - -|i - 5 -|6  5  4  5 -|5 - 3 -|2  3  2
sheng   yuan fang qin gu   dao qing cui  jie huang
生，    远 芳   侵 古 道 晴   翠  接 荒

1 -|i - 5 -|6  5  4  5 -|5 - 3 -|2  3  2  1 -|
cheng you song wang sun  qu  qi  qi man bie  qing
城． 又 送  王  孙    去，  萋 萋 满 别   情．
```

### 2.42.3 Text of the lyrics

离离原上草，一岁一枯荣.野火烧不尽，春风吹又生.
远芳侵古道，晴翠接荒城.又送王孙去，萋萋满别情.

### 2.42.4 Text of the lyrics marked with tones in Chinese pinyin

Lí lí yuán shàng cǎo yī suì yī kū róng yě huǒ shāo bù jìn
离离 原  上   草,一岁一 枯 荣. 野火 烧 不 尽,
chūn fēng chuī yòu shēng yuǎn fāng qīn gǔ dào
 春  风  吹  又  生.   远  芳  侵 古 道,
qíng cuì jiē huāng chéng yòu song wáng sūn qù
 晴  翠 接  荒    城. 又  送   王  孙 去,
qī qī mǎn bié qíng
萋萋 满 别 情.

### 2.42.5 Literal translation of the lyrics

Wilk grasses spreading over the plain, every year once flourish and once wither. Wildfires cannot burn them all; the spring breeze brings them back to life. Distant fragrance invades the ancient path, and clear greenery connects the desolate city. It sent off the prince's grandson again, filled with deep longing.

### 2.42.6 A more polished and stylistically enhanced translation of the lyrics

Wild grasses spread across the plain, every year once flourish and once wither. Wildfires burn them, but never entirely; the spring breeze brings them back to life. Their distant fragrance invades the ancient paths, and their vibrant green spread to desert places. It also bid farewell to the prince's grandson, filled with profound longing.

### 2.42.7 Translation sentence by sentence

离离原上草，一岁一枯荣.

Wild grasses spread across the plain, every year once flourish and once wither.

野火烧不尽，春风吹又生.

Wildfires burn them, but never entirely; the spring breeze brings them back to life.

远芳侵古道，晴翠接荒城.

Their distant fragrance invades the ancient paths, and their vibrant green spread to desert places.

又送王孙去，萋萋满别情.

It also bid farewell to the prince's grandson, filled with profound longing.

## 2.42.8 Brief introduction of the author of the poem

白居易（公元 772 - 846），字乐天，晚年号香山居士，河南新郑人，是唐代伟大的现实主义诗人，唐代三大诗人之一.白居易的诗歌题材广泛，形式多样，语言平易通俗.

Bai Juyi (772 - 846 AD), styled Letian and later known as Xiangshan Jushi, was a native of Xinzheng, Henan Province. He was a great realist poet of the Tang Dynasty and one of the three great poets of the Tang Dynasty. Bai Juyi's poems have a wide range of themes, diverse forms and plain and popular language.

# 2.43 Song No.43, The fisherman's song

渔歌子　唐　张志和

**Tune of the poem: The fisherman's song.**
**Author of the poem (lyrics), Tang Dynasty, Zhang Zhi He**

**2.43.0 About the score and lyrics (poem)**

This score is derived (excerpted) from the (pieces) of Tchaikovsky's Swan Lake, Neapolitan Dance and has undergone minor modifications to ensure a better alignment between the musical arrangement and the lyrics (poem).

The fisherman's life style is like that of a prince of the natural world, the cheerful, free and romantic rhythms and tunes of the music and the lyrics (the poem, original text and its translation see the following sections) are very matched each other. Thus the author incorporates this poem into that renowned musical composition.

## 2.43.1 Sheet music

$1 = C \quad \dfrac{2}{4}$

```
0  1 2  4 3 2 1 | 3  0  3 | 3  2 3  4 3 2 3 |
   西塞山前白鹭飞，  桃  花 流  水 鳜    鱼

2  1 | 1  1  1  2  7  6 | 1  7 | 7  7   7  7 |
肥.    青   莄         笠,   绿    裳

6  5 | 6  4 | 4 - | 4  4 4 | 2 2 | 2 3  4  5 4 |
衣,   斜  风   细 雨  不须归. 不

3 2 | 2  0 | 1 | 1 7  1 7 | 3 2 | 1  7 | 7  6 7 |
须   归.     青箬笠，绿  裳   衣,   斜   风

6 7 2 1 | 4 - | 4  4 4 | 4  4 | 2  4 | 2 4 | 2 4 |
细雨不须归. 不须归,   松江蟹舍蟹舍

5  4  3  2 | 2  1 | 2  1 | 2  1 | 2 1  7 6 | 1 7 |
主   人  欢,  菰饭莼羹亦   共    餐.

1 7 | 1 7 | 1 7 6 5 | 4 5 6 7 1 2 3 | 4 4 |
枫叶落, 荻花干, 醉  宿   渔   舟 不  觉  寒.
```

## 2.43.2 Sheet music with Lyrics marked in Chinese pinyin without tones

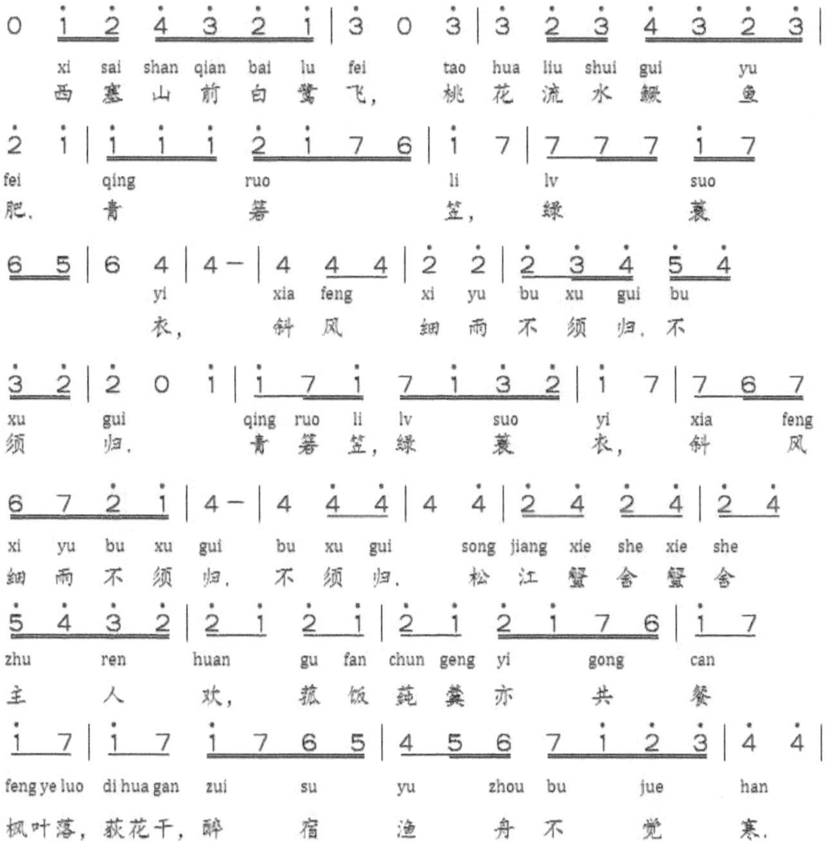

[sheet music with numbered notation and lyrics in pinyin and Chinese characters]

| | | | | | | | | | | | | | |
|---|---|---|---|---|---|---|---|---|---|---|---|---|---|
| 0 | 1 2 4 3 2 1 | 3 0 3 | 3 2 3 4 3 2 3 | | | | | | | | | | |
| | xi sai shan qian bai lu fei | tao hua | liu shui gui yu | | | | | | | | | | |
| | 西 塞 山 前 白 鹭 飞, | 桃 花 | 流 水 鳜 鱼 | | | | | | | | | | |

2 1 | 1 1 1 2 | 7 6 | 1 7 | 7 7 7 1 7
fei qing ruo li lv suo
肥, 青 箬 笠, 绿 蓑

6 5 | 6 4 | 4 — | 4 4 4 2 2 | 2 3 4 5 4
yi xia feng xi yu bu xu gui bu
衣, 斜 风 细 雨 不 须 归, 不

3 2 | 2 0 1 | 1 7 7 1 3 2 | 1 7 | 7 6 7
xu gui qing ruo li lv suo yi xia feng
须 归. 青 箬 笠, 绿 蓑 衣, 斜 风

6 7 2 1 | 4 — | 4 4 4 4 | 2 4 2 4 | 2 4
xi yu bu xu gui bu xu gui song jiang xie she xie she
细 雨 不 须 归, 不 须 归. 松 江 蟹 舍 蟹 舍

5 4 3 2 | 2 1 | 2 1 | 2 1 | 2 1 7 6 | 1 7
zhu ren huan gu fan chun geng yi gong can
主 人 欢, 菰 饭 莼 羹 亦 共 餐

1 7 | 1 7 | 1 7 6 5 | 4 5 6 | 7 1 2 3 | 4 4 |
feng ye luo di hua gan zui su yu zhou bu jue han
枫 叶 落, 荻 花 干, 醉 宿 渔 舟 不 觉 寒.

## 2.43.3 Text of the lyrics

西塞山前白鹭飞, 桃花流水鳜鱼肥.
青箬笠, 绿蓑衣, 斜风细雨不须归.
松江蟹舍主人欢, 菰饭莼羹亦共餐.
枫叶落, 荻花干, 醉宿渔舟不觉寒.

## 2.43.4 Text of the lyrics (a) marked with tones in Chinese pinyin

xī sài shān qián bái lù fēi  táo huā liú shuǐ guì yú féi
西塞山 前 白 鹭飞, 桃花流 水鳜鱼肥.

qīng ruò lì　lǜ suō yī　xié fēng xì yǔ bù xū guī
青 箬 笠, 绿 蓑 衣, 斜 风 细 雨 不 须 归.
sōng jiāng xiè shě zhǔ rén huān　gu fàn chún gēng yì gong cān
松 江 蟹 舍 主 人 欢, 菰 饭 莼 羹 亦 共 餐.
fēng yè luò　dí huā gàn zuì sù yú zhōu bù jué hán
枫 叶 落, 荻 花 干, 醉 宿 渔 舟 不 觉 寒.

### 2.43.5 Literal translation of the lyrics

In front of Xisai Mountain, white egrets fly, peach blossoms flow by the water and mandarin fish are fat. Green bamboo hat, green rain cape, no need to return in the slanting wind and drizzle.

The owner of Songjiang Crab House was happy, and he enjoys a meal with rice and soup made of water chestnuts. Maple leaves fall, reeds dry, and drunken one stay in a fishing boat without feeling the cold of weather.

### 2.43.6 A more polished and stylistically enhanced translation of the lyrics

In the presence of Xi Sai Mountain, white egrets soar through the air, peach blossoms drift along the river, and mandarin fish thrive in the water. Clad in a bamboo hat and wearing a rain cape, one finds no need to return amidst the slanting wind and drizzle.

The host of the Song Jiang Crab House was delighted, andenjoys a meal of mushroom rice and a water shield vegetable soup. Maple leaves fall, reeds dry, remain intoxicated aboard a fishing boat and fall insleep, oblivious to the cold.

### 2.43.7 Translation sentence by sentence

西塞山前白鹭飞,
In the presence of Xi Sai Mountain, white egrets soar through the air,
桃花流水鳜鱼肥.
peach blossoms drift along the river, and mandarin fish thrive in the water.
青箬笠, 绿蓑衣,

Clad in a bamboo hat and wearing a rain cape,
斜风细雨不须归.
one finds no need to return amidst the slanting wind and drizzle.
松江蟹舍主人欢,
The host of the Song Jiang Crab House was delighted,
菰饭莼羹亦共餐.
and enjoys a meal of mushroom rice and a water shield vegetable soup.
枫叶落，荻花干,
Maple leaves fall, reeds dry,
醉宿渔舟不觉寒.
remain intoxicated aboard a fishing boat and fall insleep, oblivious to the cold.

### 2.43.8 Brief introduction of the author of the poem (lyrics-b)

张志和（公元 730 年 - 810 年），字子同，浙江金华人.唐代著名道士，词人和诗人.十六岁参加科举，以明经擢第，授参军.唐肃宗赐名"志和".因事获罪贬为南浦尉，不久赦还.自此看破红尘，浪迹江湖，隐居祁门赤山镇.著有《玄真子》集.

Zhang Zhi He (730 - 810 AD), styled Zi Tong, was from Jin hua, Zhejiang Province. A renowned Taoist priest, lyricist and poet of the Tang Dynasty. At the age of sixteen, he took part in the imperial examination to be promoted and appointed as a military advisor. Emperor Suzong of Tang bestowed upon him the name "Zhihe". He was demoted to the position of Nan Pu Magistrate for a crime and was soon pardoned. From then on, he saw through the world, roamed the world and lived in seclusion in Chi Shan Town, Qi Men. He authored the collection "Xuan zhen zi".

# 2.44 Song No.44, Poems on Returning Home

回乡偶书二首 其一 唐 贺知章

**Title of the poem: One of the two Poems on Returning Home
Author of the poem (lyrics), Tang Dynasty, He Zhi Zhang**

### 2.44.0 About the score and lyrics (poem)

This score (sheet music) is derived (excerpted) from S Forster's Song: Relative of Hometown, and has undergone minor modifications to ensure a better alignment between the musical arrangement and the lyrics (poem).

The author rewrites the poem (lyrics) for the song.

### 2.44.1 Sheet music

$1 = C \quad \frac{4}{4}$

```
|3 -   2 1  3 2 | 1  i· 6  i | 5 -  3 1 | 2 - - 0 |
 少    小  离  家  老     大 回, 老   大   回,

 3 -  2 1  3 2 | 1  i· 6  i | 5   3 1 | 2  2  1 |
 乡    音  无  改  鬓     毛 衰. 鬓   毛   衰.

 7·  i  2  5 | 5· 6  5  i | i  6  4  6 | 5 - - 0 |
 儿   童 相 见   不 相  识, 儿 童 不  相  识,

 3 -  2 1  3 2 | 1  i· 6  i | 5  3 1 | 2  2  1 |
 笑    问  客  从  何     处 来. 客 从    何   处 来.
```

### 2.44.2 Sheet music with Lyrics marked in Chinese pinyin without tones

```
|3 -   2  1   3 2 | 1   i·  6   i | 5 -   3  1 | 2 - - 0 |
 shao  xiao  li   jia  lao    da  hui   lao  da  hu
 少    小    离   家    老      大  回,   老   大  回,

 3 -   2  1   3 2 | 1   i·  6   i | 5    3  1 | 2   2   1 |
 xiang yin   wu   gai  bin    mao shuai  bin   mao  shuai
 乡    音    无   改    鬓      毛  衰.    鬓    毛    衰.

 7·  i   2   5 | 5·  6   5   i | i   6   4   6 | 5 - - 0  |
 er  tong xiang jian  bu xiang  shi  er  tong  bu  xiang shi
 儿  童  相   见    不  相     识, 儿   童  不   相    识

 3 -  2  1   3 2 | 1   i·  6   i | 5   3  1 | 2   2   1 |
 xiao wen  ke    cong  he  chu  lai  ke  cong    he  chu  lai
 笑   问   客    从     何  处   来. 客  从       何   处   来.
```

### 2.44.3 Text of the lyrics

少小离家老大回, 乡音无改鬓毛衰.
儿童相见不相识, 笑问客从何处来.

### 2.44.4 Text of the lyrics marked with tones in Chinese pinyin

shào xiǎo lí    jiā lǎo dà huí    xiāng yīn wú gǎi bìn máo shuāi
少   小  离    家  老 大  回,    乡   音  无 改   鬓   毛   衰.
ér tóng xiāng jiàn bù xiāng shí    xiào wèn kè cóng hé chǔ lái
儿 童   相    见  不 相    识,    笑   问  客 从   何 处   来.

### 2.44.5 Literal translation of the lyrics

I left home when I was young and returned when I was old. My accent remained the same but my hair turned grey. Children see me but do not recognize me, smiling and asking the guest comes from where.

### 2.44.6 A more polished and stylistically enhanced translation of the lyrics

I left home in my youth and returned only in old age. Though my accent remains unchanged, my hair has turned grey. Children greet me without recognition, smiling as they inquire where the guest has come from.

### 2.44.7 Translation sentence by sentence

少小离家老大回,
I left home in my youth and returned only in old age.
乡音无改鬓毛衰.
Though my accent remains unchanged, my hair has turned grey.
儿童相见不相识,
Children greet me without recognition,
笑问客从何处来.
smiling as they inquire where the guest has come from.

## 2.44.8 Brief introduction of the author of the poem (lyrics)

贺知章（公元659年-744年），字季真，唐代著名诗人，书法家，越州永兴人.少时就以诗文知名.公元695年中乙未科状元，授予国子四门博士.后历任礼部侍郎、太子宾客等职.贺知章为人旷达不羁，八十六岁告老还乡，旋逝.诗文以绝句见长.

He Zhizhang (659 - 744 AD), styled Jizhen, was a poet and calligrapher of the Tang Dynasty. He was from Yongxing, Yuezhou. He was well-known for his poetry and prose at a young age. In the year 695 AD, he passed the imperial examination as the top scorer in the imperial examination and was awarded the title of Doctor of the Four Disciplines by Guozi. Later, he successively held positions such as Vice Minister of Rites and Guest to the Crown Prince. He Zhizhang was a carefree and unrestrained person. At the age of eighty-six, he retired and go to his hometown and passed away shortly after. Poetry and prose are known for their quatrains

# 2.45 Song No.45, Seven-character quatrain

七言绝句　唐　杜甫

**Title of the poem: Seven-character quatrain**
**Author of the poem (lyrics), Tang Dynasty, Du Fu**

**2.45.0 About the score and lyrics (poem)**

This score (sheet music) is derived (excerpted) from the Bowens's Song White Dove, and has undergone minor modifications to ensure a better alignment between the musical arrangement and the lyrics (poem).

The author rewrites the poem (lyrics) for the song.

## 2.45.1 Sheet music

$1 = C \quad \frac{4}{4}$

```
1 3 | 5  3  3  i  6 | 5  3  0  1  3 | 5  3  i  6  5 |
两 个  黄  鹂     鸣    翠 柳,    一 行  白  鹭 上 青 天.

5 - 0  1  3 | 5  3  i  6  5 | 5  3  0  1  3 | 5  5  4
       窗  含  西 岭 千 秋 雪,        门 泊  东 吴 万

2  1 | 0  5  5  5  5 | 6  6  6 - 0 | i  i  i  7 | 6  5
里 船.   窗  含  西 岭 千 秋 雪,     门 泊 东 吴 万

4  2  1  1 |
里  船.
```

## 2.45.2 Sheet music with Lyrics marked in Chinese pinyin without tones

```
1    3  | 5  3  3   i    6  | 5  3  0  1   3  | 5   3    i    6   5 |
liang ge huang li    ming   cui liu       yi hang bai  lu shang qing tian
两   个  黄   鹂     鸣     翠  柳,     一  行  白   鹭  上   青   天.

5 - 0  1     3  | 5  3   i   6   5 | 5  3  0  1   3 | 5   5   4
      chuang han  xi ling qian qiu xue       men bo dong wu  wan
       窗   含    西 岭   千  秋  雪,        门 泊  东  吴  万

2   1  | 0   5      5  | 5  5    5   5 | 6  6  6 - 0 | i   i   i   7 | 6   5
li chuan   chuang han  xi ling qian qiu xue         men bo dong wu  wan
里  船.      窗    含   西 岭  千  秋  雪,            门 泊 东  吴  万

4   2   1  1 |
li chuan
里  船.
```

### 2.45.3 Text of the lyrics

两个黄鹂鸣翠柳，一行白鹭上青天.
窗含西岭千秋雪，门泊东吴万里船.

### 2.45.4 Text of the lyrics marked with tones in Chinese pinyin

liǎng gè huáng lí míng cuì liǔ    yī hang bái lù shàng qīng tiān
　两　个　黄　鹂　鸣　翠　柳，一　行　白　鹭　上　　青　天.
chuāng hán xī lǐng qiān qiū xuě    mén bō dōng wú wàn lǐ chuán
　窗　　含　西　岭　千　秋　雪，门　泊　东　吴　万　里　船.

### 2.45.5 Literal translation of the lyrics

Two orioles sing among the green willows, and a row of white egrets soar into the blue sky. At the window one can see the thousands year never melt snow of the Western Hills, and the door is moored by the ships of the Eastern Wu that stretch for thousands of miles

### 2.45.6 A more polished and stylistically enhanced translation of the lyrics

Two orioles sing among the green willows, while a line of white egrets ascends into the azure sky. Through the window one can has a snapshot of the countless years never melt snow covered peaks of the Western Hills, and the door remains moored by ships bound for Eastern Wu, stretching thousands of miles away.

### 2.45.7 Translation sentence by sentence

两个黄鹂鸣翠柳，
Two orioles sing among the green willows,
一行白鹭上青天.
while a line of white egrets ascends into the azure sky.
窗含西岭千秋雪，
Through the window one can has a snapshot of the countless years never

melt snow covered peaks of the Western Hills,

门泊东吴万里船.

and the door remains moored by ships bound for Eastern Wu, stretching thousands of miles away.

### 2.45.8 Brief introduction of the author of the poem (lyrics)

杜甫（公元712年 - 公元770年），字子美，是唐朝著名的现实主义诗人，与李白合称"李杜".杜甫在中国古典诗歌中的影响非常深远，被后人尊称为"诗圣"，杜甫自小好学，七岁能作诗，杜甫二十岁开始了漫游生涯，游历了吴越和齐赵等地.这些经历丰富了他的生活体验，为他的诗歌创作提供了丰富的素材.杜甫742 - 756年终于得到了一些官职，安史之乱中目睹了战争的残酷和人民的苦难，759年，杜甫入川，生活相对安定，但仍心系国家和人民.在成都，在朋友的帮助下建成"杜甫草堂".随着战乱的持续，杜甫一家再次陷入漂泊之中，770年病死在湘江的一只小船中.

Du Fu (712 - 770 AD), styled Zimei, was a renowned realist poet of the Tang Dynasty. Together with Li Bai, he was known as "Li and Du". Du Fu's influence in Chinese classical poetry is extremely profound. He is respectfully called the "Poet Sage" by later generations. Du Fu was erudite. He was eager to learn from a young age and could compose poems at the age of seven. Du Fu began his wandering life at the age of twenty. These experiences enriched his life experiences and provided rich materials for his poetry creation. Du Fu finally obtained some official positions in 742-756. During the An Shi Rebellion, he witnessed the cruelty of war and the suffering of the people. In 759, Du Fu entered Sichuan. His life was relatively stable, but he still cared about the country and the people. In Chengdu, with the help of friends, the "Du Fu Thatched Cottage" was built. As the war continued, Du Fu's family once again fell into a state of wandering and died of illness in a small boat on the Xiang River in 770.

# 2.46 Song No.46, Climbing Lan Shan Mountain

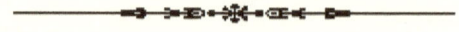

秋登兰山　寄张五　唐　孟浩然

**Title of the poem: Climbing Lan Shan Mountain and sent a letter to Zhang Wu in autumn**

**Author of the poem (lyrics), Tang Dynasty, Meng Hao Ran**

### 2.46.0 About the score and lyrics (poem)

This score (sheet music) is derived (excerpted) from the (pieces) of Turkish Folk Song：Mount Ergaz, and has undergone minor modifications to ensure a better alignment between the musical arrangement and the lyrics (poem).

Through the history and across the world, the perception and sentiment when one is climbing a high mountain are almost similar. The music and the lyrics (the poem, original text and its translation see the following sections) thus could be recombined.　Therefore the author rewrites the poem (lyrics) for the song.

## 2.46.1 Sheet music

$1 = C \quad \frac{2}{4}$

6 - | 3 - | 2 3　1 2 | 3 - | 3　3　6 | 5　#4　5 | 3 - |
北　山　白　云　里，隐者　自　怡　悦．

6 - | 3 - | 2 3　1 2 | 3 - | 3　3　6 | 5　#4　5 | 3 - |
相　望　试　登　高，心随　雁飞　灭．

5　5　5　5 | 5　#4　6 | 5 - | 2　2　2　2 | 2　1　3 |
愁　因　薄暮　起，兴　是　清秋

2 - | 2　2　2　2 | 2　1　7 | 6 - | 3 - | 2　2　2　2 |
发．时　见　归村　人，　　沙　行

2　1　7 | 6 - | 6 - | 3 - | 2 3　1 2 | 3 - | 3　3　6 |
渡头　歇．天　边　树　若　荠，江　畔

5　#4　5 | 3 - | 5　5　5　5 | 5　4　6 | 5 - | 2　2 |
洲　如　月．何　当　载酒　来，共

2　2 | 2　1　7 | 6 |
醉　重阳　节．

## 2.46.2 Sheet music with Lyrics marked in Chinese pinyin without tones

```
6 -  | 3 -  | 2  3  | 1  2  | 3 -  | 3  3  6 | 5  *4  5 | 3 - |
bei    shan   bai     yun     li     yin zhe   zi   yi    yue
北      山    白      云      里,    隐   者    自    怡    悦.

6 -  | 3 -  | 2  3  | 1  2  | 3 -  | 3  3  6 | 5  *4  5 | 3 - |
xiang  wang  shi     deng    gao    xin  sui   yan  fei    mie
相      望    试      登      高,    心   随    雁   飞    灭.

5  5  5  5 | 5  *4  6 | 5 -  | 2  2   2  2 | 2  1  3 |
chou   yin   bo   mu    qi  xing   shi      qing  qiu
愁      因    薄   暮    起,  兴    是      清    秋

2 -  | 2  2   2  2 | 2   1  7 | 6 -  | 3 -  | 2  2   2  2 |
fa     shi    jian   gui  cun   ren           sha   xing
发.     时    见    归    村    人,           沙    行

2  1  7 | 6 -  | 6 -  | 3 -  | 2  3  | 1  2  | 3 -  | 3  3  6 |
du  tou    xie    tian   bian   shu     ruo     ji    jiang pan
渡  头    歌.    天    边    树     若     茾     江   畔

5  *4  5 | 3 -  | 5  5   5  5 | 5  4  6 | 5 -  | 2  2 |
zhou ru    yue    he    dang    zai jiu   lai    gong
洲    如    月.    何    当      载 酒    来,    共

2  2 | 2  1  7 | 6 |
zui    chong yang   jie
醉    重    阳      节.
```

### 2.46.3 Text of the lyrics

北山白云里，隐者自怡悦.相望试登高，心随雁飞灭.
愁因薄暮起，兴是清秋发.时见归村人，沙行渡头歇.
天边树若荠，江畔洲如月.何当载酒来，共醉重阳节.

### 2.46.4 Text of the lyrics (a) marked with tones in Chinese pinyin

běi shān bái yún lǐ　yǐn zhě zì yí yuè xiāng wàng shì dēng gāo
北　山　白　云里，隐者 自怡悦. 相　　望　试　登高,
xīn suí yàn fēi miè chóu yīn bó mù qǐ　xìng shì qīng qiū fā
心　随　雁飞　灭. 愁　因　薄暮 起, 兴　是 清　秋发.
shí jiàn guī cūn rén　shā xíng dù tóu xiē tiān biān shù ruò jì
时 见　归 村 人,　沙 行　渡 头 歇.天　边　树 若荠,
jiāng pàn zhōu rú yuè hé dāng zài jiǔ lái　gong zuì chóng yang jié
江　畔　洲 如月.何　当　载 酒 来,　共　醉　重　阳 节.

### 2.46.5 Literal translation of the lyrics

In the white clouds of the northern mountains, the recluse finds himself content and happy. Looking at each other and trying to climb higher; their heart follows the wild geese as they fly away. Sorrow arises at dusk, while joy sprouts in the clear autumn. At that time, the people returning to the village, resting at the sand-crossing can be seen. The trees on the horizon are like chestnuts, and the islands by the river are like the moon. Why not we bring wine and get drunk together on the Chongyang Festival?

### 2.46.6 A more polished and stylistically enhanced translation of the lyrics

In the white clouds drifting over the northern mountains, the recluse finds joy in their inner heart. As we gaze at each other, we attempt to ascend higher, yet our thoughts soar with the wild geese. Sorrow emerges at dusk, while joy blossoms in the clear skies of autumn. Occasionally, the people returning to the village, crossing the sandbanks to rest can be seen. The trees on the distant horizon resemble water chestnuts, and the islets along the riverbank appear like the full moon. Why not we bring wine and share a joyful intoxication during the Chongyang Festival?

### 2.46.7 Translation sentence by sentence

北山白云里，隐者自怡悦.
In the white clouds drifting over the northern mountains, the recluse finds joy in their inner heart.
相望试登高，心随雁飞灭.
As we gaze at each other, we attempt to ascend higher, yet our thoughts soar with the wild geese.
愁因薄暮起，兴是清秋发.
Sorrow emerges at dusk, while joy blossoms in the clear skies of autumn.
时见归村人，沙行渡头歇.
Occasionally, the people returning to the village, crossing the sandbanks to rest can be seen.
天边树若荠，江畔洲如月.
The trees on the distant horizon resemble water chestnuts, and the islets along the riverbank appear like the full moon.
何当载酒来，共醉重阳节.
Why not we bring wine and share a joyful intoxication during the Chongyang Festival.

### 2.46.8 Brief introduction of the author of the poem (lyrics-b)

孟浩然（公元 689 年 - 740 年），字浩然，襄阳人，唐代著名的山水田园派诗人.40 岁时游长安，应进士举不第. 737 年张九龄招致幕府，后隐居.孟诗多写山水田园和隐居的逸兴.

Meng Haoran (689 - 740 AD), styled Haoran, was a native of Xiangyang. He was a renowned poet of the landscape and pastoral school in the Tang Dynasty. At the age of 40, he traveled to Chang 'an but failed the imperial examination. In 737, he was recruited as officer by Zhang Jiuling and later retired. Most of Meng's poems are depicting landscapes, idyllic fields and the carefree mood of seclusion.

# 2.47 Song No.47, Forever yearning

长相思　唐　白居易　及　宋　林逋

**Tune of the poem: Forever yearning.**
**Authors of the poem (lyrics), Tang Dynasty Bai Ju Yi and Song Dynasty Lin Bu**

**2.47.0 About the score and lyrics (poem)**

This score (sheet music) is derived (excerpted) from the (pieces) of American Song: Five Hundreds Miles and has undergone minor modifications to ensure a better alignment between the musical arrangement and the lyrics (poem).

A Long road, a Long yearning and a Long sense of sadness, the music and the lyrics (the poem, original text and its translation see the following sections) have similar moods, therefore the author rewrites the Chinese classical traditional poetry for the song.

## 2.47.1 Sheet music

$1 = C \quad \frac{4}{4}$

| 1　1 | 3· 3 2 1· | 3 -　2 1· | 2· 3 2 1· | 6 - - 6 1 |
汴 水 流, 泗 水 流,　　流 到 瓜 州 古 渡 头. 吴 山

| 2· 3 2 1· | 6 5· 5 5 6· 1 | 2 - - - | 2 1 1 1 |
点 点 愁. 思 悠 悠,　恨 悠 悠,　　恨 到 归 时

| 3· 3 2 1· | 3· 3 2 1· | 2· 3 2 1· | 6 - - 6 1 |
方 始 休. 方 始 休. 月 明 人 倚 楼.　　吴 山

| 2· 3 2 1· | 6 5· 5 5 6 1 | 1 - 1 1 | 3 - 2 1 |
青, 越 山 青, 两 岸 青 山 相 送 迎,　谁 知 离 别

| 1 - 0 1 | 2· 3 2 1· | 6 - - 6 1 | 2· 3 2 1· 6 |
情.　 君 泪 盈, 妾 泪 盈,　罗 带 同 心 结 未 成,

| 5· 5 5 6 1 | 1 - - - |
江 头　潮 已 平.

## 2.47.2 Sheet music with Lyrics marked in Chinese pinyin without tones

```
| 1    1   3·  3   2   1· | 3 -   2   1· | 2·  3   2   1· | 6 - - 6   1 |
  bian shui liu si shui liu         liu  dao gua zhou gu  du  tou  wu shan
  汴   水  流, 泗  水  流,        流  到  瓜  州   古  渡  头.  吴  山

  2·   3   2   1· | 6   5·  5   5  | 6·  1  | 2 - - -  | 2   1   1   1 |
  dian dian chou   si     you you   hen    you you               hen dao gui shi
  点   点   愁.    思     悠  悠,   恨     悠  悠,                恨  到  归  时

  3·   3   2   1· | 3·  3   2   1· | 2·  3   2   1· | 6 - -  6   1 |
       fang shi xiu       fang shi xiu    yue ming ren yi lou    wu  sh
       方   始  休. 方   始  休.      月  明  人   倚 楼.         吴  山

  2·   3   2   1· | 6   5·  5   5  | 6   1  | 1 - 1   1 | 3 -   2   1 |
  qing yue shan qing liang an qing shan xiang song ying shui zhi li bie qing
  青,  越  山  青, 两  岸  青  山  相  送  迎,   谁  知 离  别  情.

  1 -   0   1 | 2·  3   2   1· | 6 - -   6   1 | 2·  3   2   1·  6 |
       jun lei ying qie  lei ying      luo  dai tong xin jie wei cheng
       君  泪  盈, 妾  泪  盈,          罗  带  同  心  结  未  成,

  5·   5   5   6   1 | 1 - - - |
  jiang tou    chao yi ping
  江   头     潮  已  平.
```

### 2.47.3 Text of the lyrics (a)

### 长相思 唐 白居易

汴水流，泗水流，流到瓜洲古渡头，吴山点点愁.
思悠悠，恨悠悠，恨到归时方始休，月明人倚楼.

### 2.47.4 Text of the lyrics (a) marked with tones in Chinese pinyin

biàn shuǐ liú   sì shuǐ liú liú dào guā zhōu gǔ dù tóu wú shān diǎn diǎn chóu
汴 水 流, 泗 水 流, 流 到 瓜 洲 古 渡 头, 吴 山 点 点 愁.
sī yōu yōu   hèn yōu yōu hèn dào guī shí fāng shǐ xiū yuè míng rén yǐ lóu
思 悠 悠,  恨 悠 悠, 恨 到 归 时 方 始 休, 月 明 人 倚 楼.

### 2.47.5 Literal translation of the lyrics (a)

The Bian River flows and the Si River flows, flowing to the ancient ferry terminal of Guazhou city, with a touch of melancholy on Wushan Mountain. Thoughts linger on and on, regret lingers on and on. Regret only ceases when it's time to return. Under the moonlight, people lean against the tower.

### 2.47.6 A more polished and stylistically enhanced translation of the lyrics

The Bian River flows into the Si River, eventually reaching the ancient ferry terminal of Guazhou city. A sense of melancholy lingers amidst the Wu Mountains. Thoughts persist, and so does resentment, only to subside when the time for return arrives. The bright moon leans gently against the tower.

### 2.47.7 Translation sentence by sentence

汴水流，泗水流，
The Bian River flows into the Si River,
流到瓜洲古渡头，
eventually reaching the ancient ferry terminal of Guazhou city.

吴山点点愁.
A sense of melancholy lingers amidst the Wu Mountains.
思悠悠，恨悠悠，
Thoughts persist, and so does regret,
恨到归时方始休，
only to subside when the time for return arrives.
月明人倚楼.
The bright moon leans gently against the tower.

### 2.47.8 Brief introduction of the author of the poem (lyrics-a)

For details, please refer to section 2.42.7 of this book, we do not repeat here.

### 2.47.9 Text of the lyrics (b)

**长相思宋林逋**

吴山青，越山青，两岸青山相送迎，谁知离别情.
君泪盈，妾泪盈，罗带同心结未成，江头潮已平.

### 2.47.10 Text of the lyrics (b) marked with tones in Chinese pinyin

wú shān qīng yuè shān qīng liǎng àn qīng shān xiāng song yíng
吴 山 青，越 山 青，两 岸 青 山 相 送 迎，
shui zhī lí bié qíng jūn lèi yíng qiè lèi yíng
谁 知 离 别 情.君 泪 盈，妾 泪 盈，
luó dài tong xīn jié wèi chéng jiāng tou cháo yǐ píng
罗 带 同 心 结 未 成，江 头 潮 已 平.

### 2.47.11 Literal translation of the lyrics (b)

Wu Mountain is green, Yue Mountain is green, the green mountains on both banks bid farewell and welcome each other. Who knows the parting feelings? Your tears are welling up, my tears are welling up. The knot of our hearts has not yet connected, but the tide at the river's head has already subsided.

## 2.47.12 A more polished and stylistically enhanced translation of the lyrics (b)

The Wu Mountains are verdant; the Yue Mountains are equally green. The lush hills on both riverbanks seem to bid farewell and offer welcome in turn. Who can truly comprehend the depth of parting sorrow? Your tears flow, as do mine. Before the knot of our hearts could form, the tide at the river's mouth had already receded.

### 2.47.13 Translation sentence by sentence

吴山青，越山青，
The Wu Mountains are verdant; the Yue Mountains are equally green.
两岸青山相送迎，
The lush hills on both riverbanks seem to bid farewell and offer welcome in turn.
谁知离别情.
Who can truly comprehend the depth of parting sorrow.
君泪盈，妾泪盈，
Your tears flow, as do mine.
罗带同心结未成，
Before the knot of our hearts could form,
江头潮已平.
the tide at the river's mouth had already receded.

### 2.47.14 Brief introduction of the author of the poem (lyrics-b)

林逋（公元 967 - 1028）字君复，浙江人.幼时刻苦好学，通晓经史百家.喜恬淡，不趋荣利.隐居杭州西湖，结庐孤山.每逢客至叫门，即命童子纵鹤放飞. 作诗随就随弃，从不留存.宋仁宗赐谥"和靖先生".

Lin Bu (967 - 1028 AD), styled Junfu, from Zhejiang Province. When he was young, he was diligent and studious, well-versed in the classics, history and various schools of thought. I prefer tranquility and do not seek fame and fortune. Living in seclusion by West Lake in Hangzhou and building a cottage on a solitary mountain. Whenever guests arrive, knock the door, he then order boy to set the cranes flying freely for a while. Poems are written and discarded at will, never retained. Emperor Renzong of the Song Dynasty bestowed upon him the posthumous title of "Mr. Hejing"

# 2.48 Song No.48, Though the turtle lives long

龟随寿　东汉　曹操

**Title of the poem: Though the turtle lives long**
**Author of the poem (lyrics), Eastern Han Dynasty, Cao Cao**

### 2.48.0 About the score and lyrics (poem)

This score (sheet music) is derived (excerpted) from the (pieces) of Johann Strauss II's Emperor Waltz and has undergone minor modifications to ensure a better alignment between the musical arrangement and the lyrics (poem).

Emperor should be politician, emperor is also human being, they also need to lead ordinary lives and have a lot of ordinary thinking.

The music and the lyrics (the poem, original text and its translation see the following sections) have similar artistic conceptions, therefore it is well worth to try to combine the lyrics and the music. Thus the author incorporates this poem into that renowned musical composition.

## 2.48.1 Sheet music

$1 = C \quad \frac{4}{4}$

| 3  5· 5 | 4 − − | 3  5  3 | 2 − − | 4  6· 5 | 5 − − |
  神 龟 虽 寿，     犹 有 竟 时.     腾 蛇 乘 雾，

| 4  5  4 | 3 − − | 3  5· 5 | 4 − − | 3  6  3 | 2 − − |
  终 为 土 灰.     老 骥 伏 枥，     志 在 千 里.

| 6  1· 5 | 7 − 6 | 5  4  2 | 1 0 0 | 1  3 − | 3  7 − |
  烈 士 暮 年， 壮 心 不     已.    盈 缩 之 期

| 7· 2  2  2 | 6 − − | 7  2 − | 2  6 − | 6· 1  1  1 |
  不 但 在     天.   养 怡 之 福，  可 得 永 年.

| 5 − − | 4  3· 7 | 2  1· 6 | 6 − 5 | 1 0 0 |
         幸 甚 至 哉， 歌 以     咏 志.

## 2.48.2 Sheet music with Lyrics marked in Chinese pinyin without tones

```
| 3  5·  5 | 4 - - | 3  5  3 | 2 - - | 4  6·  5 | 5 - - |
  shen gui sui shou    you you jing shi   teng she cheng wu
  神   龟  虽  寿,     犹   有  竟  时.   腾   蛇  乘   雾

  4  5  4 | 3 - - | 3  5·  5 | 4 - - | 3  6  3 | 2 - - |
  zhong wei tu hui    lao ji  fu li     zhi zai qian li
  终   为  土  灰.    老  骥  伏  枥,   志  在  千  里.

  6  1·  5 | 7 - 6 | 5  4  2 | 1 0 0 | 1  3 - | 3  7 - |
  lie shi mu nian zhuang xin bu    yi    ying suo  zhi qi
  烈  士  暮  年,  壮    心  不    已.   盈   缩   之  期,

  7·  2  2  2 | 6 - - | 7  2 - | 2  6 - | 6·  1  1  1 |
  bu dan zai   tian     yang yi   zhi fu   ke  de yong
  不 但  在    天.      养  怡    之  福,   可  得  永

  5 - - | 4  3·  7 | 2  1·  6 | 6 - 5 | 1 0 0 |
  nian    xing shen zhi  zai ge yi      yong zhi
  年      幸   甚   至   哉,  歌 以      咏   志.
```

### 2.48.3 Text of the lyrics

神龟虽寿，犹有竟时.腾蛇乘雾，终为土灰.
老骥伏枥，志在千里.烈士暮年，壮心不已.
盈缩之期，不但在天.养怡之福，可得永年.
幸甚至哉，歌以咏志.

### 2.48.4 Text of the lyrics marked with tones in Chinese pinyin

shén guī suī shòu yóu yǒu jìng shí　téng shé chéng wù
　神　龟　虽　寿，犹　有　竟　时. 腾　蛇　乘　雾，
zhōng wèi tǔ huī lǎo jì　fú lì　zhì zài qiān lǐ　liè shì mù nián
终　为　土灰.老　骥　伏枥，志　在　千　里. 烈 士 暮　年，
zhuàng xīn bù yǐ　yíng suō zhī qī　bù dàn zài tiān yǎng yí zhī fú
壮　心 不已. 盈 缩 之 期，不但　在 天. 养 怡 之 福，
kě dé yǒng nián xìng shèn zhì zāi　gē yǐ yǒng zhì
可得　永　年. 幸　甚 至 哉，歌 以 咏 志.

### 2.48.5 Literal translation of the lyrics

Though the divine turtle lives long, it still has its time to end. The snake that soars through the mist eventually turns to dust. An old steed, though tethered in the stable, still has the ambition to travel a thousand miles. The martyr, in his old age, still has an unyielding spirit. The period of waxing and waning is not only in the sky. Cultivating good fortune can lead to eternal life. How fortunate it is! Songs are used to express one's aspirations.

### 2.48.6 A more polished and stylistically enhanced translation of the lyrics

Though the divine turtle enjoys a long life, it still meets its end. The soaring serpent rides the mist but ultimately turns to dust. An old steed, though tethered, still aspires to travel a thousand miles. A true hero, even in old age, never relinquishes his ambition. The timing of fortune and misfortune is not solely determined by heaven. Contentment and peace can lead to eternal life. How fortunate! I sing to express my aspirations.

## 2.48.7 Translation sentence by sentence

神龟虽寿，犹有竟时.
Though the divine turtle enjoys a long life, it still meets its end.
腾蛇乘雾，终为土灰.
The soaring serpent rides the mist but ultimately turns to dust.
老骥伏枥，志在千里.
An old steed, though tethered, still aspires to travel a thousand miles.
烈士暮年，壮心不已.
A true hero, even in old age, never relinquishes his ambition.
盈缩之期，不但在天.
The timing of fortune and misfortune is not solely determined by heaven.
养怡之福，可得永年.
Contentment and peace can lead to eternal life.
幸甚至哉，歌以咏志.
How fortunate, I sing to express my aspirations.

## 2.48.8 Brief introduction of the author of the poem (lyrics)

曹操（公元155年 - 220年），字孟德，小字阿瞒，沛国谯（今安徽亳州）人.东汉末年杰出的政治家，军事家，文学家.三国中曹魏政权的开创者，其子曹丕称帝后，追尊为武皇帝.曹操精兵法，诗歌抒发自己的政治抱负，并反映汉末人民的苦难生活，慷慨悲凉，开启并繁荣了建安文学.

Cao Cao (155 - 220 AD), courtesy name Meng De, childhood name Aman, from Bozhou, Anhui Province. He was an outstanding politician, military strategist, and litterateur of the late Eastern Han Dynasty, the founder of the State of Wei during the Three Kingdoms period, and later posthumously honored as Emperor Wu. Cao Cao excelled in poetry, expressing his political aspirations and reflecting the hardships of the people at the end of the Han Dynasty. His style was grand and heroic, passionate and tragic, initiating and flourishing the literature of the Jian'an era.

# 2.49 Song No.49, Enjoy Wines while going down Zhongnan Mountain

下终南山过斛斯山人宿置酒　唐　李白

**Title of the poem: Enjoy Wines while going down Zhongnan Mountain to spend the night with the recluse at mountain Hu**
**Author of the poem (lyrics), Tang Dynasty, Li Bai**

### 2.49.0 About the score and lyrics (poem)

This score (sheet music) is derived (excerpted) from the (pieces) of Verdi's Woman are fickle and has undergone minor modifications to ensure a better alignment between the musical arrangement and the lyrics (poem).

If one set different poem to the music, it can express different meaning and mood that differ from Woman are fickle. For example English author Fritz rewrites a new poem to it: Over the Summer Sea, thus rewrite into a lyrical song.

The music of the Over the Summer Sea is similar to the lyrics (the poem, original text and its translation see the following sections) especially in the rhythmic sense, therefore it is well worth to try to combine the lyrics and the music. Thus the author rewrites the poem (lyrics) for the song.

## 2.49.1 Sheet music

$1 = C \quad \frac{2}{4}$

3 3 3 | 5 4 2 | 2 2 2 | 4 3 1 | 3 2 1 |
暮 从 碧 山 下, 山 月 随 人 归. 却 顾 所

1 7 7 | 2 1 6 | 6 5 5 | 3 3 3 | 5 4 2 |
来 径, 苍 苍 横 翠 微. 相 携 及 田 家,

2 2 2 | 4 3 1 | 3 2 1 | 1 7 7 | 2 1 6 |
童 稚 开 荆 扉. 绿 竹 入 幽 径, 青 萝 拂

6 5 5 | 3 2 1 | 1 7 7 | 2 1 6 | 6 6 5 |
行 衣. 欢 言 得 所 憩, 美 酒 聊 共 挥.

2 3 2 2 | 5 2 | 3 4 3 3 | 6 3 | 5 6 5 5 |
长 歌 吟 松 风, 曲 尽 河 星 稀. 我 醉 君

6 5 | 4 5 4 3 2 | 1 0 |
复 乐, 陶 然 共 忘 机.

## 2.49.2 Sheet music with Lyrics marked in Chinese pinyin without tones

```
3   3   3 | 5   4   2 | 2   2   2 | 4   3   1 | 3   2   1 |
mu  cong      bi shan xia shan yue   sui ren gui que  gu
暮  从        碧  山  下， 山  月    随  人  归. 却  顾

1   7   7 | 2   1   6 | 6   5   5 | 3   3   3 | 5   4   2 |
suo lai jing cang cang heng cui wei   xiang xie ji  tian   jia
所  来  径， 苍  苍  横  翠  微      相  携  及  田     家，

2   2   2 | 4   3   1 | 3   2   1 | 1   7   7 | 2   1   6 |
tong zhi kai jing fei       lv  zhu ru  you     jing qing luo
童   稚 开  荆  扉.        绿  竹  入  幽        径， 青  萝

6   5   5 | 3   2   1 | 1   7   7 | 2   1   6 | 6   6   5 |
fu  xing yi  huan yan de  suo      qi  mei jiu liao gong  hui
拂  行  衣. 欢  言  得  所         憩， 美  酒 聊  共      挥.

2   3   2   2 | 5   2 | 3   4   3   3 | 6   3 | 5   6   5   5 |
chang  ge  yin song feng qu      jin he xing xi      wo    zui jun
长    歌  吟  松  风， 曲       尽 河  星  稀.      我    醉  君

6   5 | 4   5   4   3   2 | 1   0 |
fu  le  tao   ran gong wang ji
复  乐， 陶    然   共  忘   机.
```

### 2.49.3 Text of the lyrics

暮从碧山下，山月随人归.却顾所来径，苍苍横翠微.
相携及田家，童稚开荆扉.绿竹入幽径，青萝拂行衣.
欢言得所憩，美酒聊共挥.长歌吟松风，曲尽河星稀.
我醉君复乐，陶然共忘机.

### 2.49.4 Text of the lyrics (a) marked with tones in Chinese pinyin

mù cóng bì shān xià shān yuè suí rén guī què gù suǒ lái jìng
暮　从　碧　山下，山　月　随人　归. 却顾　所来　径，
cāng cāng héng cuì wēi　 xiāng xié jí tián jiā　 tong zhì kāi jīng fēi
苍　苍　横　翠　微. 相　携　及田　家，童　稚　开荆　扉.
lǜ zhú rù yōu jìng　 qīng luó fú xíng yī huān yán dé suǒ qì
绿竹入幽径，青　萝拂行衣. 欢　言　得　所憩，
měi jiǔ liáo gòng huī cháng gē yín sōng fēng qū jǐn hé xīng xī
美酒聊共挥. 长　歌吟松　风，曲尽河星稀.
wǒ zuì jūn fù lè　 táo rán gong wàng jī
我醉君复乐，陶然　共　忘　机.

### 2.49.5 Literal translation of the lyrics

At dusk, from the green mountain, the moon follows one's return. Looking back at the path I came from, it was vast and verdant. Together with the farming family, childhood opens the door of prosperity. Green bamboo leads into a secluded path, and blue lilies caress the traveler's clothes. We find a place to rest in joy and enjoy fine wine together. A long song sings of the pine breeze; when the melody ends, the stars in the river become few. I am intoxicated and you are happy again, and in a state of bliss, we forget the time together.

### 2.49.6 A more polished and stylistically enhanced translation of the lyrics

At dusk, the moon follows one back from the verdant mountains.

Looking behind, the path taken stretches vast and green. Hand in hand, we go together down to the farming family, childhood ushers in prosperity. Green bamboo leads into a secluded path, and blue lilies gently brush against the traveler's garments. We find a place to rest joyfully and share fine wine. A long song echoes the breeze through the pines; when the melody ends, the stars above the river begin to fade. I am intoxicated, and you are joyful bliss, we forget the passage of time.

### 2.49.7 Translation sentence by sentence

暮从碧山下，山月随人归.
At dusk, the moon follows one back from the verdant mountains.
却顾所来径，苍苍横翠微.
Looking behind, the path taken stretches vast and green.
相携及田家，童稚开荆扉.
Hand in hand, we go together down to the farming family, childhood ushers in prosperity.
绿竹入幽径，青萝拂行衣.
Green bamboo leads into a secluded path, and blue lilies gently brush against the traveler's garments.
欢言得所憩，美酒聊共挥.
We find a place to rest and chat joyfully and share fine wine.
长歌吟松风，曲尽河星稀.
A long song echoes the breeze through the pines; when the melody ends, the stars above the river begin to fade.
我醉君复乐，陶然共忘机.
I am intoxicated, and you are joyful bliss, we forget the passage of time.

### 2.49.8 Brief introduction of the author of the poem

Refer to section 2.03.7 of this book, we do not repeat here.

# 2.50 Song No.50, Recording the Dreams on the night

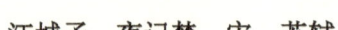

## 江城子　夜记梦　宋　苏轼

**Tune of the poem: Guys of Riverside Town. Title of the poem:
Recording the Dreams (nightmare) on the night
Author of the poem (lyrics), Song Dynasty, Su Shi**

### 2.50.0 About the score and lyrics (poem)

This score (sheet music) is derived (excerpted) from the (pieces) of Chopin's Funeral March and has undergone minor modifications to ensure a better alignment between the musical arrangement and the lyrics (poem).

Chopin's Funeral March is a profound meditation on death, grief, and the human condition. When you are listening to it, the Funeral March continues to move listeners with its poignant expression of sorrow and its reminder of the inescapable reality of death. Through this work, Chopin has left us with a timeless reflection on the nature of life and loss.

If we use the above description about Chopin's Funeral March to describe Su Shi's poem: Recording the Dreams on the Night, we will find no other words more appropriate. Thus the author incorporates this poem into that renowned musical composition.

## 2.50.1 Sheet music

$1 = C \quad \frac{4}{4}$

| 6  6· 6  6  6 | 5  3· 5  6 - | 5· 6  7  6  5 |

十 年 生 死　　两 茫　 茫,　不　 思　 量,

| 6·#4  3  2 - | 3  6  3  3  7  6  5 | 6  3  2  1 - |

自　 难 忘. 千 里 孤 坟,　无　 处 话 凄 凉.

| 2· 3  6  0  6  0 | 3  2  1  7  6 - | 6  2  1  7  6 |

纵 使 相　 逢　 应　 不　 识, 尘 满 面,

| 2  6  1  7  6 - | 6  2  1  7  6 | 2  6  1  2  3 - |

鬓 如 霜.　　夜 来 幽 梦 忽　 还　 乡,

| 3  6  5  4  3 | 6  3  2  1 - | 2· 3  6  0 #4  0 |

小 轩 窗,　正 梳 妆.　　相 顾 无　 言,

| 3  2  1  7  6 - | 3  6  5  4  3 | 6  3  2  1 - |

惟 有 泪 千 行. 料 得 年　 年 断 肠　 处

| 2· 3  6  0 #4  0 | 3  2  1  7  6 - |

明　 月　 夜, 短　 松　 冈.

## 2.50.2 Sheet music with Lyrics marked in Chinese pinyin without tones

```
| 6  6·  6   6    6 | 5   3·  5   6 - | 5·  6   7   6    5 |
  shi nian sheng si     liang mang mang  bu      si  liang
  十  年   生    死     两    茫   茫,   不      思   量,

| 6·  *4   3   2 - | 3   6   3   7 | 6   5 | 6   3   2   1 - |
  zi  nan  wan qian  li  gu  fen wu         chu hua  qi  liang
  自  难   忘, 千    里  孤  坟,  无         处  话   凄   凉.

| 2·  3   6   0   6   0 | 3   2   1   7 | 6 - | 6   2   1   7   6 |
  zong shi xiang    feng      ying  bu  shi         chen man  mian
  纵   使  相        逢       应    不   识,         尘   满   面,

| 2   6   1   7   6 - | 6   2   1   7 | 6   2   6   1   2   3 - |
  bin ru  shuang           ye  lai  you meng  hu       huan    xiang
  鬓  如  霜.              夜  来  幽   梦    忽        还      乡,

| 3   6   5   4   3 | 6   3   2   1 - | 2·  3   6   0   *4   0 |
  xiao xuan chuan zheng shu zhuang        xiang dui  wu        yan
  小   轩   窗,    正   梳   妆.          相    顾   无        言,

| 3   2   1   7   6 - | 3   6   5   4 | 3 | 6   3   2   1 - |
  wei you lei qian hang    liao de  nian    nian duan chang  chu
  惟  有  泪  千   行.      料  得  年    年    断   肠     处,

| 2·  3   6   0   *4   0 | 3   2   1   7 | 6 - |
  min      yue     ye       duan    song    gan
  明      月      夜,      短     松     冈.
```

### 2.50.3 Text of the lyrics

十年生死两茫茫，不思量，自难忘.千里孤坟，无处话凄凉.
纵使相逢应不识，尘满面，鬓如霜.
夜来幽梦忽还乡，小轩窗，正梳妆.相顾无言，惟有泪千行.
料得年年断肠处，明月夜，短松冈.

### 2.50.4 Text of the lyrics (a) marked with tones in Chinese pinyin

shí nián shēng sǐ liǎng máng máng bù sī liang zì nán wàng
十 年 生 死 两 茫 茫，不思量，自 难 忘.
qiān lǐ gū fén wú chǔ huà qī liáng
千 里 孤 坟 无 处 话 凄 凉.
zong shǐ xiāng féng yīng bù shí chén mǎn miàn bìn rú shuāng
纵 使 相 逢 应 不 识，尘 满 面，鬓 如 霜.
yè lái yōu mèng hū huán xiāng    xiǎo xuān chuāng zhèng shū zhuāng
夜来 幽 梦 忽 还 乡， 小 轩 窗， 正 梳 妆.
xiāng gù wú yán    wéi yǒu lèi qiān háng
相 顾 无 言，惟 有 泪 千 行.
liào dé nián nián duàn cháng chù míng yuè yè    duǎn sōng gāng
料 得 年 年 断 肠 处，明 月 夜，短 松 冈.

### 2.50.5 Literal translation of the lyrics

Ten years have passed, and we are separated by life and death. I don't think about it, but I can never forget it. A solitary grave a thousand miles away, with no place I can talk about the desolation. Even if we meet again, we should not recognize each other. My face is covered with dust and my hair is as white as frost. One night, in a deep dream, I suddenly returned home. By the small window, I was grooming myself. We are looking at each other in silence, only a thousand tears flow. Year after year, at the place where one's heart breaks, will be on a moonlit night, on a short pine hill.

## 2.50.6 A more polished and stylistically enhanced translation of the lyrics

A decade has passed, separated by life and death. Though I do not deliberately think of you, I cannot forget. A solitary grave lies a thousand miles away, with no place to express my desolation. Even if we were to meet again, we might not recognize each other. My face is covered in dust, my hair as white as frost. One night, in a deep dream, I suddenly returned home. You sat by the window, combing your hair. We gazed at each other in silence, tears flowing endlessly. Year after year, where the heart breaks, is a moonlit night atop a hill of short pines.

### 2.50.7 Translation sentence by sentence

十年生死两茫茫，不思量，自难忘.
A decade has passed, separated by life and death. Though I do not deliberately think of you, I cannot forget.
千里孤坟，无处话凄凉.
A solitary grave lies a thousand miles away, with no place to express my desolation.
纵使相逢应不识，尘满面，鬓如霜.
Even if we were to meet again, we might not recognize each other. My face is covered in dust, my hair as white as frost.
夜来幽梦忽还乡，小轩窗，正梳妆.
One night, in a deep dream, I suddenly returned home. You sat by the window, combing your hair.
相顾无言，惟有泪千行.
We gazed at each other in silence, tears flowing endlessly.
料得年年断肠处，明月夜，短松冈.
Year after year, where the heart breaks, is a moonlit night atop a hill of short pines.

### 2.50.8 Brief introduction of the author of the poem

For details, please refer to section 2.08.7 of this book.

# 2.51 Song No.51, The reeds

兼葭　先秦　选自诗经　孔子

**Title of the poem: The reeds**
**Author of the poem (lyrics), Spring and Autumn period, Confucius**

### 2.51.0 About the score and lyrics (poem)

This score (sheet music) is derived from a Singapore folk song has undergone minor modifications to ensure a better alignment between the musical arrangement and the lyrics (poem).

Living on a island facing the sea, there is both yearning for the distant and a touch of sadness. Both the music and the lyrics (the poem, original text and its translation see the following sections) has similar tone, therefore rewrites the poem (lyrics) for the song is appropriate.

## 2.51.1 Sheet music

$1 = C \quad \frac{4}{4}$

| 6̇ 5 6̇ 6̇ 0 | 1̇ 1̇ 6̇ 5 0 | 3 5 6̇ 6̇ 0 |
蒹 葭 苍 苍， 白 露 为 霜． 所 谓 伊 人，

| 5̇ 6 3 2 0 | 3 5 3 2 0 | 5 3 6̇ 2 0 |
在 水 一 方． 溯 洄 从 之， 道 阻 且 长．

| 3 5 3 2 0 | 5 3 5 6 0 | 2 1̇ 1̇ 1̇ |
溯 游 从 之， 宛 在 水 中 央．

## 2.51.2 Sheet music with Lyrics marked in Chinese pinyin without tones

| 6̇ 5 6̇ 6̇ 0 | 1̇ 1̇ 6̇ 5 0 | 3 5 6̇ 6̇ 0 |
jian jia cang cang  bai lu wei chuang  suo wei yi ren
蒹 葭 苍 苍， 白 露 为 霜． 所 谓 伊 人，

| 5̇ 6 3 2 0 | 3 5 3 2 0 | 5 3 6̇ 2 0 |
zai shui yi fang  su hui cong zhi  dao zu qie chang
在 水 一 方． 溯 洄 从 之， 道 阻 且 长．

| 3 5 3 2 0 | 5 3 5 6 0 | 2 1̇ 1̇ 1̇ |
su you cong zhi  wan zai shui  zhong yang
溯 游 从 之， 宛 在 水 中 央．

### 2.51.3 Text of the lyrics

蒹葭苍苍，白露为霜.所谓伊人，在水一方.
溯洄从之，道阻且长.溯游从之，宛在水中央.

### 2.51.4 Text of the lyrics (a) marked with tones in Chinese pinyin

jiān jiā cāng cāng bái lù wèi shuāng suǒ wèi yī rén
蒹　葭　苍　苍，白露为　　霜．所　谓伊人，
zài shuǐ yī fāng sù huí cóng zhī　dào zǔ qiě zhǎng
在　水一　方.溯洄　从　之，　道阻且　长.
sù yóu cóng zhī　wǎn zài shuǐ zhōng yāng
溯游　从　之，宛　在水　　中　　央.

### 2.51.5 Literal translation of the lyrics

The reeds are lush and green, the white dew turns to frost. The fair lady I think resides on the other side of the water. Tracing back and following it, the road ahead is long and arduous. Following it, one feels as if in the middle of the water.

### 2.51.6 A more polished and stylistically enhanced translation of the lyrics

The reeds are luxuriant and verdant; the white dew has turned to frost. The graceful lady I long for resides across the water. Tracing back along the river to find her, the path is arduous and distant. Pursuing her, one feels as though she is right in the center of the water.

### 2.51.7 Translation sentence by sentence

蒹葭苍苍，白露为霜.
The reeds are luxuriant and verdant; the white dew has turned to frost.
所谓伊人，在水一方.
The graceful lady I long for resides across the water.
溯洄从之，道阻且长.

Tracing back along the river to find her, the path is arduous and distant.
溯游从之，宛在水中央.
Pursuing her, one feels as though she is right in the center of the water.

**2.51.8 Brief introduction of the author of the poem (lyrics-b)**

For details, please refer to Section 2.14.7 of this book, we do not repeat here.

# 2.52 Song No.52, Songs of Eight famous people in Drinking

---

饮中八仙歌（节选）　唐　杜甫

**Title of the poem: Songs of Eight famous people in Drinking**
**Author of the poem (lyrics), Tang Dynasty, Gu Fu**

### 2.52.0 About the score and lyrics (poem)

This score (sheet music) is derived (excerpted) from the (pieces) of Gossyk'sGavot Dance and has undergone minor modifications to ensure a better alignment between the musical arrangement and the lyrics (poem).

Bothe the music and the lyrics (the poem, original text and its translation see the following sections) has cheerful, relaxed, free and unrestrained rhythm and melody, they are quite matched each other. Thus the author incorporates this poem into that renowned musical composition.

## 2.52.1 Sheet music

$1 = C \quad \frac{4}{4}$

| 5̇ 6̇ 5̇ 3̇ | 4̇ 5̇ 4 2 | i i i 0 | 4̇ 5̇ 4 2̇ |
|---|---|---|---|
| 知 章 骑 马 | | 似 乘 船， | 眼 花 |

| 3̇ 4̇ 3̇ 1̇ | 2̇ 5 5 0 | 2̇ 4̇ 3̇ 5̇ | 4̇ 3̇ 2̇ 1̇ |
| 落 井 水 底 眼. | 宗 之 | 潇 洒 | |

| 7 2̇ 4̇ 0 | 3̇ 5̇ 4 6 | 5 4 3̇ 2̇ | 1̇ 3̇ 5̇ 0 |
| 美 少 年. | 举 觞 白 | 眼 望 青 | 天. |

| 6̇ 5̇ 5̇ 4̇ | 4̇ 3̇ 3̇ 2̇ | 2̇ 4̇ 6̇ 0 | 5̇ 3̇ 7 1̇ |
| 苏 晋 长 斋 | 绣 佛 前， | 醉 中 | |

| 4̇ 2̇ 6 7 | i i i 0 | 3 3 4 4 | 5̇ 1̇ 7 1̇ |
| 往 往 爱 逃 禅. | 李 白 斗 酒 | 诗 百 | |

| 5̇ 0 | i i 2 2 | 3̇5̇4̇5̇ 6̇5̇4̇3̇ | 2̇ 5 7̇ 5̇ |
| 篇， 长 安 市 上 | 酒 家 | 眠， | |

| 6 i̇ 6 6 | 6 5 i̇ 5 | 5 5 | 4 5 3 5 | 2̇ |
| 天 子 呼 来 | 不 上 船， | 自 称 臣 是 | 酒 |

| 2̇3̇4̇3̇ 2 0 | 4 4̇3̇2̇1̇ | 7 i̇ | i̇ 5̇ i̇ 0 | 4̇ |
| 中 仙. 张 旭 | 三 杯 | 草 圣 传， | 脱 |

| 4̇3̇2̇1̇ 7 i̇ | i̇ 5̇ i̇ 0 | 6 1̇7̇6̇5̇ | 4̇ 6̇ | 6̇ 4̇ |
| 帽 露 顶 王 公 前， | 挥 毫 | 落 纸 如 云 | |

| 6̇ 0 | 5̇ 5̇6̇5̇4̇ 3̇ 5̇ | 5̇ 5̇ 5̇ 0 |
| 烟. 挥 毫 落 纸 如 云 烟. |

## 2.52.2 Sheet music with Lyrics marked in Chinese pinyin without tones

| 5 6 | 5 3 | 4 5 | 4 2 | 1 1 1 0 | 4 5 | 4 2 |
| zhi | zhang | qi | ma | si cheng chuan | yan | hua |
| 知 | 章 | 骑 | 马 | 似 乘 船, | 眼 | 花 |

| 3 4 | 3 1 | 2 5 5 0 | 2 4 | 3 5 | 4 3 | 2 1 |
| luo | jing | shui di mian | zong | zhi | xiao | sa |
| 落 | 井 | 水 底 眠. | 宗 | 之 | 潇 | 洒 |

| 7 2 4 0 | 3 5 | 4 6 | 5 4 | 3 2 | 1 3 | 5 0 |
| mei shao nian | ju | shang | bai | yan | wang qing | tian |
| 美 少 年, | 举 | 觞 | 白 | 眼 | 望 青 | 天, |

| 6 5 | 5 4 | 4 3 | 3 2 | 2 4 | 6 0 | 5 3 | 7 1 |
| su | jin | chang | zhai | xiu | fo | qian | zui zhong |
| 苏 | 晋 | 长 | 斋 | 绣 | 佛 | 前, | 醉 中 |

| 4 2 6 7 | 1 1 1 0 | 3 3 | 4 4 | 5 1 | 7 1 |
| wang wang | ai tao chan | li bai | dou jiu | shi | bai |
| 往 往 | 爱 逃 禅. | 李 白 | 斗 酒 | 诗 | 百 |

| 5 0 | 1 1 | 2 2 | 3 5 4 5 | 6 5 4 3 | 2 5 | 7 5 |
| pian | chang an | shi shang | jiu | jia | mian |
| 篇, | 长 安 | 市 上 | 酒 | 家 | 眠, |

| 6 1 | 6 6 6 | 5 1 5 | 5 5 | 4 5 | 3 5 | 2 |
| tian zi | hu lai bu | shang | chuan | zi cheng | chen shi | jiu |
| 天 子 | 呼 来 不 | 上 | 船, | 自 称 | 臣 是 | 酒 |

| 2 3 4 3 | 2 0 | 4 | 4 3 2 1 | 7 1 | 1 5 | 1 0 | 4 |
| zhong | xian | zhang xu | san bei | cao sheng chuan | tuo |
| 中 | 仙. | 张 旭 | 三 杯 | 草 圣 传, | 脱 |

| 4 3 2 1 | 7 1 | 1 5 | 1 0 | 6 1 7 6 5 | 4 6 | 6 4 |
| mao | lu ding wang gong qian | hui hao | luo zhi | ru yun |
| 帽 | 露 顶 王 公 前, | 挥 毫 | 落 纸 | 如 云 |

| 6 0 | 5 5 6 5 4 | 3 5 | 5 5 | 5 0 |
| yan | hui hao | luo zhi ru | yun yan |
| 烟. | 挥 毫 | 落 纸 如 | 云 烟. |

### 2.52.3 Text of the lyrics

知章骑马似乘船，眼花落井水底眠.宗之潇洒美少年，举觞白眼望青天，苏晋长斋绣佛前，醉中往往爱逃禅.李白斗酒诗百篇，长安市上酒家眠，天子呼来不上船，自称臣是酒中仙.张旭三杯草圣传，脱帽露顶王公前，挥毫落纸如云烟.

### 2.52.4 Text of the lyrics marked with tones in Chinese pinyin

zhī zhāng qí mǎ sì chéng chuan yǎn huā luò jǐng shuǐ dǐ mián
知　章　骑马似乘　　船，眼　花落井　水底眠.
zōng zhī xiāo sǎ měi shào nián jǔ shāng bái yǎn wàng qīng tiān
宗　之潇洒美少　年，举　觞　白眼　望　青　天，
sū jìn cháng zhāi xiù fó qián zuì zhōng wǎng wǎng ài táo chán
苏晋　长　　斋　绣佛前，醉　中　　往　　往　爱逃　禅.
lǐ bái dǒu jiǔ shī bǎi piān cháng ān shì shàng jiǔ jiā mián
李白斗酒诗百篇，长　　安市　上酒家　眠，
tiān zǐ hū lái bù shàng chuan zì chēng chén shì jiǔ zhōng xiān
天子　呼来不上　　船，自　称　　臣是酒　中　　仙.
zhāng xù sān bēi cǎo shèng chuan tuō mào lù dǐng wáng gōng qián
张　　旭三杯草圣　　传，脱帽　露顶　王　公　前，
huī háo luò zhǐ rú yún yān
挥　毫落纸如云　烟.

### 2.52.5 Literal translation of the lyrics

Zhi Zhang rode a horse as if in a boat, his eyes blurred as he fell asleep at the bottom of a well. Zong Zhi, a carefree and handsome young man, raises his cup and looks up at the blue sky with white eyes. Before Su Jin's long study to embroider Buddha statues, he often loved to escape Zen when drunk. Li Bai composed a hundred poems while drinking wine. He slept at a tavern in Chang 'an City. When the emperor called him, he did not board the ship and called himself a fairy among wines. Zhang Xu Three Cups of the Sage of Cursive Script，takes off his hat and exposes his head before the prince. His brush moves on the paper like clouds and smoke.

## 2.52.6 A more polished and stylistically enhanced translation of the lyrics

Zhi Zhang rode a horse as if gliding in a boat, his vision blurred until he fell asleep at the bottom of a well. Zong Zhi, a carefree and dashing young man, raised his cup and gazed upward at the blue sky with an air of defiance. Su Jin, in his quiet study, embroidered before the Buddha. When inebriated, he often neglected his meditation. Li Bai composed a hundred poems after drinking a cup of wine and once slept at a tavern in Chang'an City. When the emperor summoned him, he refused to board the royal vessel, proudly calling himself a celestial being among drinkers. Zhang Xu, known as the Three Cups of the Sage of Cursive Script, removed his hat and stood bareheaded before the prince. With his brush, he writes and move on the paper as if conjuring clouds and smoke.

### 2.52.7 Translation sentence by sentence

知章骑马似乘船，
Zhi Zhang rode a horse as if gliding in a boat,
眼花落井水底眠.
his vision blurred until he fell asleep at the bottom of a well.
宗之潇洒美少年，
Zong Zhi, a carefree and dashing young man,
举觞白眼望青天，
raised his cup and gazed upward at the blue sky with an air of defiance.
苏晋长斋绣佛前，
Su Jin, in his quiet study, embroidered before the Buddha.
醉中往往爱逃禅.
When inebriated, he often neglected his meditation.
李白斗酒诗百篇，
Li Bai composed a hundred poems after drinking a cup of wine，
长安市上酒家眠，
and once slept at a tavern in Chang'an City.
天子呼来不上船，

When the emperor summoned him, he refused to board the royal vessel,

自称臣是酒中仙,

proudly calling himself a celestial being among drinkers.

张旭三杯草圣传,

Zhang Xu, known as the Three Cups of the Sage of Cursive Script,

脱帽露顶王公前,

removed his hat and stood bareheaded before the prince.

挥毫落纸如云烟.

With his brush, he writes and move on the paper as if conjuring clouds and smoke.

**2.52.8 Brief introduction of the author of the poem (lyrics-b)**

See section 2.24.7, we do not repeat here.

# 2.53 Song No.53, Song of Divination

卜算子　南宋　严蕊

**Tune of the poem: Song of Divination.**
**Author of the poem (lyrics), Southern Song Dynasty, Yan Rui**

### 2.53.0 About the score and lyrics (poem)

This score (sheet music) is derived from the Cuban song of Children of Havana, and has undergone minor modifications to ensure a better alignment between the musical arrangement and the lyrics (poem).

A Child of Havana Composed by Li Jefu, also known as Beautiful Havana, this song was written in China in 1962 to show solidarity with the Cuban Revolution.

This song is often mistaken for a Cuban one. The song is tinged with a hint of sadness. The author rewrites the poem (lyrics) for the song.

### 2.53.1 Sheet music

$1 = C \quad \frac{2}{4}$

| 1 2 3　 2 1 | 3 - | 5 6 i　 7 6 | 5 - | 3 3 3
不 是　 爱 风 尘, 似 被　 前 缘 误. 花 落

| 2 1 | 6 6 6　 5 4 3 | 1 2 3　 2 7 | 1 - |
花 开 自 有　 时,　 总 赖　 东 君 主

| 1 2 3　 2 1 | 3 - | 5 6 i　 7 6 | 5 - | 3 3 3
去 也　 终 须 去, 住 也　 如 何 住. 若 得

| 2 1 | 6 6 6　 5 4 3 | 1 2 3　 2 7 | 1 -
山 花 插 满　 头,　 莫 问　 奴 归 处.

### 2.53.2 Sheet music with Lyrics marked in Chinese pinyin without tones

| 1 2 3　 2 1 | 3 - | 5 6 i　 7 6 | 5 - | 3 3 3
bu shi　 ai feng chen　 si bei　 qian yuan wu　 hua luo
不 是　 爱 风 尘, 似 被　 前 缘 误. 花 落

| 2 1 | 6 6 6　 5 4 3 | 1 2 3　 2 7 | 1 - |
hua kai zi you　 shi　 zong lai　 dong jun zhu
花 开 自 有　 时,　 总 来　 东 君 主

| 1 2 3　 2 1 | 3 - | 5 6 i　 7 6 | 5 - | 3 3 3
qu ye　 zhong xu qu　 zhu ye　 ru he zhu　 ruo de
去 也　 终 须 去, 住 也　 如 何 住. 若 得

| 2 1 | 6 6 6　 5 4 3 | 1 2 3　 2 7 | 1 -
shan hua cha man　 tou,　 mo wen　 nu gui chu
山 花 插 满　 头,　 莫 问　 奴 归 处.

### 2.53.3 Text of the lyrics

不是爱风尘，似被前缘误.花落花开自有时，总赖东君主.
去也终须去，住也如何住.若得山花插满头，莫问奴归处.

### 2.53.4 Text of the lyrics (a) marked with tones in Chinese pinyin

bú shì ài fēng chén　sì bèi qián yuán wù huā luò huā kāi zì yǒu shí
不　是　爱　风　尘，　似被　前　缘　误.花　落　花　开 自　有　时，
zǒng lài dōng jūn zhǔ　qù yě zhōng xū qù　zhù yě rú hé zhù
总　赖　东　君 主.　去 也　终　须　去，住 也如何　住.
ruò dé shān huā chā mǎn tóu　mò wèn nú guī chǔ
若　得　山 花　插　满 头，莫　问　奴 归 处.

### 2.53.5 Literal translation of the lyrics

It's not that I love the dust of the world, but rather that I'm misled by a predestined past. Flowers fall and bloom at their own time; it all depends on the Eastern monarch. If one goes, one must go; if one lives, one must live. If you have mountain flowers all over your head, don't ask where you have returned.

### 2.53.6 A more polished and stylistically enhanced translation of the lyrics

It is not that I cherish the dust of the mundane world, but could be that I was misled by a predestined past. Flowers bloom and fall according to their own time, all depending on the Eastern monarch. If one must depart, one must go; if one remains, one must live. If mountain flowers crown my head, do not inquire where I have returned.

### 2.53.7 Translation sentence by sentence

不是爱风尘，
It is not that I cherish the dust of the mundane world,
似被前缘误.

but could be that I was misled by a predestined past.
花落花开自有时，
Flowers bloom and fall according to their own time,
总赖东君主.
all depending on the Eastern monarch.
去也终须去，
If one must depart, one must go,
住也如何住.
if one remains, one must live.
若得山花插满头，
If mountain flowers crown my head,
莫问奴归处.
do not inquire where I have returned.

### 2.53.8 Brief introduction of the author of the poem (lyrics-b)

严蕊（公元 1160 - 1215），原姓周，字幼芳，南宋中叶女词人.出身低微，自小习乐礼诗书，后沦为台州营妓，改严蕊为艺名.琴，棋，歌，乐，书，画，诗词具佳.南宋淳熙九年，朱熹巡行台州，弹劾唐仲友，其中论及唐与严蕊风化之罪，下令抓捕严蕊，施以鞭笞，逼其招供.严说："身为贱妓，纵合与太守有滥，科亦不至死；然是非真伪，岂可妄言以污士大夫，虽死不可诬也."此事朝野议论.后朱熹改官，岳霖任提点刑狱，有意释放严蕊，问其归宿.严蕊作此《卜算子》.岳霖判令从良.

Yan Rui (1160 -1215 AD), originally surnamed Zhou, styled Youfang, was a female poet of the Southern Song Dynasty. Born into a humble family, she began studying music, etiquette, poetry, and calligraphy at a young age. Later, she became a courtesan in Taizhou and adopted the stage name Yan Rui. She was proficient in playing the zither, chess, singing, music, calligraphy, painting, and poetry.In the ninth year of the Chunxi era of the Southern Song Dynasty, Zhu Xi visited Taizhou and impeached Tang Zhongyou. In the process, he accused Tang and Yan Rui of corruption and ordered her arrest and public whipping to extract a confession. Yan Rui responded, "As a lowly courtesan, even if I had an affair with the governor, I should not face capital punishment. How can one recklessly defame a scholar-official without evidence? Even at the cost of death, I will not confess falsely." This case sparked widespread debate throughout the court and the nation. Later, Zhu Xi was promoted to a new post, and Yue Lin was appointed as the director of criminal justice. He intended to release Yan Rui and inquired about her fate. Yan Rui composed this "Song of Divination" Yue Lin ordered her to reform.

# 2.54 Song No.54, Full River Red

满江红　南宋　岳飞

**Tune of the poem: Full River Red**
**Author of the poem (lyrics), Southern Song Dynasty, Yue Fei**

**2.54.0 About the score and lyrics (poem)**

This score (sheet music) is derived (excerpted) from the (pieces) of Marseille (Marseillaise，La Marseillaise), the French national anthem composed in 1792 during the French Revolution. The poem (verse) is derived from Yue Fei's poem Full River Red. Both poem and music have undergone minor modifications to ensure a better alignment between the musical arrangement and the lyrics (poem).

This Marseillaise is appropriate globally for all humankind in inspiring people to fight for freedom and democracy, national liberation and for a just cause. The author of this book likes this piece of music very much.

The Yue Fei's poem（verse Full River Red）is full of the fighting spirit of sacrificing one's life for the country with loyalty, which perfectly aligns with the fighting spirit of the Marseillaise, therefore the author rewrites the poem (lyrics) for the song.

## 2.54.1 Sheet music

$1 = C \quad \frac{4}{4}$

```
5· 5· 5 | 1  1  2  2 | 5· 3  1· 1  3· 1 | 6  4 —
怒 发 冲 冠，  凭    栏    处    潇 潇 雨 歇.

2· 7 | 1 — 0  1· 2 | 3· 3  3  3  4· 3 | 3  2  0
抬 望 眼，   仰 天 长 啸，  壮 怀 激 烈.

2· 3 | 4· 4  4  5· 4 | 3 — 0  5· 5 | 5  3· 1
三 十 功 名 尘 与  土，   八 千 里 路

5  3· 1 | 5 — 0  5  5· 7 | 2 — 4  2· 7  7 | 2  1
云 和  月，   莫 等 闲，白 了 少 年 头， 空 悲

7 — | 6  1· 1  1  7· 1 | 2 — 0  7 | 1· 1  1  2· 3 |
切.  靖 康 耻， 犹 未  雪.    臣 子 恨， 何  时

7 — 0  1· 7 | 6· 6  6  1  7· 6 | 6  5  0  0  5  5 |
灭.  驾 长 车  踏 破 贺 兰 山 缺.    壮 志

5 — 5· 5  3· 1 | 2 — — 0  5  5 | 5 — 5· 5  3· 1 |
击 杀 敌 酋 首，    誓 让 强 虏  血 还

2 — — 5 | 1 — — 2  3 — — 0 | 4 — 5  6 | 2 — — 6 | 5 —
血.  待 从 头  收 拾    旧  山 河，  朝

0  3  4· 2 | 1 — 1· 0 |
天  阙.
```

## 2.54.2 Sheet music with Lyrics marked in Chinese pinyin without tones

```
5  5·  5  | 1  1  2   2 | 5·  3  | 1·  1   3·  1 | 6   4  -
nu fa chong guan    ping  lan    chu      xiao xiao yu  xie
怒  发  冲  冠,       凭    栏     处,      潇    潇   雨   歇.

2·  7 | 1  -  0  | 1·  2 | 3·  3   3   3 | 4·  3 | 3   2   0
tai wang yan         yang tian chang xiao   zhuang huai   ji    lie
抬   望   眼,         仰    天    长    啸,    壮     怀    激    烈.

2·  3 | 4·  4   4 | 5·  4 | 3  -   0 | 5·  5 | 5   3·  1
san shi  gong ming chen yu      tu        ba qian  li   lu
三   十   功   名    尘   与     土,       八  千    里   路

5   3·  1 | 5  -   0 | 5   5·  7 | 2  -   4 | 2·  7   7 | 2   1
yun     he          yue      mo deng xian bai le shao nian tou    kong bei
云       和           月,     莫   等   闲, 白  了   少   年   头,   空    悲

7  -  | 6   1·  1   1 | 7·  1 | 2  -   0 | 7 | 1·  1   1   1 | 2·  3
qie    jing kang chi you wei      xue         chen zi hen he        shi
切,    靖    康   耻,  犹   未    雪.         臣    子  恨,  何       时

7  -   0 | 1·  7 | 6·  6   6   1 | 7·  6 | 6   5   0   0   5   5 |
mie       jia chang che    ta po he lan shan que           zhuang zhi
灭.        驾   长    车    踏 破 贺 兰   山    缺.           壮     志

5  -   5·  5   3·  1 | 2  -  -   0   5   5 | 5  -   5·  5   3·  1 |
ji       sha di  qiu shou         shi rang qiang lu     xue huan
击       杀  敌   酋   首,          誓   让    强    虏     血   还

2  -  -   5 | 1  -  -   2 | 3  -  -   0 | 4  -   5   6 | 2  -  -  6 | 5 -
xue       dai cong tou shou shi           jiu    shan he       chao
血.        待   从   头   收   拾           旧     山    河,      朝

0   3   4·  2 | 1  -   1·  0 |
              tian    que
              天      阙
```

### 2.54.3 Text of the lyrics

怒发冲冠，凭栏处，潇潇雨歇.抬望眼，仰天长啸，壮怀激烈.
三十功名尘与土，八千里路云和月.莫等闲，白了少年头，空悲切.
靖康耻，犹未雪.臣子恨，何时灭.驾长车踏破贺兰山缺.
壮志击杀敌酋首，誓让强虏血还血.待从头收拾旧山河，朝天阙.

### 2.54.4 Text of the lyrics (a) marked with tones in Chinese pinyin

nù fà chōng guān ping lán chù　xiāo xiāo yǔ xiē tái wàng yǎn
怒 发 冲 冠，凭 栏 处, 潇 潇 雨 歇. 抬 望 眼，
yǎng tiān cháng xiào zhuàng huái jī liè
仰 天 长 啸， 壮 怀 激烈.
sān shí gōng míng chén yǔ tǔ　bā qiān lǐ lù yún hé yuè
三 十 功 名 尘 与 土, 八 千 里 路 云 和 月.
mò děng xián bái le shào nián tóu　kōng bēi qiè
莫 等 闲, 白 了 少 年 头， 空 悲 切.
jìng kāng chǐ yóu wèi xuě chén zǐ hèn　hé shí miè
靖 康 耻， 犹 未 雪. 臣 子 恨， 何 时 灭.
jià cháng chē tà pò hè lán shān quē
驾 长 车 踏破 贺 兰 山 缺.
zhuàng zhì jī shā dí qiú shǒu shì rang qiáng lǔ xuè huán xuè
壮 志 击杀 敌酋 首，誓 让 强 虏 血 还 血.
dài cóng tóu shōu shí jiù shān hé　cháo tiān què
待 从 头 收 拾 旧 山 河， 朝 天 阙.

### 2.54.5 Literal translation of the lyrics

With hair standing on end in rage, I leaned on the railing and the drizzling rain ceased. Looking up, I let out a long howl to the sky, filled with intense emotions. Thirty years of fame and fortune, dust and earth, eight thousand miles of journey, clouds and moon. Don't idle away your youth; your hair will turn white and you will only be filled with sorrow. The humiliation of Jingkang has yet to be avenged. When will the hatred of a subject cease! Drive a long chariot through the gaps of Helan Mountain.

With lofty aspirations, I slay the enemy's chieftain, Swear to make the invaders pay for their blood. When I start to tidy up the old mountains and rivers from the beginning, I face the celestial gate.

## 2.54.6 A more polished and stylistically enhanced translation of the lyrics

With hair bristling in fury, I leaned against the balustrade, and the drizzle gradually ceased. Gazing upward, I raised a prolonged cry toward the heavens, overwhelmed by intense emotions. Thirty years of fame and fortune have turned to dust and earth; eight thousand miles of journeying lie behind me, beneath clouds and moonlight. Do not waste your youth in idleness; when your hair turns white with age, only sorrow will remain. The humiliation of Jingkang remains unavenged. When shall the resentment of a loyal subject finally subside? I will drive a long chariot to attack through the passes of Helan Mountain. With resolute ambition, I vow to slay the enemy's leader and swear to make the invaders pay for their blood. Only when I restore the once lost mountains and rivers shall I stand before the Celestial Gate.

### 2.54.7 Translation sentence by sentence

怒发冲冠，凭栏处，潇潇雨歇.
With hair bristling in fury, I leaned against the balustrade, and the drizzle gradually ceased.
抬望眼，仰天长啸，壮怀激烈.
Gazing upward, I raised a prolonged cry toward the heavens, overwhelmed by intense emotions.
三十功名尘与土，八千里路云和月.
Thirty years of fame and fortune have turned to dust and earth; eight thousand miles of journeying lie behind me, beneath clouds and moonlight.
莫等闲，白了少年头，空悲切.
Do not waste your youth in idleness; when your hair turns white with age, only sorrow will remain.
靖康耻，犹未雪.臣子恨，何时灭.

The humiliation of Jingkang remains unavenged. When shall the resentment of a loyal subject finally subside.

驾长车踏破贺兰山缺.

I will drive a long chariot to attack through the passes of Helan Mountain.

壮志击杀敌酋首，誓让强虏血还血.

With resolute ambition, I vow to slay the enemy's leader and swear to make the invaders pay for their blood.

待从头收拾旧山河，朝天阙.

Only when I restore the once lost mountains and rivers shall I stand before the Celestial Gate.

### 2.54.8 Brief introduction of the author of the poem

岳飞（公元 1103 年 - 1142 年），字鹏举.

Yue Fei (1103 - 1142 AD), styled Pengju.

For details, please refer to section 2.35.7 of this book, we do not repeat here.

# 3 Discussions

## 3.1 About the talent

When attempting to set music to lyrics or vice versa, safely speaking, one must examine whether the emotional curves of the poetry and music align closely. First, check whether the emotional tones of the two works are compatible, and then assess whether their structural turning points correspond. If both are compatible, the lyrical adaptation is likely to succeed, potentially resulting in a work of remarkable craftsmanship.

Over the past century, numerous musicians and scholars have aspired to incorporate classical Chinese poetry into the realm of classical music and art song. Yet, why have such efforts largely failed to produce enduring results? The fundamental reason lies in the fact that these individuals often lack a deep understanding of either poetry or music. Some may not grasp the essence of poetic expression at all, while others may fail to capture the emotional tone of a particular musical piece or lack musical knowledge altogether. Consequently, it becomes nearly impossible for them to perceive the unique and shared characteristics between a specific poem and a corresponding musical fragment or composition.

Frankly speaking, only the one that possesses a genuine understanding of both music and poetry and has mastered their essential elements, then undertake and complete the endeavor. Sono choice but only the author can undertake the job.

## 3.2 About the translation

Translating ancient poetry is by no means a simple task. Ancient Chinese poems are a rich art treasure, as well as a vast, deep, and gorgeous world.

For a long time, Chinese and foreign translators and scholars have been consistently discussing whether Chinese classical poems are translatable and if they are, then how should they be translated.

In fact, Chinese classical poetry is written in vernacular Chinese rather than in classical Chinese.

This book does not aim to achieve extreme accuracy in conveying the original meaning of classical poetry, as such a goal is inherently subjective and limitless. Instead, this book provides two types of translations: a literal version and a literary adaptation, both intended for reference purposes.

## 3.3 Regarding the pinyin annotation of Chinese characters

In the musical notation provided in this book, only one version with Chinese pinyin annotations (without tone marks) is included. When one is singing, the tones of Chinese characters must conform to or follow up the musical melody rather than strictly adhering to their original tonal values.

The original text of the Chinese pinyin poems with tones is listed separately after it.

## 3.4 About the sequence arrangement of the songs

The sequence of songs in this book is arranged randomly, although this was not an intentional design. It was later considered, however, that a random arrangement might produce a more favorable effect, perhaps this arrangement may always bring surprises to readers, who knows.

The final piece in the score of this book is "Full River Red", a poem composed by the renowned ancient Chinese national hero Yue Fei. This selection is intended to express hopes that nations around the world that have suffered invasion and territorial occupation, as well as those that are still being invaded, to successfully defeat or repel the invaders and recover their lost territories, at the earliest possible time.

# 4 Background story of this project

Before the age of five, the author witnessed several bookshelves filled with bound classical literature at home.

In fact, the author's father was secretly arrested and imprisoned in the year the author was born (1961), and his whereabouts were kept confidential. During this period, secret agents visited the author's home multiple times and confiscated several sacks of bound books and diaries belonging to the author's grandfather, without providing any explanation.

When the ten-year cultural upheaval began, nearly all privately owned bound books were forcibly burned, leaving no trace behind.

As stated in (1966 - 1977), books were not borrowed from public or school libraries. There were no classical literary works such as Tang poetry or Song ci poetry available on bookshelves. Xinhua Bookstore (the only type of bookstore at the time) did not carry any classical literature. Therefore, the author had no opportunity to engage in literary pursuits during his youth.

Over a decade later, it was not until the autumn of 1977, the second year after the death of one special person, that the authorities returned some materials that had been confiscated during the earlier searches, including two volumes of poetry collections in traditional Chinese binding. One was "Wonderful and Fine Poems" compiled by Qing Dynasty scholars, and the other was "The Complete Poems of Li Changji (Li He)." The author was deeply moved and began to appreciate the elegance and subtlety of classical Chinese poetry. Eight years later, the gradual reprints of classical anthologies such as the "Three Hundred Tang Poems" and the "Thousand Poems" gave the author more opportunities to read ancient literature. However, since the author was dedicated to studying science and engineering, classical literature remained a personal hobby.

As for Western classical music and foreign songs, including those from the former Soviet Union, they became increasingly scarce after 1966. During the height of the cultural catastrophe, Western and Soviet music were labeled as remnants of reactionary feudalism. Individuals found secretly possessing records or listening to Western classical music without authorization were subject to criticism, physical punishment, imprisonment, or even death. These were not isolated incidents.

Thus, during the more than ten years of this cultural catastrophe, people were extremely cautious about classical poetry and Western music, often unaware of the existence of these timeless artistic achievements.

The first Western musical piece that deeply moved the author was Schubert's "Army March" in 1981. From that point on, the author developed a strong appreciation for classical music, although he had limited time for deliberate listening.

The idea of setting Western classical music to ancient Chinese poetry first emerged in 1985, during the author's second year of graduate studies. With a more flexible schedule, many students spent time after dinner learning to play the guitar. At that time, the author felt that the lyrics of guitar songs were often vulgar and lacked elegance, and the music was mostly pop-oriented. He questioned whether musical appreciation had to remain at such a superficial level. Could there not be a more refined approach? He proposed to his classmate, who was also guitar instructor of the classmate, whether they could attempt setting lyrics to some classical music pieces and try singing them. Initially, the author was prosoed Haydn's symphonies, such as "The Surprise" and "The Clock." However, the "guitar instructor" was unimpressed and admitted lacking the necessary skills. This made me very disappointed and helpless, but I didn't completely give up this creative idea immediately. Could I attempt it by myself?

It was not until 2003, after returning to China following several years abroad, that the author finally found time to conduct music-related research. During this period, he calmly and confidently incorporated over twenty classical poems into Western classical music and re-adapted classical poetry into foreign songs. However, he faced the challenge of having no platform for public dissemination. For the next two decades, preoccupied with earning a living and conducting scientific research in other fields, he set aside his literary work.

By 2025, both the author and his peers had retired. In the years leading up to and following his retirement, he focused on literary archaeology, scientific methodology, and modern physics. After publishing a total of seven books with different themes through the American Academic Press, he originally intended to take a break and retire from research.

On June 6, 2025, during a gathering of old classmates, the author discussed cultural and artistic issues with a former classmate, Zhang Dali (张大立). Zhang suggested that the author continue exploring the authorship of the classical novel "Dream of the Red Chamber," aiming to clarify in mainland China that the true author may not be the commonly accepted one.

However, the author believed that in many academic fields, mainland China is not the ideal place to pursue objective truth. After much persuasion, the author has to say that he would rather explore music-related hobbies, such as learning the electronic piano or guzheng. Pausing briefly, he added that he could also focus on creating and innovating musical compositions. Zhang asked, "What do you mean?" The author replied that he intended to combine Chinese classical poetry with Western classical music. This idea intrigued the group, who found it novel and surprising. After a moment's thought, someone asked, "Do you have any completed examples you consider successful?" The author immediately replied, "Yes!" So, why not demonstrate one?

He suggested Dvořák's Humoresque. Another classmate, Xu Donglai (许东来), who was familiar with classical music, immediately hummed the melody and asked, "Is this the piece?" The author confirmed. This piece perfectly matched a humorous and teasing poem by Su Shi, a great Song Dynasty literary figure, titled "Butterfly Lovers." The author softly recited Su Shi's poem to the melody (as detailed in section 2.13 of this book). Several classmates found the combination novel and impressive, though they requested another example.

The author then cited Toselli's Serenade, which, when paired with Li Zhiyi's Song Dynasty poem "Longing for Each Other," produced an extremely elegant effect. The author recited the lyrics to the melody (as detailed in section 2.12), which deeply impressed the group, generating excitement and enthusiasm.

They believed that such creative reinterpretations not only offer aesthetic pleasure but also possess unexpected cultural and social benefits. If promoted, they could benefit audiences both domestically and internationally, appealing to people of all ages.

In the midst of their enthusiasm, the group discussed freely until the early hours of the morning, exploring ways to produce more such works and strategies for their promotion.

In the following days, the group met several times to continue discussions. During one session, Zhang Dali requested the author to perform two additional pieces that had already been adapted with lyrics and music. These were the works (included in sections 2.03 and 2.27) of this book. Zhang Dali was deeply impressed, stating that if performed by talented young singers, the effect would be extraordinary—refreshing, visually pleasing, emotionally touching, and heartwarming. This further solidified the group's determination to promote this cultural heritage, both domestically and internationally.

Therefore, the author proposed compiling the completed works into a collection, clearly documenting the sources of the lyrics and music, and recognizing this project as a natural outcome of the accumulation of human literary and artistic civilization. Some foundational research and explanation are necessary. The most fundamental task is to organize and write the material into a book. The core content includes works that integrate classical poetry into traditional classical music, as well as adaptations of classical poetry into classic songs. Suitable publishers and book categories should be identified to facilitate publication, serving as foundational materials and intellectual property for future promotion and development.

From June to early August, through the dedicated efforts of the author, Zhang Dali, Xu Donglai, and others, the first volume of this collection was completed. They then sought a suitable publisher, hoping for prompt publication. The author initially considered the American Academic Press (AAP), so he searched for submission guidelines and submitted the manuscript.

This is the general account of the true story behind this book, spanning several decades.

It should be emphasized that regardless of the future success or failure of this work, without the some classmate reunion and their encouragement on June 6, 2025, the author would not have been motivated to complete this collection of song research.

Liu Kedian (the author)<br>
Aug 06 2025

# Postscript and acknowledgments

This book represents a pioneering effort, and I believe it will stand as a unique and unparalleled contribution to its field.

This work is not only beneficial to overseas students of Chinese language and culture, but also to scholars who appreciate both traditional Chinese culture and classical music. Furthermore, it serves as a valuable intellectual resource with both aesthetic and practical significance for music enthusiasts and poetry lovers on the Chinese mainland and foreigners. However, as the author and several assistants are not full-time researchers in music or literature, and due to time constraints, limited expertise, and the constraints of available software and hardware tools, this book may not be entirely flawless. Nevertheless, these limitations should not detract from the usability and artistic value of the musical compositions presented.

This book may be considered as the first volume in a potential series. The publication of a second volume will depend on various factors, including the reception of this work and the availability of resources.

The author would like to express sincere appreciation for the numerous publications that have become available during the relatively open academic period since 1978.

On behalf of this work, the author would like to extend special gratitude to two former college classmates, Zhang Dali and Xu Donglai, who provided substantial support in terms of materials and technical tools during the preparation of this book. For example, they assisted in downloading and installing music production software, as well as in selecting and purchasing necessary hardware. Due to the lack of dedicated funding for acquiring professional music software and hardware, we relied on relatively simple, freely available software with limited functionality, resulting in a final product that meets basic usability standards.

These two individuals also contributed valuable materials and insights regarding musical content and melodies. For instance, they suggested using Tchaikovsky's "June: Barcarolle." Initially, I believed the piece carried a melancholic tone that would be difficult to pair with poetry. Similarly, when studying Yue Fei's regulated verse "Small Overlapping Hills," I found its mood to be similarly somber, making it challenging to find a suitable musical accompaniment. Upon further experimentation and arrangement, however, it was discovered that these two elements were, in fact, highly compatible. This realization led to the creation of Section 2.35.

Ultimately, this book is offered as a present to lovers of classical music and classical poetry around the world, and as a little gift to appreciate the helps and encouragement of these two classmates, Zhang Dali and Xu Donglai (张大立 and 许东来).

Liu Kedian (刘可滇)
August 14, 2025

www.ingramcontent.com/pod-product-compliance
Lightning Source LLC
Chambersburg PA
CBHW030107010526
44116CB00005B/130